Building Beloved Communities

Building Beloved Communities

The Life and Work of Rev. Dr. Paul Smith

HILDI HENDRICKSON

The University of Georgia Press   Athens

Designed by Erin Kirk
Set in Minion

The paper in this book meets the guidelines for
permanence and durability of the Committee on
Production Guidelines for Book Longevity of the
Council on Library Resources.

Most University of Georgia Press titles are
available from popular e-book vendors.

Printed in the United States of America
25   24   23   22   21   C   5   4   3   2   1

Library of Congress Cataloging-in-Publication Data
Names: Hendrickson, Hildi, 1961– author.
Title: Building beloved communities : the life and work of Rev. Dr. Paul Smith /
    Hildi Hendrickson.
Description: Athens : The University of Georgia Press, [2021] | Includes
    bibliographical references and index.
Identifiers: LCCN 2021010560 | ISBN 9780820359618 (hardback) |
    ISBN 9780820359625 (ebook)
Subjects: LCSH: Smith, Paul, 1935– | Presbyterian Church—Clergy—Biography.
    | African American clergy—Biography. | African American Presbyterians—
    Biography. | Race relations—Religious aspects—Presbyterian Church. |
    African American clergy—Political activity. | African American
    Presbyterians—Political activity.
Classification: LCC BX9225.S545 H46 2021 | DDC 285.092 [B]—dc23
LC record available at https://lccn.loc.gov/2021010560

Contents

Photographs

Author's Note

This is the story of an extraordinary man who has dedicated his life to building the "beloved communities" heralded by Martin Luther King Jr. Schooled in the ethics and techniques of the civil rights era, Rev. Dr. Paul Smith is a translator among groups of estranged people, a courageous healer of hatred and suffering, a man of God whose ministry knows no bounds. Through his example, we can learn to become the kind of people who create a more just and compassionate society.

After the fashion of his mentor and colleague, the visionary theologian Rev. Dr. Howard Thurman, Dr. Smith has created vital, multiracial congregations in four different cities over the course of a sixty-year career. With uncommon honesty and compassion, Smith has helped engender the face-to-face experiences and lasting relationships through which bigotry and distrust can actually be defused.

Smith faces down prejudice with courage, compassion, and humor. As a mediator, he walks straight into conflict. As a preacher, he publicly grapples with his own anger over the racism he continues to encounter to this day. He freely shares the insights he gains through journaling, introspection, engagement, and prayer. As a pastor, Dr. Smith practices unreserved equanimity, giving parishioners, friends, colleagues, and even rivals and opponents the courage to face anger, conflict, illness, and death.

Though I am an anthropologist, our work has much in common. Smith believes as I do that human relationships are the antidote to bigotry and hatred. As capably as anyone in my profession, Dr. Smith practices the radical humility, deep listening, and agile translation that create understanding among people who know little about each other. Smith works in what anthropologist Victor Turner called the "liminal" spaces—the zones of transition and transformation between the well-worn social identities we settle into and defend. Dr. Smith knows, as I do, that these are places of risk, discovery, and joy. They are spiritual places where we need to spend time to fully appreciate our common humanity.

I first met Dr. Smith at a fund-raising dinner in 2001 at the university where I taught and where he was a trustee. After collaborating on projects like bringing Ambassador Andrew Young to campus to speak to students, I invited Dr. Smith to join me in teaching a senior seminar on nonviolence. Our rapport was so organic and powerful that we team-taught that course four times over the next several years. It was while teaching with him that I saw the impact his stories have on people. He shares the beauty, the humor, and the pain of human experience in language that makes people feel at home. When I suggested he get his stories written down, he challenged me to take up the task. This was unexpected; I thought, at first, what could a white, female, Buddhist academic bring to the biography of a civil rights–era Black Christian minister? But what I didn't know then was how much we share down deep. As he has done with many others, he saw something in me that I did not yet see in myself.

Since I took up this project in 2014 and began my first interviews with him, I have become Dr. Smith's de facto archivist. Beginning with a large cardboard box stuffed with books, papers, and photographs, Smith has given me free access to the letters, church programs, published writing and notes, newspaper articles, and other mementos he and his family have collected throughout his long, eventful life. Organizing this trove of historical artifacts and finding the chronological thread running through them is where this fascinating work began.

With characteristic openness and self-assurance, Dr. Smith has also given me unfettered access to the more than eighty journals he has written since the late 1950s. These documents constitute an extraordinary record of a working minister's thoughts, emotions, joys, and struggles over more than six decades. Weaving passages from the journals into this narrative make it part memoir, part biography. The quotes allow the reader to hear Smith's voice and to look over his shoulder as he comes of age and carries his passion for social justice into his work as a minister, a professor, a corporate consultant, and a family man.

Dr. Smith has also encouraged me to contact anyone among his family, friends, and colleagues that I wished to speak to. Unless otherwise noted, I recorded and transcribed all the interviews that are quoted in this book. It has been a privilege to meet and get to know some of the exceptional people in Paul Smith's world. They have constantly inspired me in this work. It is my hope that, when this book is finished, the recordings and transcriptions along with the rest of Smith's collected papers can be housed in a place where they will be available to other scholars.

Writing this book has demanded a healthy investigation of my own beliefs, prejudices, and racial preconceptions. Making a close study of the details of Dr. Smith's life has afforded me invaluable insight into my own upbringing, family history, and place in the power structure. Living in the fiction of "whiteness" in America has allowed me to be ignorant of so much. I now see and feel more acutely how often and how deeply this country fails to live up to its ideals. I am grateful for this ongoing education. Being given the chance to write this story has indelibly changed my understanding of myself, of American history, and of the possibilities for America's future.

Dr. Smith has a special gift for creating uncommon collaborations like ours. While nurturing lifelong ties within his own community, Smith has carried the loving wisdom of his family, the Black church, and African American experience into predominantly white institutions including the Presbyterian church, seminaries, colleges, and the corporate world. He has worked within such institutions in a quietly subversive way, insisting that they grow and change in the direction of King's "beloved community" ideal. In the corporate sector, he was one of many in the early 1960s who worked to persuade white businesses to open their doors to qualified Black candidates. As such, he was an early practitioner of what came to be known as "diversity and inclusion consulting."[1] This involved honing and applying his powerful mediation skills.

Dr. Smith has also been a force for reform within the Christian church itself. While never giving up on the institution, he has used his presence, his personality, and his professionalism to create a daily reckoning with the church's deeply rooted bigotry. He has not allowed bureaucratic or sectarian concerns to limit the healing work of his ministry. He has insisted that social justice must be central to Christian religious life, and he has opened his arms to all spiritual seekers, whether within the Christian world or beyond it.

Most unusually, Dr. Smith has used his many gifts to *make real* the all-inclusive peace- and justice-loving communities Dr. King held up as the ideal. In Smith's congregations, people of differing racial, ethnic, economic, and cultural backgrounds have created lasting relationships and alliances. He has taught people to grow and work together as equals more strongly united by their collective values than separated by their differences. And he has shown people how to do the internal and external work that allows them to cross boundaries and open their hearts to each other.

Dr. Smith's deepest lessons come through his pastoring. Over the years we have known each other, I have had occasion to feel the effects of this compassionate service firsthand in times of both joy and grief. Perhaps most meaningfully, he officiated at my wedding in 2011. In helping others confront the common human conditions of loss, illness, and death, Dr. Smith shares with everyone the healing realism, faith, and resilience of Black cultural experience. Vanquishing cynicism, he inspires people to follow Dr. Thurman in "listening for the sound of the genuine" in themselves and others, and in following that sound wherever it leads.[2]

If Americans want a more unified future, we have to learn from the complex truth of our collective past. Dr. Smith can be our guide, inspiring us to expand our hearts, to defuse conflict, to celebrate difference, and to insist on equal justice for all.

Building Beloved Communities

CHAPTER 1

Answering Dr. King's Call

On March 9, 1965, when he boarded a plane bound for Selma, Alabama, Paul Smith knew he was headed for a direct confrontation with hatred. Like most people in the country, he had heard that nonviolent protesters attempting to march from Selma to the state capitol in Montgomery had been subjected to brutal violence. National television programming two days earlier had been interrupted by news footage showing well-dressed, pious marchers being beaten to the ground and tear-gassed by baton-wielding state and local law enforcement officers. The raw brutality directed at disciplined and resolute citizens shocked Americans from Main Street to Washington, D.C. Yet Smith did not hesitate when Rev. Dr. Martin Luther King Jr. sent telegrams on Monday, March 8, asking clergy to join him in the march to Montgomery. The thirty-year-old Black minister with an active congregation, a wife, and two young children knew he had to answer Dr. King's call.

As director of race and religion for the Presbytery of St. Louis, Rev. Smith was leading a delegation of white ministers from Ferguson, Missouri, a town that has become synonymous with renewed racial strife after the killing there of young Michael Brown by a white police officer in 2014. Rev. Carl Dudley, Smith's white copastor at Berea Presbyterian Church, was at Smith's side. Typically for Smith and Dudley but atypically for the rest, they were flouting authority in making the trip. The governing boards of their congregations had told them they could lose their jobs if they went to join Dr. King at the protests. Though King was gaining national prominence, his refusal to stop staging public protests was causing major consternation among government officials, law enforcement, and clerical leadership across the country.

Smith had met Dr. King and wholeheartedly believed in the righteousness of his cause. As has so often happened in Smith's life, his certainty and enthusiasm carried others forward. Even some who did not go on the journey showed they knew what kind of support the travelers would need. As Smith recalls:

> I remember our going to Ferguson the night before we were to fly to Selma. At the end of dinner, our host, who was one of the families of Ferguson Presbyterian Church participating in our exchange program, said to us: "We unfortunately will not be able to join you and our minister on the trip to Selma. However, we want you to know you have our spiritual, financial and prayerful support should you need us. Do what you believe is right for everyone and know that we have lawyers primed to come to Alabama should you be arrested."[1]

Dr. King's telegram, which had gone out through the National Council of Churches network across the country, constituted a direct appeal to clergy. He made a powerful case: "No American is without responsibility. All are involved in the sorrow that rises from Selma to contaminate every crevice of our national life. . . . I call, therefore, on clergy of all faiths, representatives of every part of the country, to join me for a ministers' march to Montgomery on Tuesday morning, March 9th."[2]

Having decided to answer Dr. King's call, Rev. Smith and his colleagues quickly learned there were no seats on the regularly scheduled flights to Selma that day. Roughly eight hundred clergy from twenty-two states were rushing to Alabama to put themselves on the line for justice.[3] Fortunately, Archbishop Joseph Ritter of the St. Louis Catholic Church called August Anheuser Busch Jr., a scion of the local beer company, and asked for help. In a matter of hours, Paul, his colleagues, and thirty-five other ministers were bound for Alabama in Busch's DC-9. Everyone knew they were on a collision course with the fury of the white South.

What transpired that Sunday in Selma is now seen to have been a watershed for the country. Though people could not know it at the time, the complex, long-term, and multilayered reality of the "movement" was reaching a crescendo. The efforts and sacrifice of countless volunteers over many years had finally won the full attention of the nation, the White House, and the press. What everyone witnessed thanks to the media was the undeniable contrast between resolute marchers and furious, club-swinging law enforcement personnel. Ordinary people and congressional legislators, governors, and police officers, Black people and white—everyone who cared about freedom and justice—could see that change could no longer wait.

The political activity at Selma was built on the outcomes of decades of organized resistance, sacrifice, failure, and triumph. Twenty years earlier, groups like the Congress of Racial Equality (CORE), made up of Black and white people, women and men, had formed to undertake nonviolent protest in the name of equality. The earthshaking 1954 *Brown v. Board of Education* U.S. Supreme Court decision made the "separate but equal" racial approach to public education illegal and set in motion protests, court cases, and violent confrontations between people who saw integration as just and those who emphatically did not.

In 1955, fourteen-year-old Chicagoan Emmett Till, on summer vacation in Money, Mississippi, was kidnapped, tortured, and killed after a white woman accused him of whistling at her. Years later, the woman recanted and said he had not deserved his fate. The boy was taken from his relatives' home during the night and beaten until he died. His body was strapped to a piece of mechanical equipment and thrown into a river. The horrible condition of the boy's face as he lay in his open casket caused national revulsion.

Not long afterward, Rosa Parks and others refused to give up their seats on city buses in Montgomery, Alabama. The successful Montgomery Bus Boycott was accomplished by working women in particular who were willing to walk to work through a long, cold winter.

In 1957, after the boycott, Dr. King and others founded the Southern Christian Leadership Conference (SCLC), one of the most influential activist organizations of the era. In 1960, younger leadership with their own ideas about nonviolent resistance formed the rival Student Nonviolent Coordinating Committee (SNCC). Sometimes together and at other times at odds, these groups planned increasingly organized campaigns of civil disobedience and nonviolence around the South, creating legal challenges to discriminatory laws. In 1961, CORE launched the Freedom Riders campaign to force the integration of the interstate transportation system. At bus stations in cities across the South, outright murderous violence awaited those attempting to integrate national bus lines.

Some of the worst violence occurred in Birmingham, Alabama, which Dr. King characterized as "probably the most thoroughly segregated city in the United States."[4] In the late 1950s and early 1960s, the bombing of Black homes and churches had become so commonplace that some called the city "Bombingham." Eugene "Bull" Connor, the city's public safety commissioner, became legendary in the region for his brutal treatment of nonviolent local and national activists.

After a young John F. Kennedy was elected in 1960 to succeed President Dwight Eisenhower, free access to the vote became a particularly active battlefront in the struggle for equal rights. Systematic efforts by activists to register Black voters in cities and small towns all over the South resulted in even more terrible violence.

A partial accounting of events in 1963 alone shows how one event after another relentlessly shocked the national conscience. The year opened with newly elected Governor George Wallace of Alabama declaring in his inaugural address his belief in "segregation now, segregation tomorrow, segregation forever."[5] That spring, the Birmingham campaign of daily demonstrations against segregation got underway, organized by Rev. Fred Shuttlesworth and the SCLC. In April, after Dr. King was arrested and jailed at one protest, he wrote and published his famous "Letter from Birmingham Jail," articulating the movement's intention to not comply with unjust laws and decrying the absence of support for the civil rights struggle from white clergy. In May, Bull Connor's decision to use attack dogs and fire hoses against peacefully protesting teenagers made international news and caused a national uproar. On June 11, Governor Wallace barred the doors of the University of Alabama in a failed attempt to keep Black students from enrolling.

The very next day, World War II veteran and National Association for the Advancement of Colored People (NAACP) voting rights organizer Medgar Evers was gunned down in front of his family by a white supremacist in the driveway of his Mississippi home. (It took thirty years for his killer to be brought to justice.) In August, the nonviolent and intensely hopeful March on Washington for Jobs and Freedom brought masses of people and impassioned speakers to the reflecting pool between the Washington Monument and the Lincoln Memorial. A few weeks later, President Kennedy had to use the National Guard to enforce the integration of Birmingham city schools. On September 15, four girls aged eleven through fourteen were killed by a bomb detonated at the 16th Street Baptist Church in Birmingham on a Sunday morning. In November, Kennedy himself was shot and killed in Dallas, Texas.

The following year, CORE workers Michael Schwerner and James Chaney, along with summer volunteer Andrew Goodman, went missing while assisting the voter registration campaign in Mississippi, a state notorious for its segregation and the subjugation of Black citizens. When the young men's buried bodies were found days later, the fact that they had been murdered for their earnest and lawful political work horrified the nation.

All this was part of the lead-up to Selma about a year later. After the 16th Street Baptist Church bombing, voting rights campaigns and demonstrations intensified in Alabama. Selma was chosen as a point of concentration for protest, though activists had seen it as a hopeless cause. In 1964 and early 1965, local activists like Amelia Boynton helped to organize thousands around Selma who were arrested at nonviolent demonstrations and jailed. Workshops helped train activists on how to endure taunting, intimidation, physical violence, and incarceration. Ordinary people learned to take a toothbrush to demonstrations, knowing they were headed to jail, sometimes for days before they could be bailed out. Though being behind bars was especially frightening for law-abiding people of color, prayer and rousing song helped keep their fears at bay.

It was the particularly wrenching death of one of these bighearted protesters that launched the first attempt to march from Selma to Montgomery. On the evening of February 18, 1965, Jimmie Lee Jackson, a local church deacon in his midtwenties, walked out of a church with his family to demonstrate for voting rights in nearby Marion, Alabama. In what was clearly a staged attack, a mass of state troopers and auxiliary police told the marchers to turn back and then set upon them as the streetlights suddenly went dark. An angry white crowd looked on as dozens of people were beaten. When the violence fell on his eighty-two-year-old grandfather, Jackson attempted to pull his family to safety in a nearby café. Pursued inside by state troopers, Jackson's mother was attacked as she tried to defend her father. When Jackson stepped up to shield his mother, two troopers set upon him, one of whom shot him twice in the stomach. Jackson was beaten as he lay on the ground outside after he tried to escape the café. The local and national press spread news of the wanton brutality the next morning.

When Jackson died in a local hospital eight days later, complications from the gunshot wounds were given as the official cause of death. However, in 1979, one of the Black doctors at the hospital, Dr. William Dinkins, revealed to researchers for the *Eyes on the Prize* television documentary that Jackson had been recovering well when two white doctors took him back into surgery.[6] He protested, but the other doctors insisted. In surgery, Dr. Dinkins noticed that Jackson appeared to be getting too much anesthetic and told the anesthesiologist to give him more oxygen. The other doctor defiantly declared that Jackson needed more anesthetic, and a few minutes later, Jackson stopped breathing.

Even without knowing about the final insults to which Jackson had been subjected, activists in the region were stunned and infuriated by the nature and extent of the violence in Marion. Only a few days later, after large funeral ceremonies had been held for Jackson in Marion and Selma, James Bevel of the SCLC, among others, called for marchers to take their outrage directly to Governor Wallace in Montgomery. Bevel, John Lewis, and local minister Hosea Williams were among those chosen to lead the marchers. Sheriff Jim Clark and Major John Cloud of the state troopers led the forces that awaited them on the other side of the Edmund Pettus Bridge.

Named for a Confederate general (like so many features in the southern landscape), the steeply arching iron bridge soars over the Alabama River dozens of feet below. Knowing the history, it is chilling to walk from the foot of the bridge up toward the unknown. You cannot see anything on the other side until you reach the very crest of the bridge, where you are completely exposed. On March 7, 1965, when about six hundred marchers first attempted to cross, what came into view was a veritable army of state troopers with clubs, whips, and gas masks backed up by the sheriff's deputies, many of them on horseback. After crossing the bridge, the protesters sang and prayed before quietly refusing to disperse. Fatefully, Major Cloud and Sheriff Clark ordered their men to advance. Their forces fell en masse upon the unresisting protesters in a crashing wave of swinging weapons and charging horses. Witnesses say that protesters screamed and dodged blows, while a white crowd behind the troopers cheered.

John Lewis, the young chairman of SNCC, led the protesters and was the first to go down under vicious blows to the head. Middle-aged Amelia Boynton, the first Black woman to run for office in the state, was knocked unconscious to the sidewalk. Men, women, and children scrambled to get out of the way of the fists, clubs, and horses until tear gas enveloped them all. The marchers retreated and were chased all the way back to Brown Chapel African Methodist Episcopal (AME) Church and other places of refuge. After the melee was over, more than ninety people needed treatment at nearby medical facilities.[7] Images of what came to be known as "Bloody Sunday" were broadcast and published around the country and all over the world.

Preparations continued for a second attempt to cross the bridge on Tuesday, March 9. Everyone had seen the kind of physical punishment that almost certainly awaited. Still, several thousand willing volunteers, Black people now joined by many more whites, lined up two-by-two behind Dr. King, who had been on his way back to Selma when the first march commenced. Resolutely, the ranks mounted the bridge again to face a greatly expanded sea of law enforcement as well as dozens more reporters. It was about three o'clock in the afternoon. This time, though, as the marchers paused near the far end of the bridge, law enforcement was told to draw back. Dr. King had been made acutely aware that by setting off down the highway he would be for the first time violating a federal order, not a local one, and so he had been convinced not to cross the bridge. Surprising everyone, he abruptly told the marchers to turn back and return to the church. Witnesses say that the masses of protesters at the front of the line met those farther back like opposing walls of water.

This was the drama into which Rev. Smith, Dudley, and the other St. Louis clergy plunged. Because of the large number of flights trying to reach Selma that day, their plane had been diverted to a small airfield outside of town. It appears that the group arrived in the early afternoon, just about the time that Dr. King was leading the "turnaround" on the bridge. Historian Taylor Branch mentions "two new planeloads of clergy from the Midwest"[8] arriving at that point. Smith remembers lining up to march but not being able to get near the bridge due to the crush and confusion. So his group went to Brown Chapel, about ten blocks away.

The chapel, like many Black churches in the South, had become the meeting place for those gathering to mobilize for social action. Smith remembers Dr. King speaking, the masses of people, and the sense of danger in the air. "Everyone went straight to the church. It was packed, hot; there was no A/C. You were wondering whether somebody might throw a bomb in there. There was no security sweep of the church or the areas downtown."[9]

Inside, Dr. King was attempting to shore up his forces and mollify SNCC leaders in particular who felt betrayed by the aborted march. Some were angry that it was only with more white people in their ranks that violence appeared to have been averted. Others expressed gratitude for the renewed forces and the outside support. Andrew Young of the SCLC told the group that there hadn't been much choice. After the morning's court order was issued prohibiting them from carrying on the march, "if we had run into that police line, they would have beaten us up with court approval."[10] The afternoon wound down with more speakers and attempts to buoy the crowds with song.

There was more violence to come. Revs. Smith and Dudley ran headlong into their own trial by fire as they left to find their plane. As colleagues and friends, the two men were used to working and socializing together. But on a day crackling with racial tension, there were some who didn't like seeing a Black man and a white man walking together for any reason. Smith and Dudley soon became aware that a hostile crowd was gathering around them.

> We were about 150 yards from the church. Carl and I looked up and we were being surrounded by about 50 or more angry white people, mostly men, who began shouting at us and calling us names. They referred to Carl as an "N" lover as they got closer and closer to us. There was some minor pushing and shoving, but Carl and I had had nonviolence training, which was a prerequisite for clergy like us who were directly involved in the movement. I was not terribly frightened at first, but as they got closer to us, it became clear that Carl and I could be harmed.[11]

Frustrated that they could not get a rise out of their victims, the tension in the crowd rose. Finally, one man's hatred boiled over, and he spat in Paul's face.

What Rev. Smith learned in that moment has shaped the rest of his life. "For one moment Carl froze because he knew I had been violated. As well as we knew each other, he had no idea how I would respond to [that]. And in a nanosecond, I thought to myself, 'I am going to die or get hurt badly because I am going to knock this guy in the mouth!'"[12]

Smith was furious at being so crudely challenged, but he had been trained not to react. In the next instant, he thought of his wife and children—and what it would mean to leave them alone. His second daughter had been born just a few weeks earlier. He knew that as a Black man who physically fought back, he might end up in jail or dead. Smith realized he had an impulse to retaliate that he wasn't sure he could control, and that made him dangerous. Whatever sort of self-control that had allowed John Lewis to walk headlong into a beating and not fight back, Smith now knew he did not possess. Nonviolent direct action on the front lines could not be his place in the struggle. Instead, he was going to spend the rest of his days finding ways to fight for what he knew was right without allowing his rage to consume him. Smith now jokes that in that moment, he realized he was better suited for a desk job. But he had no regrets. Heeding their training, Smith says, the ministers looked at each other, turned, and ran. The laughter of the thugs followed them; someone said, "Look at those niggers run."[13]

Dudley has written about what happened next.

> Suddenly we realized that a man in a pickup truck was headed right toward us, and he was not going to stop until he ran us over. We ran, and fast. We jumped over a ditch, and so did the truck. Then we saw a gas station, so we ran through the pumps (the truck could not follow) and into the office of the gas station. But then we saw that the three men who worked there were just as unfriendly as the truck driver. I remember the look in their eyes—surprised [at] our sudden entry, and openly angry with us "outsiders," Black and White together supporting civil rights. We did not look long, and we did not chat. Paul and I went out the back door as fast as we had come in the front. If there had not been a back door, we would have made one! The threat in their eyes burned hot, unmatched only by the courage we had seen among us.[14]

Dudley concludes, "Like soldiers surviving combat, this encounter with hatred and possible harm has sealed our friendship as brothers for the rest of our lives."[15]

It is fortunate that Paul and Carl did not try to reason with their attackers, because that very night, a white Unitarian minister from Boston felt the full force of white southern bigotry on Selma's back streets. Like the St. Louis group, Rev. James Reeb and more than fifty other Unitarians had arrived too late to join the attempt to cross the bridge. They decided to stay the night and were soon welcomed into a Black restaurant nearby. Reemerging after dark, they were accosted by several white men armed with clubs. While two colleagues were kicked and punched in the face, Reeb was clubbed in the head so violently that he later died from the injuries. That evening, Dr. King spoke to a crowd at Brown Chapel, thanking the remaining out-of-town clergy for their efforts and asking for prayers for Rev. Reeb and his fellows.[16] By the next morning, President Lyndon Johnson and the nation had heard that a white minister had been savaged in Selma at the hands of white thugs, and another wave of shock and outrage swept across the land.

Meanwhile, Smith had made his way back to the airfield to discover the pilots had a new concern. There were rumors that there might have been attempts to sabotage the airplanes by putting sand in the gas tanks. While Smith waited for the pilot to look over the Busch plane, the sky blackened with what looked like a severe thunderstorm. They managed to take off but were quickly grounded in Birmingham by the weather. Smith then found three lawyers from a Presbyterian church in Alton, Illinois, near St. Louis, who had to be in court the next morning. Together, they rented a car, intending to drive the six hundred miles back home.

With lawless rage thick in the air, however, just being Black and white men together in a car was dangerous. As they drove through the dark rural landscape that night, they heard on the radio about the attack on James Reeb and the other Unitarian ministers. Smith admits that "it was the only time I think I was literally afraid of being in the South because the Ku Klux Klan was on the loose and showing up in strange ways trying to intimidate us. En route to St. Louis, we were not protected by the National Guard who [were later] sent to Selma by the president."[17]

As it neared midnight, Paul asked his companions to drop him off at the home of a family he knew in Athens, Alabama, near the Alabama-Tennessee border. It is quite possible that his decision spared them all confrontation, injury, and even death. They were completely alone on a rural road in hostile territory where anyone might be looking for an opportunity to unleash his or her anger. As Paul walked up to the darkened house, his companions were anxious, wondering who would open the door where there seemed so much to fear in the dark. But the residents quickly recognized Rev. Smith and drew him in to safety. All of the men eventually made their way home unscathed.[18]

The third and successful attempt to cross the Pettus Bridge and march to Montgomery came thirteen days later. By that time, court battles and high-tension political maneuvering by Dr. King, President Johnson, and other government officials had been decided in the marchers' favor. Critical to this was the speech given by Johnson on the evening of March 15 to a joint session of Congress. In the wake of the appalling events at Selma, Johnson made the case for voting rights legislation before a huge national TV audience, saying:

> About this there can and should be no argument. Every American citizen must have an equal right to vote. . . . What happened in Selma is part of a far larger movement which reaches into every section and State of America. It

is the effort of American Negroes to secure for themselves the full blessings of American life. Their cause must be our cause too. Because it is not just Negroes, but really it is all of us, who must overcome the crippling legacy of bigotry and injustice.[19]

Everyone was stunned when Johnson ended his address by saying, "And we *shall* overcome."

The protesters set out from Selma for the third and final time on March 21, with federal troops and the National Guard in place to ensure that the march could proceed without violence. The activists crossed the bridge successfully and endured a rainy and uncomfortable four-day trek to Montgomery, where they were joined by thousands of others. In front of the imposing building at the crest of a hill that had previously served as the capital of the Confederacy, Dr. King spoke, famously asking how long people of color would have to wait to freely exercise their right to vote and participate in the political process. Black entertainers including Harry Belafonte, Sidney Poitier, and Dick Gregory roused the crowd to new heights of joy and hope. Sadly, even the euphoria of that day was marred by news of violence. Ku Klux Klan members killed a middle-aged Michigan woman named Viola Liuzzo who was at the wheel of her car on the Jefferson Davis Highway that evening. Her crime had been helping to ferry back to Selma some of the stalwart marchers who had finally made it to Montgomery.

While civil rights laws had been passed in 1957, 1960, 1963, and 1964, it took yet another piece of legislation—the Voting Rights Act of 1965—to fully address persistent barriers to enfranchisement. The Voting Rights Act prohibited state and local entities from devising discriminatory obstacles to registration and voting. It also laid out a process of government oversight in parts of the country where such obstructionist methods had been the norm. Thereafter, Black people were able to register and vote, many for the first time in their lives.

Remarkably, Rev. Paul Smith, representing the Presbytery of St. Louis, was in the room at the White House the day President Johnson signed this most consequential bill into law. John Lewis, who became a revered and long-serving member of Congress, was also present that day. Lewis later wrote that the signing "represented a high point in modern America, probably the nation's finest hour in terms of civil rights. . . . It was certainly the last act for the movement as I knew it. Something was born in Selma during the course of that year, but something died there too. The road of nonviolence had essentially run out. Selma was the last act."[20]

Only a few short days later, the most destructive rioting ever seen in this country broke out in the Watts neighborhood of Los Angeles. Thirty-four died, hundreds were injured, and thousands were arrested. Lewis had seen this coming because so many deep problems remained: "The lack of concern on the part of the American public and the lack of concern and courage of the federal government breed bitterness and frustration. Where lack of jobs, intolerable housing, police brutality and other frustrating conditions exist, it is possible that violence and massive street demonstrations may develop."[21]

Though there have been monumental breakthroughs, most notably having a Black president in the White House from 2009 until 2017, many of the same deep, structural problems continue to plague us. Levels of economic inequality have ballooned to new heights. Ordinary Americans are still fighting to find affordable housing, health insurance, and decent jobs. After the death of Michael Brown in 2014 and later George Floyd in 2020, massive street protests brought media attention to the unending stream of Black deaths at the hands of law enforcement. The election of President Donald J. Trump has emboldened new generations of racist and xenophobic extremists to publicly proclaim their views. Before his death on July 17, 2020, John Lewis surely saw the terrible irony that the exact same statement could be made today, more than fifty years later.

Even the principles enshrined in the Voting Rights Act are being debated anew. In 2013, a conservative Supreme Court greatly weakened the Act by removing the federal oversight requirement for voting districts that had historically discriminated against some of their citizens. In the *Shelby County v. Holder* decision, Chief Justice John Roberts wrote for the majority that the extraordinary measures enacted to address the "insidious and pervasive evil" of racial discrimination in voting were unnecessary, since "the conditions that originally justified these measures no longer characterize voting in the covered jurisdictions."[22]

Many were not surprised when Roberts was quickly proven wrong. Since that key Supreme Court decision, state lawmakers have unabashedly created obstacles to exercising political power in Texas, North Carolina, Alabama, and other states.[23] Stricter voter ID laws have been enacted; days, times, and methods for voting have been curtailed; and new maps have been drawn with almost mathematical precision to disempower some while benefiting others. Before the 2018 elections, twenty-three states enacted laws making it more difficult to vote.[24] Meanwhile, the Trump administration has railed against "illegal" voting, and the only recent provable case of it occurred in his own party.[25] As civil rights historian Robert Pratt has observed, "it would appear that the lessons of Selma have yet to be learned."[26]

In order to understand these contradictory realities, we need to look more carefully at the details of our shared history. One compelling way to do that is to follow the life story of someone who has been there, with his eyes open, through it all.

CHAPTER 2

On Granny's Porch

South Bend, Indiana, was a thriving industrial town when Paul Smith was born in September 1935. Smith grew up surrounded by a loving family, and his character was shaped in particular by his mother's mother, a powerful personality. "Granny" was the lodestar in Smith's life; from his point of view as a child, the world revolved around her.

> I was very mischievous as a youngster and always in trouble . . . my grandmother's house was 10 minutes away . . . I don't care what I had done bad or wrong, if I got to my grandmother, she would say, "Leave that boy alone!" My parents could never, ever discipline me if she was around. She saw something in me I couldn't see in myself until much later.
>
> She ran a rooming house. Her name was Odie Overby. In the evening, she sat in a rocking chair on her porch. There was a little chair right next to her where I sat. . . . Everyone knew Mrs. Overby. So, when people were coming home from work, they would stop and say hello. Doctors, lawyers, people from [the] pool hall. . . .
>
> She'd say to people going by, "Come up and sit a spell. How's your family?" Everyone knew her. Guys would tip their hat. . . . It made no difference what station a person had in life . . . Granny was the go-to person. She talked to everybody. And I sat next to my grandmother, listening to these stories.[1]

Looking back, Rev. Smith believes he learned how to engage and comfort people by watching his grandmother interact with neighbors in this vibrant community. Her wisdom was extended to all, and it seemed to touch everyone who reached for it. "There was something wonderful and magical about the way Granny listened. The people she listened to always seemed

Odie Wingo Overby, Indiana
Dunes, Indiana, 1940.
Courtesy of the Smith Family.

restored and refreshed. Little did I realize at the time that this would be her wonderful legacy to me."[2]

Odie Wingo Overby acquired her worldly perspective over the course of a long and eventful life. She was born in 1883 in Cuba, Kentucky, a tiny town in the extreme southwestern corner of the state known as the "Jackson Purchase."[3] In 1851, when the mighty Illinois Central Railroad began connecting Chicago to the South,[4] the rails bypassed Cuba while bringing prosperity to other towns in the region. Locally, it is thought that nearby Wingo was founded around 1854 by a man named Jerman Wingo who had the foresight to allow the railroad to run its tracks across his land.[5] Wingo began selling goods there, and the town that coalesced eventually took his name.

Two of Smith's cousins have traced Odie's lineage back to a mixed-race relationship tied to this town. The family believes that Odie's father Ferdinand ("Paw Paw") was named Wingo because Jerman was his father. The family has located public records that show an enslaved woman named

Maria or Mirah was the mother of Ferdinand and his older brother George. While Jerman was married to a white woman with whom he had eleven other children, it appears that he took responsibility for Ferdinand and his brother.

Smith's cousin Bernard Streets remembers Odie's mother Nancy Wingo, known as "Mammy," talking about this. "Mammy Wingo told me Paw Paw's father was his owner and that his father always looked out after him and his siblings as best he could. She said Paw Paw is a 'true Wingo' and that his surname was taken because he was his white father's son and not simply because he was the slave, [a] piece of property and just tacked on the owner's name. Mammy often stated that Paw Paw was 'blood kin' of the Wingos."[6]

The Graves County government website appears to corroborate the story, though the site's sources and authorship are opaque. An online description of the town of Wingo notes that, "As Kentucky came into the Union as a slaveholding state, Mr. and Mrs. [Jerman] Wingo could own slaves and had several. Many of them took his name and were willed land when he died. Even after they were freed, many of them refused to leave Mr. Wingo."[7]

Odie and her mother further asserted that Ferdinand was directly related to a Cherokee chief named Wingo. Dr. Smith says he knew Odie was part Cherokee but had never heard the details. Another family story, however, alludes to a surprising level of mutual respect and sociability among members of this heterogeneous clan. Streets recalls Mammy saying that every summer, the entire Wingo family, "white, colored, Indian, and all mixtures would gather for a kinfolks' picnic."[8]

While people of African descent in this country can often trace cross-racial/cross-cultural ancestry, holding annual reunions of these kin is not known to have been common at the time. But Smith's ancestors seem to have been unusual in many ways. Odie's parents were not farmers like most of their neighbors; instead, they ran a boarding house for people of color somewhere in the environs of Cuba and Wingo, perhaps on land inherited from Jerman Wingo. Sometime after the turn of the twentieth century, the family moved to the popular Kentucky spa town of Dawson Springs where their successful inn, the "Wingo House," launched the family into the middle class.

The inn attracted wealthy people of color who came to enjoy the salubrious effects of the local hot springs. Streets was told that business was good.

Our great-grandparents had a small staff of housekeepers, yardmen, kitchen helpers, and a wagon driver who would go to the railroad station there and collect the guests and transport them to the guesthouse. Paw Paw Ferd was a gourmet chef, known widely for his tasty cuisine creations. . . . Mammy was the business manager and supervisor of staff, as well as the bookkeeper. She taught herself accounting and obviously was good at it, because other establishments hired her to officially audit their books. She told me that the other business owners trusted her work and paid her well.[9]

Streets remembers Mammy saying to him, "These quality white folks never called me by my first name. They always addressed me as 'Mrs. Wingo.'"[10]

Remarkably, a six-month diary written by Nancy and Ferd's daughter Odie between December 1901 and May 1902 has survived for nearly 120 years.[11] This treasure, written when Odie was eighteen years old, was given to Rev. Smith by his mother's sister, Odie Mae. Receiving this gift in his forties may very well have helped reinforce Smith's own journal-writing practice. But on its own, the diary constitutes a unique window into the mind and world of a young woman of color at the turn of the twentieth century.[12]

Some of the first entries written in early December 1901 give a sense of Odie's preoccupations and her buoyant spirit:

Arose 15 to 7 o'clock dressed & cleaned up the house ate breakfast & left for school thinking this was examination day. Left my book at home to my surprise. Miss Lou made Carrie & I go back home & get them. Mailed Ed Holland letter. Willie gave me a tablet for examination. Oh; Diary he is the most adorable fellow. Diary I am as happy as a lark & Pearl says she is as happy as a jay.

   B. Wingo[13]

                                                        Dec 6 weather cloudy

Arose & dressed for school & Carrie was so long about coming I had to go after her. On our way to school met Mr. Duke had a few words with him. Wonder why Burnett doesn't write? How glad I am to see this snow. I have been playing snowball isn't it fine sport Pearl? I dreamed I was making love[14] with Mr. Mallery. Will it ever come true? No never; well I don't know.

   B.[15]

                                                        Dec 7, 1901 weather cloudy

Arose at 7 o'clock with a very sick headache though I feel some better now. I helped Mamma iron, carried the clothes home. Went to the train to see

Mr. Mitchel[l]. Papa brought me a letter from my dear friend Ellie. Oh; how glad. Oh; say Diary I have been trying an old saying: cut [your finger] nails seven Sundays & the young man comes on the 7 Sunday will be your H. Oh: say wouldn't it be funny if no one comes, then I guess I will be an old maid.[16]

Dec 8 weather cloudy

Aros[e] & dressed for S.S.[17] [H]ad a very good S.S. Rev. Grey of Hopkinsville preached at 11, o'clock. Intended to preach Sunday night but the rain prevented it. Dr. Flemister came today to see Miss Larkins & she is as happy as a Lark. I have just answered Dutch & my jewel's letter.

Bee[18]

The three most common subjects Odie mentions in the diary are letter writing, "going to town," and meeting the railroad trains. Presumably, much of this hustle and bustle revolved around guests in her parents' house. Odie mentions exchanging letters, visits, gifts, and photographs with over a hundred people in the course of the six-month diary. She writes most often about her parents, aunts and uncles, and her grandmother, but dozens of other people are mentioned by name multiple times. Another fifty individuals are mentioned once. Sixteen different ministers are named in the entries, as are twelve girls who may have been relatives or friends.

Odie attended school and church and had a busy social life including regular "prayer," "literary," "society," and "watch" meetings. In addition to household chores, Odie's responsibilities included helping her mother with sewing, washing, and ironing. It is likely that at least some of this work was for the boarders who were staying at the house. She also mentions working for wages at a local hotel.

The young Miss Wingo also had time for leisure. Among the pastimes Odie mentions are reading; singing and playing music; playing checkers, dominoes, and croquet; looking at magazines; and going walking with friends and family. Twice, she writes about having her fortune told. Odie and her friends sat for at least two photographic portraits that are still in the possession of Dr. Smith's family.[19] She mentions two popular novels by name—Thelma and Two Orphans.

Odie was particularly excited by the railroad; she mentions trains or train personnel more than a dozen times in the diary. Odie slips easily into a distinctive argot when she talks about the intriguing young men who worked on the rails. She calls them "the kids" and "the Dining Car boys." She obviously gets a thrill out of "cutting a dash with the R.R. boys."

Odie Wingo (right),
Dawson Springs,
Kentucky, 1899.
Courtesy of the Smith
Family.

Odie writes of towns like Hopkinsville, Paducah, Madisonville, Mayfield, and Cadiz, which are within an eighty-mile radius of where she was born and raised. However, she also mentions cities like Louisville, Chicago, Atlanta, and Denver. This suggests that Odie had awareness of and/or communication with people across a broad expanse of the American Midwest.

Viewed through the narrow window of these diary entries, Odie Wingo's teenage life revolved around home, church, school, and work. She mentions one or two moments of sadness during the months she wrote in the diary, but she does not appear to have wanted for anything material, and she appears to have been surrounded by an active and congenial community.

Odie Wingo was a light-skinned member of the Black community, and few facts are known about the ways this shaped her life. She says nothing in the diary that even hints at the fact that she was living in a part of Kentucky that became known for its violence and racism in the decades after the Civil War.[20] Kentucky never joined the Confederacy, and white Kentuckians fought on both sides of the Civil War. After the war, particularly in the rich farmlands of the Jackson Purchase, there was sharp disagreement about whether the federal government could abolish slavery. Due to resistance from slaveholders in the state, the Thirteenth Amendment giving full citizens' rights to formerly enslaved people was not ratified, and slavery continued to be legal for decades. This left the status of formerly enslaved people dangerously ambiguous.[21]

After the war, newly freed people of color in Kentucky began exercising their rights by voting, running for office, starting businesses, and pursuing professional careers. Black people began to sit on juries, to become doctors and lawyers in small but significant numbers, and to hold public office. There was a Black city councilman in nearby Hopkinsville between 1895 and 1907, and "others . . . served as deputy sheriff, county coroner, and county physician."[22]

These developments did not sit well with many whites, however, particularly in the Jackson Purchase region, which had strongly supported secession from the Union in contrast to the rest of the state.[23] Many migrants to the Purchase had family in Tennessee and the Carolinas, and their large-scale Kentucky plantations growing cotton and tobacco tied them economically to the South. It appears they had southern attitudes about race as well.[24] Rather stunningly, the Thirteenth, Fourteenth, and Fifteenth Amendments were only formally ratified in the state in 1976.[25]

Prosperous Black families came to be viewed as an economic threat in late nineteenth- and early twentieth-century Kentucky.[26] The lawlessness and violence that ensued included "whitecapping"—using threats, destruction of property, and violence to coerce people deemed "undesirable" to flee from their homes. At least 350 known lynchings were perpetrated across Kentucky between 1860 and 1939, and many others no doubt went unreported.[27] Some three-quarters of these lynching victims were people of color. Nearly half of these killings occurred between 1875 and 1899 while Odie was growing up. More ominously, two counties in the Jackson Purchase, Fulton and Odie's own Graves County, were among those statewide that had the highest total number of lynchings.[28]

Furthermore, there is evidence that Mayfield, the Graves county seat, "richly deserved its reputation as a hostile place for blacks."[29] In December 23, 1896, for instance, a *New York Times* article blared, "All Mayfield Under

Arms: Excitement over the Kentucky Race War."[30] A Black resident had been lynched, and a note pinned to his body listed others who would be next if they did not leave town. One of those listed armed himself and shot back when the vigilantes came to find him. This stoked rumors of armed Black mobs converging on Mayfield.[31] The *Times* article mentions Wingo as one of the places where "the negroes had massed . . . 250 in number, and . . . every one had some sort of weapon."[32] As the news of these armed gatherings spread, the white population responded by barricading their homes and passing out weapons. A special train was organized to bring white reinforcements from Fulton to Mayfield.

The *Times* reported the next day that three people had been killed and several houses burned down. However, cooler heads ultimately prevailed.

> Fears of further race troubles are rapidly passing away. At a mass meeting last night [a] petition, signed by over 100 Negroes, asking for peace, was read. The excitement was appeased and many of the armed citizens and volunteers from surrounding towns returned to their homes. . . .
>
> Will Suett, the negro killed yesterday morning at the railroad station, had just returned from St. Louis to spend Christmas at home. His death was declared unprovoked, and the white citizens are now raising a fund to support his aged mother.[33]

In her diary, Odie mentions nothing about violent conflict close to home. While it is hard to imagine she did not know about such recent events, it is difficult to assess the way mob violence would have affected a teenager at the time. A young woman's diary might be the place where she would write about what frightened her—or, alternately, it could be the perfect place to banish such thoughts. What *can* be said is that the irrepressible diary writer asserts herself as a girl surrounded by friends and family, secure in her community and unafraid of the wider world.

Odie's congenial upbringing and vibrant personality seem to have carried her into a happy marriage. Her first husband was John "Johnny Boy" Wells Johnson, who had been born in Cadiz, Kentucky, in 1879. Odie was twenty-five and John close to thirty when they married. The couple moved to Chicago where they had a daughter, Evangeline, in 1909.

Streets says that Granny told him Johnson surprised her with the deed to land where they hoped to build a house. Yet very early in their marriage, they were instead confronted with a tragedy—the death of their first child.

Wedding party of John Johnson and Odie Wingo, Dawson Springs, Kentucky, 1908.
Courtesy of the Smith Family.

Census data and a death record show that Evangeline died in March 1911, at
the age of two and a half. It is not clear what caused her death, but she died
in Chicago and was buried in Dawson Springs.

This may have been the first real crisis of Odie's life. There is no record of
her thoughts in this difficult period. However, the strength of her marriage
shows in the fact that she and Johnson went on to have two more daughters—Josephine (Paul Smith's mother) in February 1912 and Odie's name-
sake Odie Mae in November 1913. John Johnson's occupation was given as
"Post Office clerk" on the death record of his first daughter, so it seems the
couple had some financial resources to lean upon.

This young family of four did not get to enjoy their life together for very
long, however. Within a few years, they were swept into a global-scale ca-
tastrophe. In 1918, a devastating flu pandemic hit cities around the world,
and John Johnson became one of the millions who died though he was not
yet forty. While Odie survived the crisis, Johnson's death left her alone at
thirty-five with two daughters under the age of seven.

Shortly thereafter, Odie returned to Dawson Springs to rebuild her life. At least there, her parents could help care for her daughters while she sought ways to earn a living. One measure of her courage and determination is shown in how, as a widowed mother, Odie went on to graduate from West Kentucky Industrial College for Negroes in Paducah and is said to have worked in local schools as a teacher.

Odie also married again. The family has an old photographic portrait of Winstead Overby that shows him to be a handsome, well-dressed man. It appears that he and Odie met in Dawson Springs and then moved the family to South Bend, Indiana, sometime around 1922. Streets relates that Odie wanted her daughters to call Overby "Daddy." However, Streets was told that the girls could never bring themselves to comply. How Overby felt about being a stepfather is not known.

Overby owned a rambling house with a porch at 134 Birdsell Street on the western side of South Bend. Sited on a triangular piece of land bounded by Birdsell, Orange Street, and West Colfax Avenue, the house was only about a block and a half from the center of an African American business district located at Birdsell and Liston streets. A local historian has called the area "a complete city neighborhood in which businesses, single homes and apartment buildings were mixed in with schools, churches and other public buildings."[34] There were funeral parlors, several hotels, restaurants, and a theater.

Corroborating Paul Smith's memories, the historian reports that on Birdsell and Washington streets, "a two-story brick building housed Ford's barbershop and Hank's Pool Hall on the ground floor. Above these, the African American political leadership of South Bend met."[35] A new NAACP office came into being at Pilgrim Baptist Church in 1919.[36] Odie herself helped found the Greater St. John Missionary Baptist Church, which was situated two blocks from her home, in July 1922. The neighborhood was less than a mile from the manufacturing plants of companies like Studebaker, Singer Sewing Machines, and Oliver Chilled Plow. These attracted European immigrants and Great Migration families from the South. The New York Central and South Shore railroad lines connected this part of the city to Chicago and beyond.

For several years, the family thrived in this cosmopolitan environment. However, their halcyon days did not last. In November 1927, an accident shattered their world. A local newspaper story gives the details.

NEGRO KILLED BY FREIGHT TRAIN

Winstead S. Overby, age 62, coloured, 134 North Birdsell St. died at 5:22 o'clock this morning as a result of injuries sustained when he was struck a few minutes before by a New York Central (Illinois division) freight train at the Arnold Street crossing and run over subsequently by a yard engine which was following the train. Mangled, he still showed signs of life when the police ambulance reached the scene but died on his way to the St. Joseph's Hospital. It was sleeting at the time and it is believed that he did not see the train. He was on his way to work at the time of the accident. Surviving are his widow . . . and two children.[37]

In this way, Odie once again lost her husband, and her family was again shaken to its core. It seems especially sad that the trains Odie had found so exciting as a teenager caused this devastating loss. A receipt saved by the family shows that Mrs. Overby paid one of the local morticians $250 in full for her husband's funeral two days later.

Odie married again ten years later to Claybron Merriweather, but the family believes that he was much older than she and that the marriage did not last long. The fact that Odie used Overby's name after Merriweather died suggests where her heart lay.

For many of her later years, Odie lived in the house on Birdsell Street. She later told grandson Bernard that Overby had "been a very nice man and that she was appreciative that he had left her a nice, big house."[38] That critical resource allowed her to be self-sufficient and to bring her mother to live with her as well. Mammy died in 1958 at age ninety-three, having outlived Ferd by twenty years. Mrs. Odie Wingo Overby herself died in 1975 at age ninety-one.

In contrast to—and perhaps because of—the loss and upheaval experienced by his grandmother and his mother, Rev. Smith's own childhood was quiet and stable. On September 20, 1935, when he was born, Odie was in her fifties and her house on Birdsell Street was the center of the family's life. Paul's sister Marlene remembers that the house had two bedrooms upstairs, one bedroom downstairs, and two apartments attached out back. Paul recalls, "Granny was the matriarch of the family and all the family gatherings were at her house because it was so large and could handle all of us. Granny was my Sunday school teacher and the pastor at the church respected her very much. . . . She tutored all of us."[39]

The family had reason to celebrate when Odie's daughter Josephine Johnson married Leonard Smith in October 1929. Their first daughter Joan was born a year later. The family lived on North Carlisle Street, ten short blocks from Odie's home. The Smiths raised five children in all: Joan, Marlene, Leonard, Paul, and William. As the two oldest, Joan and Marlene formed a natural unit. They were followed by another duo, Lennie and Paul. Then came Willie, the youngest, who was doted on by Marlene. Their bond was such that the two were not allowed to sit together in the back of the car, because they would "carry on" so much.

Smith remembers that as a child, whenever he visited his grandmother, she made sure the children went to visit Mammy's room to say hello. Their great-grandmother often gave them some coins from her purse. Being the oldest boys, Lennie and Paul spent extra time at Granny's house. They looked after the yard, the chickens, and the coal furnace. The boys had to stop by each morning to clean out the ashes and load in new coal, and they "banked" the coals each night. It was strictly understood that the *only* time they were allowed to go into the pool hall down the street was when Granny sent the boys to buy chewing tobacco—her "spark plugs."

Both Granny's mettle and the community's feelings about her are clear in another story Smith tells about Granny's house. "Somebody tried to get her to buy a furnace one time, a charlatan," he said. "When she found out she was being cheated, she confronted the guy and he beat her up. Well, when the guys at the pool hall heard about it, they went out and found the guy and kicked the daylights out of him!"[40] Smith says they looked out for Mrs. Overby more carefully after that.

Odie was regularly listed in census records as "Negro," but in 1930, she appears to have been counted as "White." Odie's light skin later helped her get a job at Sears. Smith says he doesn't remember her ever purposefully "passing" as white, but Paul's wife Fran recalls Odie saying that nobody at the job asked her "what she was" and she just didn't say. The fact that she walked to work from her home in the Black neighborhood never came up. One year, she took grandson Paul to Sears to pick out a bike. He says, "They didn't know she was Black. They asked if she wanted it on account. She said, 'What's that?' Black people didn't have credit! She paid cash in full for the bike."[41]

At age eleven or twelve, Paul expressed an interest in being baptized, and Odie used her forceful personality and connections to make it happen. This meant asking for help from the rival Baptist church nearby.

I was not baptized in my home church. We didn't have a baptistery, a pool. I was baptized at the church down the street. The minister there lived at Granny's until he had a house. . . . If you didn't have a baptistery, you were baptized in the St. Joe River.

So, I was baptized at Pilgrim Baptist church. My parents didn't know it until Granny told them. Granny was there, my whole family. Granny told my parents it was going to happen. Granny set it up. She said, "This is my grandson and he *will* be baptized."[42]

Today, very few of the buildings Paul Smith knew as a child remain. Granny's house, his parents' house, the Black business district, the pool hall—all have been torn down. The stout brick "natatorium," an indoor swimming facility nearby,[43] has been repurposed as a Civil Rights Heritage Center run by Indiana University at South Bend. Locally, some objected to housing the museum in a building that had been segregated from its opening in 1922 until 1950. A successful fight to desegregate the natatorium was led by prominent Black residents including lawyers J. Chester and Elizabeth Fletcher Allen.[44] To Paul and Lennie, what mattered most was being the first Black kids completely free to use that big pool.

The hulking, empty factory buildings with gigantic chimneys that can still be seen a few miles away were once the heart of South Bend's economy. Starting around the time of World War I, South Bend became an industrial city attracting immigrants and southern Blacks alike. As one local historian has noted, "When white immigration declined after 1914, scores of Black laborers from the South arrived to take their places in the factories of Studebaker, Singer, and Westinghouse. Census numbers grew from 604 in 1910 to more than 1219 by 1920."[45]

By 1930, there were about 3,400 Black people out of a total population of 100,000 in South Bend.[46] By the time Paul turned five, World War II had begun, and industrial cities were brimming with work. Smith remembers impressive gentlemen like Mr. Graham, who worked at Bendix Brakes, and Mr. Poindexter, who lived next door and worked in the foundry of Studebaker. Though he was still a child, Smith remembers a relatively well-integrated community.

In the factories, Blacks and whites worked together. Black men worked in the foundries; they did the most dangerous jobs. If there was a job stamping papers, say, a white person would get that job. If you were Black, you looked for a job at Studebaker's or Bendix—you couldn't get one at Singer. But everyone lived in the same community. [It] was as mixed as any place I have ever lived.

There were immigrants from Yugoslavia, Poland, all over . . . their mentality permeated the place for me and my classmates.[47]

A Black sociologist who lived in Smith's South Bend neighborhood earlier in the century clarifies that Singer, Westinghouse, and Oliver Chilled Plow all employed Black workers along with Studebaker.[48] Other eyewitnesses have testified to the fact that the immigrant whites and southern Blacks got along well since "they were all newcomers."[49] A scholar of Black history in Indiana sums up the period that Paul remembers: "For most blacks in Indiana, both older residents and newcomers, the war years were a period of hope and rising expectations."[50]

South Bend differed from other industrial cities in the state. In 1930, Black residents in South Bend made up only about 2% of the total population compared to 12% in Indianapolis and 18% in Gary.[51] It has been noted that pre–World War I, South Bend had no Black neighborhood, de facto or otherwise, and "blacks had been accepted in the same restaurants and other places of public accommodation patronized by whites."[52] South Bend never built segregated high schools like those in Gary and Indianapolis.

The presence of Notre Dame gave South Bend a distinctive character. Its students famously chased the Ku Klux Klan away in 1924 when the Klan, which was anti-Catholic, attempted to hold a rally in downtown South Bend.[53] Father Theodore Hesburgh, who was president of the university between 1952 and 1987, was well known for joining civil rights protests with Dr. King and Rabbi Abraham Heschel.[54] South Bend's J. Chester Allen was one of two Black representatives elected to the state legislature in 1938, and he became a visible and respected champion of Black citizens' rights statewide.[55]

It was fortunate that Smith's grandmother and parents arrived some years ahead of the crowd; they secured good homes in a city that became badly overcrowded during and after World War II. Later migrants had few options for housing. The federal government built some housing for workers necessary to the war effort, but the construction was meant to be temporary. With the influx of more and more Great Migration immigrants from the South, including 5,600 in the year 1940, slumlike conditions developed in some Black housing districts downtown.[56] Meanwhile, housing segregation all over the city became more pronounced as it became clear to white residents that incoming workers intended to stay.[57]

People like lawyers J. Chester and Elizabeth Allen pushed back. In the mid-1950s, they led a group that formed a corporation in secret, bought land, and built houses for African Americans who bought in to the project.[58]

The resulting middle-class housing development became known as "Better Homes of South Bend." A whole generation of kids benefited from growing up there, and most of the houses are still occupied.

All this made it likely that Odie Overby's rooming house had a steady supply of customers. Paul's parents were people of modest means, but they too lived comfortably. Paul remembers a racially and economically flexible community.

> My classmates were more white than Black probably. . . . A couple of white people joined our church—they were teachers. They had a lot to do with my going to college. One of them, Mrs. Bolden, became good friends with my parents and my aunts. She would come check in with my parents about how I was doing in school. . . . Even our high school basketball team was as integrated as any today.
>
> I never felt like an outsider racially. We had white people in our homes; we were in theirs. . . . We were not afraid of white people or intimidated. When we were in the rich neighborhoods at lunchtime, we went inside and sat at the table with everybody else. We were all there together, immigrants, white and Blacks.[59]

Paul's father Leonard was too short to be hired for factory work. Instead, he became a master cleaner in the Holmes' Silver Crystal China Shop. Smith says, "Our store was where white families registered their daughters who were getting married. We all worked there at one time or other. Mr. Holmes had two children of his own. His wife kept everything in order. They both loved my dad. He helped my dad get a car—went down to the car dealership with him to make sure he didn't get mistreated."[60]

In addition to their regular jobs, "Smitty" and Josephine catered parties in the big houses and fancy neighborhoods across the river on the east side of town.

> My dad had had very little formal education. Twyckenham Drive was the rich part of town where it was all white people. We went to those homes and made good money working for those families.
>
> Now that I think about it, class-wise there was no reason for my daddy to be there with those people. But everyone knew my parents, respected them, trusted them—Knute Rockne and the corporate people. In fact, [my parents] helped recruit the other people who worked [in those homes]. The crème de la crème—my mother and father knew them and were known by them.[61]

Leonard did not have the elite education his sons would one day receive, but like his mother-in-law Odie, he played a central role in a community that had long been politically aware. Smith remembers meetings held over the barbershop and pool hall.[62]

> My father was one of the organizers. They met in the doctor's offices upstairs every Saturday. I asked my dad, "Why are all these Black men gathering?" My father said, "Because we're talking about making changes."
>
> This was about 1945. I went with my father and brothers to these meetings. You knew something important was going on. Think about it! It was serious. It was spirited. My father had the least amount of education. But it was his job to tell the Knute Rocknes that [the local men] had met, and [the corporate folks] needed to come talk with that group.... We had a lot of hand-me-down clothing, but everyone respected my dad.[63]

Paul was recognized in school for both athletic and musical talent. A "Pupil's Report" in June 1947 from South Bend's General Arts Studio notes of the twelve-year-old: "Paul is one of our best pupils. Encourage him all you can for he has a good future in music."

He also displayed such a gift for preaching that he was offered his own church at sixteen. Like John Lewis who preached and held funerals for the family chickens as a young boy,[64] Paul's parents said he pretended to be preaching from the time he was about eight years old. He was quickly recognized for his abilities and supported in his ambitions, not just by his parents but also by the other adults around him. He recalls:

> I would walk into the barbershop with my dad and two brothers, and people would say, "Smitty, have your son say something to us." And I would.
>
> I was often asked to recite poetry, read scripture, and give a message early on in my life. Remember, the Black church and community was a place of nurture and opportunity for all of us. If you even *thought* you wanted to be something, the community was there to encourage you on. I do not remember much about my early topics except they always had to do with inspiring people to reach their potential; they were messages of hope in the midst of despair and I often used the Psalms and the Gospels for my texts.[65]

His sister Marlene remembers that after the family went to Sunday service, Paul often disappeared to preach elsewhere. Rev. Bernard L. White, the new minister at St. John's when Paul was growing up, took it upon himself to mentor young men like Paul. He allowed the boys who showed promise into the pulpit to "try it out." Rev. White was young and energetic, and St. John's thrived under his leadership. Paul recalls that the reverend's ministry "addressed the racial and political issues of the day, including challenging the white political structure."[66] NAACP meetings were held at St. John's, and national civil rights leaders visited to speak.

Given the brutal realities of African American history in this country, it should be no surprise that Black church services and preaching have developed powerful, distinctive characteristics. In an update of a classic 1970 text,[67] Rev. Henry H. Mitchell cites the preacher's use of the vernacular, a focus on the listener's survival needs, the preacher's close identification with the listener, and the use of call and response interplay as key components of a Black preaching style. The Black preacher is allowed broad freedom of expression, whatever might be needed to allow their "inner fervor" to surface.[68] Listeners seek an emotional experience; they want to be "stirred . . . stretched, helped and fed."[69] They are attuned to the ways a creative preacher makes the Word come alive on a given day. Audience participation is central, Mitchell says: "When [relevant] content and imaginative delivery grips a congregation, the ensuing dialogue between preacher and people is the epitome of creative worship."[70] He notes further that services should end with celebration and reach for transcendence: "The Black congregation is one of the most dynamic and healing places known to humanity."[71]

Jason E. Shelton and Michael O. Emerson, a Black and white team of sociologists, have much more recently identified what they see as five "building blocks" that make Black Protestant faith at the group level distinctive.[72] These include valuing the experiential over the doctrinal, seeing faith as central to survival, being open to the mystery in life, being attuned to the miraculous in the everyday, and being explicitly committed to social justice and equality for all.

Such qualities were already surfacing in Paul's teenage years, attracting the attention of leaders from other Black Baptist churches.

> It was almost like recruiting. When I would speak, the recruiters would be there. And the people would say, "That kid is going somewhere! We better get that kid now!"
>
> They'd say, "Why go to college? You don't need to go to college. We'll take care of you. We got it. What do you need? A car? We'll give you a car. Money? We have money. What else do you need?" And Granny said, "You *need* an education!"[73]

Paul was thrilled with the way he was treated when invited to preach in Cassopolis, just over the state line in Michigan. But this was not what Odie and Josephine had in mind for him. "I was *not* going to be a Jack Leg preacher! That is a term for Black ministers who had little or no formal education but were charismatic and great speakers. My parents and my grandmother would hear none of that. I had a gift, but it needed to be honed. [They] were saying, 'You need to want more. You can't settle [for] being some boy wonder.'"[74]

Smith's family and his community pushed him into a wider world. He believes that the Allens were instrumental in helping him get into Talladega College. Elizabeth Allen's father had been a builder for the American Missionary Association, and both he and his daughter had graduated from Talladega. With their encouragement, Smith won an academic scholarship that made it possible for him to attend their alma mater.

Ever caring and pragmatic, Granny wanted to be the last to speak to the young man before he got on the train to go south to college. Paul recalls, "I'm sixteen. She was the grandmother who doted on me, my Sunday school teacher. My mother and father are on the train getting my seat, and Granny said, 'Leonard, Josephine, why don't you go? I'd like to talk to my grandson.' They got off the train."[75]

Odie had three parting contributions to make, Smith recalls. First, she gave her grandson $25. The fact that tuition at Talladega for the year was $350 suggests just how sizeable this gift was. Then she asked him, without warning and in rather blunt language, if he knew about sex. He says, "I almost fainted. I said, 'Well no,' because I didn't really know. I almost fainted!"[76]

Granny made sure he understood—if you don't know what you're doing, don't blunder into anything you will regret. She then imparted a final piece of wisdom that revealed she was not as nonchalant about race as she had appeared to her grandson: "Don't get involved with anyone darker than you!"[77]

CHAPTER 3

Riding the Hummingbird into the Fire

In September 1952, just before his seventeenth birthday, Paul Smith packed his bags and left his family for the first time, boarding the Illinois Central Railroad bound for Talladega College in Alabama. While his grandmother had ridden the train north toward the urban opportunities of Chicago and South Bend, Smith was riding "The Hummingbird" south into the heartland of Jim Crow. He would soon encounter the first virulent racial bigotry of his life.

His college was one of what are now known as the HBCUs—Historically Black Colleges and Universities. Most of these were built and staffed after the Civil War by northern abolitionist church groups like the American Missionary Association. Great Migration parents wanted their children and grandchildren to attend these prestigious institutions, but it meant sending their loved ones back to the regions they had worked so hard to leave behind. The older people were aware of the ironies involved and anxious about the teenagers' safety. By Paul's account, his mother and father were "terrified."

The parents of these college-bound students had good reason to be afraid. It was only three years later that Emmett Till was murdered in central Mississippi, two hundred miles to the west. Till might one day have ridden the Hummingbird to college himself. Instead, he was tortured and died at age fourteen. After that, it may only have been the protection provided by A. Philip Randolph's unionized train porters that made it possible for Black parents to put their sons and daughters on a train going south.[1]

Like many young men on those journeys, though, Smith's focus was on new challenges, new surroundings, and pretty girls. He had not thought much about the fact that interstate transportation was segregated.

Paul Smith,
South Bend,
Indiana, 1952.
Courtesy of the
Smith Family.

I got on the Hummingbird in Chicago; I went by myself. And what's important about the Hummingbird is that on that train there were kids from Illinois,
Indiana. . . . We had our own cars. The porters looked out for us. We got on
with forty or fifty kids going to Tennessee State, Fisk, Alabama A and M, and
all those southern schools. . . .

    I didn't know enough to be scared. I was falling in love—I'd never *seen* so
many pretty girls! The idea was to get a seat next to one of them. We used
to say [you'd] fall in love in Chicago, then you'd get to Indianapolis and see
somebody finer than the first one—and fall in love again. And then you'd get
to Nashville, and you'd be in love again.[2]

Sleeping in their seats because Black people were not permitted to ride
in sleeper cars, the students arrived at the train station in Birmingham,
Alabama, the next morning. They had two immediate obstacles to

overcome. First, they needed to negotiate the several miles between the train station and the Trailways bus depot. That part of the journey had even Paul concerned. Though it would be several years before the Freedom Riders would meet savage violence at that bus station, Birmingham was already known as a racist hornets' nest. Passing through the station, Paul saw his first "Whites Only" signs and noted that the facilities for people of color were particularly foul.[3] From there, students had to ride the segregated bus fifty-four more miles to the college.

With typical insouciance, Paul made a friend who could help—Claudette Beck, who was already a sophomore at Talladega.

> The [bus] station was for whites only. It was my first experience with segregation, being in that Trailways station. Claudette guided me through the station with my big footlocker with all my worldly goods. . . . You were taking your life in your hands to ride those buses, you know. That bus was invariably 90 percent Black. If there were white people on the bus, they were all the way up front. Probably scared of us. There were too many of us. . . . But I had enough sense that I didn't do anything to bring attention to [myself]. I was thinking, "This is one fine sister! She can help me anytime she wants to."[4]

Talladega College has a long history and a powerful origin story that is detailed on the school's website.[5] Only a few months after the Civil War ended, two former slaves, William Savery and Thomas Tarrant, proposed to build a school for people of color in Talladega, their hometown. The American Missionary Association and a former Union general leading the Alabama's Freedman's Bureau helped the community acquire land and an existing building. Ironically, Savery, Tarrant and other enslaved people had helped build that structure for a white Baptist institution before the war. "Thus," the website emphasizes, "a building constructed with slave labor for white students became the home of the state's first private, liberal arts college dedicated to servicing the educational needs of blacks."[6] Talladega first enrolled students in 1867. By the end of the century, similar HBCUs were educating students all over the South.

When Paul Smith arrived in 1952, Talladega was a small, steadfast oasis in the ominous social and physical landscape of the Jim Crow South. The wood-frame and brick campus buildings are well spaced around the crossroads of West Battle Street and what is now called Martin Luther King Jr. Drive. West Battle, the main road through the campus, runs east-west and slopes down to the east as it leaves the campus gates to join the main road leading to the town of Talladega. Outside those gates in Smith's day, there

Savery Library, Talladega College, Talladega, Alabama. Photo by the author.

was a little roadhouse called "High Pockets" that students frequented when they wanted to eat something other than cafeteria food. Smith notes, however, that they "had to enter through the back door, of course."[7] Down that road, one might also encounter hostile white locals or see their cars driving conspicuously by outside the campus.

Despite its proud history, Talladega had its own brand of bigotry. Smith relates that he had to include a photograph with his application to the college and says, "If I had been blacker, I might not have gotten in." He says that "light, bright, and damn near white" was how some Black onlookers would have described his college classmates. Despite the way it echoed the classism and racism of white elites, use of the phrase was commonplace, Smith says.[8]

Inside the gates, Talladega was thriving in 1952. It had just hired its first African American president. An Alabamian and alumnus of Talladega, Rev. Dr. Arthur D. Gray had earned his PhD at the Chicago Theological Seminary in 1934.[9] This deeply impressed Smith.

> Going to Talladega—that was really a cultural shock. The college was the
> Black intelligentsia. I was shocked to see so many white teachers there at this

small Black college. The student body was all Black—there may have been a white student or two there. . . . The president of the college was Black. . . . He was a Congregational minister, had served in Chicago before becoming president of Talladega . . . those Black ministers were not like the Black ministers I grew up with. [Gray was] very sophisticated, very well spoken, no shouting, no theatrics in his preaching—very grounded.[10]

Talladega's faculty consisted of highly educated Blacks and whites who felt it was their Christian duty to ensure that Black students in the South had access to a sound education. "I had never had any instruction in high school from anybody Black. Never. . . . So now I get to Talladega, sixteen years of age and here are all these Black PhDs who are my professors. The president of the college is a Black Congregational minister. And now the white professors, who were in the predominance, clearly had my best interests at heart. I had not seen that before."[11]

Several professors soon recognized Paul as a gifted student and went to extra lengths to teach him. Peg Montgomery was a professor of English who worked with him closely. Ma Gibson, a teacher of classics, met with Paul once a week at her cottage on campus. Paul read aloud to her so that he could learn to speak well. Those teachers sacrificed more than just their time; for them, the Deep South was hostile territory too. Rev. Smith says the white teachers who lived on campus with their families were at times no safer outside the campus gates than the Black students they served.

Most important in Paul's development was Dr. John Bross, a white professor of psychology and religion. Bross was raising a family on campus, and Paul joined them for dinner nearly every Friday night. Bross took Paul to lectures and conferences, introducing him to a wider academic, religious, and political world. Their connection was affirmed when Bross preached the ordination sermon years later at Paul's first pastorate in Buffalo, New York.

But not all the teachers were so impressed with Smith.

The Biology teacher [was] a PhD, single, very attractive. And you did not play around in her class, you hear me? You did not play around in her class. She was saying, "I am a PhD; this is how I got to where I am. And you have to get to where I am, and I am going to help you get there. You are in my class. You will study, you will learn, you will do x, y and z." I had never had a Black professor say that to us.

[She'd say,] very nicely, "Mr. Smith, Mr. Epps? So, you didn't do your homework today? Can you tell me why?" [He'd answer,] "I was at basketball practice." [She'd say,] "What will basketball practice do for you?" And you have to answer! . . . They knew the key to our success was to go the path they had gone on.[12]

Despite his abilities and the support he received, Smith's first year at Talladega was difficult. He was very young to be plunging into college life. A letter typed to his father sometime that first semester reveals how much his thoughts were still of home.

> Paul Smith
> Talladega College
> Stone Hall, Rm. 206

Dear Daddy,

How is everything? Today we are having the entrance exams, and we have to have them for three days. My typewriter came today but my trunk has not come yet. I'm still very lonesome and I hope that I'll get over it soon. The check is to be written for $182. Tell Leonard and them to please write me and tell mother to tell Willy to take the library books to Catherine's house. In a half hour our exams will begin. Tell Willy to get me Julius Mason [*sic*] address, and some of the other kids too.

The upperclassmen were in our dorm trying to paddle us, but our Counselors wouldn't let them. Last night we had a freshman get together with all the teachers there, and we had to introduce ourselves and show some kind of a talent, and it was real swell. I met two girls on the train that were going to same place that I was, and they are real cute. After the get together, the upperclassman ran us all the way home. They told us that we will have to put up with all this until Thursday. I haven't much more to say so I guess I'll close now with all my love. Don't forget to tell them to write me. Bye now. They have a chapel here for the students to attend.

Your loving son,
Paul Smith[13]

Rev. Smith can say now what he surely could not then—that it was the social side of college that was troublesome. Even though he was a tall, athletic northerner who made friends easily, he was in some ways still innocent. "I wasn't ready for girls! I thought I was. But at college, I'd see these girls every day. We went to the movies on campus, since they were segregated in town. It was freshman year. [I was] with a girl at the movies. And suddenly she put her hand on my leg. No high school girl had ever done that! It was exciting but I was scared."[14]

During the next academic year, 1953–54, Smith stayed home and worked. It was one of the very few detours on his road to adult life. He took some classes at the South Bend campus of Indiana University "to stay sharp." And it helped. He says, "I found my groove that year I was out. When I got back, I was ready."[15] Meanwhile, his stories of college life had convinced older brother Lennie that he was missing out. In the late summer of 1954, both boys got on the train in Chicago and roared off to become "Dega" men.

Talladega College is located in the wooded heart of Alabama, close to Montgomery, Birmingham, and other small cities that were becoming battlegrounds in the struggle for social justice. In 1952, the year Paul first enrolled in college, Authurine Lucy was housed and educated at Talladega while the fight went on in court to get her admitted as the first Black person at the University of Alabama at Tuscaloosa. One of her lawyers, Arthur D. Shores, was chairman of the board at Talladega, and he made sure she kept up with her studies while the case dragged on. He told the other students, "This is a safe haven for her. Be nice to her."[16] Paul remembers seeing her in the dining hall.

But fellow students were not the only ones alert to her presence. Paul recalls that Authurine "stayed at the president's house. That's when the Klan came. They gathered down the hill . . . we saw them there getting ready to do something about Authurine being on campus. . . . The Klan couldn't get at her in Tuscaloosa, so they wanted to try while she was at Talladega."[17] In the end, Talladega students, like those at Notre Dame, banded together near the campus gates to show they were not going to allow anyone dangerous into their midst. Authurine was safe, at least for the time being.

Off campus, the landscape was claimed and defined by whites who felt no need to disguise their hostility and often seemed to relish confrontation. Paul had come to Talladega on an academic scholarship but was welcomed onto the basketball team. This meant traveling to other Black colleges to compete. Packed together into a car, Black students and their coach had to negotiate a veritable minefield between safe havens. Meals were not a problem, as the coach took them to the homes of alumni or Black church folk in the region. But they couldn't avoid taking breaks and stopping for gas:

> When we had to use the bathrooms, we could not of course use the one inside the gas station because it was reserved for whites. Outhouses were always in the back of the station, and they were reserved for Black folks.

On one occasion, we had to go through the gas station to get to the back door [and] the outhouse. As we waited our turn, we [looked] over the candy, nuts, and sodas—which we could not purchase—over the counter. [Then] I realized the men who were sitting outside of the gas station had come inside to check on us. They were basically speaking nasty words to us and as they were walking towards us, I realized we would be surrounded by them in a few moments. A sudden panic rose in all of us, and within seconds we headed towards the back door and eventually found our way to the waiting car being filled with gasoline....

My brother and I will never forget that experience and the fear which quickly engulfed us. We were targeted because we were Black college students hopefully on our way to becoming successful—and they were not.[18]

Attorney Shores came to the rescue in another close encounter with violence during Smith's college years. The team was traveling to play against Miles College, another Black school near Birmingham. The distance was less than sixty miles, but the interstate highway system had not yet been built, so the trip took several hours. Despite driving carefully to avoid trouble in the city of the notorious Bull Connor, the team's car slid into the rear of a car ahead of them that had stopped abruptly.

The white person in the car ... jumped out with fire in his eyes, calling us the "n" name and threatening to beat us all to death. As we began getting out of the car ... he realized he outnumbered us, and he began to be a bit more conciliatory.... [Then] a bus pulled up beside the accident and opened the door and the bus driver said to the white driver, "I saw what happened and it was those niggers' fault." The bus and passengers remained until the police arrived.

Now I was really frightened, but the coach kept his cool.... [He] invoked the name of the civil rights attorney from Birmingham ... who had represented many prominent Black folks in Birmingham—this gained us some respect. [Soon] Mr. Arthur Shores showed up at the scene ... and within a few minutes we were back in our cars on our way to Miles College. I can see the faces ... and I can still hear the shouting of the white man. I realize how fortunate I am to still be here today.[19]

Smith did not go home for Christmas his senior year. Instead, Dr. Bross arranged for Smith and two other Black students to attend a conference at Davidson College in North Carolina, more than 350 miles away. Founded by Presbyterians in 1837 and quite liberal today, Davidson at that time was an all-white institution.

We three—two Black guys and one Black girl—drove with Bross to the conference. When we got there, they had the area cordoned off with police cars.
People shouted nasty names at us. They split us up [for sleeping arrange-
ments]. I was in a room with someone who had never, ever been that close to
a Black person. He was not happy at first. . . .

That was one of the first interracial conferences for Black and white students. We ate together, lived together. That was 1957. The objective was to put
Black and white students together from a religious perspective so we could
all get used to each other.[20]

Smith remembers the experiment as a success. The young people discovered they were not so different after all, and there was no further confrontation. Smith asserts that, after Davidson, "I knew integration was possible."[21]

Dr. Bross and other faculty wanted their students to know as much as
possible about the history unfolding around them. In the spring of 1957,
Talladega professors took students to Montgomery every Friday to hear the
speakers that Rev. Martin Luther King Jr. was inviting to the Dexter Avenue
Baptist Church. At the time, the young minister was serving in his only
full-time pastorate in the little brick church a mere block from the massive
white pillars of the Alabama State House. Smith heard speakers including Rev. King, Vernon Johns, Adam Clayton Powell, and Ralph Abernathy
a stone's throw from where the Selma marchers would make their stand
a few years later. Smith says the eloquence and power of those speakers
spurred him to work even harder on his own oratorical style. The visitors
from Talladega did not go unnoticed, however; one Friday, their car was
splashed with acid while the students were in the church.

Also in senior year, Smith was elected to lead a new chapter of the NAACP
on campus. This happened accidentally, he says, because he asked the most
questions in the planning meetings. Nonetheless, his speaking abilities and
leadership potential were being recognized. He recalls his duties: "We kept
up with the activities of other campus chapters. There were conferences
to go to—we'd get on a bus and go to Atlanta. It kept us abreast of what
was happening nationally in Washington, New York, Chicago . . . [with]
the fight to grant us our rights. It was the premier African American organization."[22] Smith's personal contact with Rev. King began in May 1957. As
Paul remembers it, his fraternity had asked King to visit Talladega to speak
and spend a few days. Andrew Young had come to the campus because he
wanted to meet King. Young's own account adds some details: "The Alpha
Phi Alpha fraternity chapter at Talladega College in Alabama provided my

first opportunity to meet Martin Luther King. Alpha Phi Alpha was my fraternity at Howard University, and the president of Talladega, Arthur Gray, was an Alpha and a Congregational minister. I accepted Gray's invitation in the spring of 1957 to speak. . . . When I arrived, I discovered I was one of two speakers; Martin King was the other. I looked forward to hearing him speak and to meeting him with great anticipation."[23]

A popular, multitalented, and industrious young man, Paul himself pledged Alpha Phi Alpha in 1955. For the speakers' visit in 1957, Smith was one of the Alphas who escorted them around campus. In the course of fulfilling those duties, Young concurs that it was Smith who actually introduced Young and King to each other. Young, of course, later became King's deputy in the Southern Christian Leadership Conference, and their partnership changed American history.

It is not surprising that a fraternity brought the three together. Founded by African Americans at Cornell University in 1906, Alpha Phi Alpha is the oldest fraternity for men of color in the country. While there are many other highly respected Black fraternities and sororities, the history and membership list of Alpha Phi Alpha are unmatched.

The impact of these voluntary organizations over the past century cannot be overstated. Going beyond what their white counterparts have generally aspired to, Black fraternities and sororities have long created "a lasting identity, a circle of lifetime friends, a base for future political and civic activism . . . a forum, postcollege, through which some of the best-educated blacks in America can discuss an agenda to fight racism and improve conditions for other less-advantaged blacks."[24]

Writer, lawyer, and Black elite insider Lawrence Otis Graham contextualizes the rise of these organizations. Shut out of white fraternities and sororities for decades, Black students at both the HBCUs and the best white colleges have joined together in powerhouse social, intellectual, and political networks of their own. Alpha Phi Alpha became part of what are called "the Divine Nine"—major fraternities mostly founded in the first quarter of the twentieth century. While Graham notes that the groups have been criticized for creating class divisions within the Black community, he points out that from the late 1950s on, fraternity brothers united with non-members in civil rights protests.[25]

The Talladega meeting of the three young Alphas is a perfect example of the powerful potential inherent in these elite fraternal societies.[26] Speaking invitations extended to rising public figures like King and Young helped

Martin Luther King Jr. with Paul Smith (right back), John Bross (right) and others at Talladega College, Alabama, 1957. Courtesy of the Smith Family.

circulate political ideas and information. The speaker circuits linked the HBCUs to each other and to other academic institutions. It was through this system that Paul repeatedly heard his most influential mentor, Rev. Dr. Howard Thurman.

Those few days with Martin King in 1957 made a deep impression on Smith. He later wrote: "I will never forget that experience; his depth, his warmth, his piercing eyes; his folded hands. This surely was a man of God."[27]

Young, on the other hand, was very disappointed.[28] He had traveled to Talladega from rural Thomasville, Georgia, where he was managing two churches and a voter registration drive. Having heard a great deal already about King, Young had hoped they could talk politics, theology, and philosophy. It turned out that King needed a break from the spotlight and wanted to talk mainly about his newborn child. Young only later realized how exhausted King was. King was busy polishing the speech he delivered a few days later at an important early march, the Prayer Pilgrimage, in Washington, D.C.[29]

College drew Paul and Lennie into powerful social networks that continue to be important in their lives today. Along with classmates, professors, and fraternity brothers, both men met their future wives at Talladega. Paul met

Frances ("Fran") Pitts in June 1956, as he was about to begin his senior year. Her father, mother, and two uncles had graduated from Talladega. Fran's mother was visiting the campus that summer to attend her class reunion, and Fran was going to enroll as a freshman that fall. Paul had a coveted job waiting tables in the private dining room for President Gray, the faculty, and the administration. It was there that he first caught a glimpse of Fran when he waited on her and her mother.

Frances must have been memorable to most of the young men she encountered. Born in Soperton, Georgia, she was the smart, beautiful, eldest child in a successful middle-class family. Fran had grown up on the grounds of Fort Valley State College, an HBCU southeast of Atlanta where her father had been a math teacher. Her family shared basic values with Paul's but also came with a different set of expectations. Hers was an educated household where opera and theater were appreciated. As she puts it, "I was used to a university atmosphere."[30]

Located outside the white town, the Fort Valley campus was a safe haven in hostile territory. However, the Black neighborhood did not receive the same services as the areas where white people lived. The roads near the college were not paved, and they often became muddy and dangerous. Fran says, "One time our car slid off the road into a ditch. My father decided he had had enough. He went to the meeting of the [town leadership]; they knew who he was. They said he wasn't supposed to be there and asked him what he wanted. And he said, 'I pay taxes in this town. I want my goddamn street paved!' So, they paved the street but just as far as our house."[31] The paving stopped about a foot past a tree at the corner of their property.

Paul got to know Fran during that school year and fell deeply in love. Already a well-known senior, he had begun preaching in the churches on campus, including the formidable DeForest Chapel. As Smith recollects, "I was the man!" He had many friends on campus, some of whom he is in touch with to this day. But he had made his choice.

One evening in April 1957, Paul enlisted the aid of his fraternity brothers to jump from behind the bushes in front of Silsby Hall and sing Fran a love song. When he presented her with the Alpha Phi Alpha pin he had paid $35 to buy, Fran did not refuse it. In those days, that meant marriage was likely to be ahead. As Fran recalls:

My parents were in the Congregationalist Church and Talladega was a Congregational school. So, it was all familiar. They went to Talladega as well as my father's brothers. It was in my background to marry clergy; it was acceptable and appropriate. Education and profession mattered in terms of who you would marry.

I'm an old-fashioned girl. People of my generation, when you got married, you were supposed to support your husband in whatever he did. That's what you did. The same with getting married right out of college—it was the day after graduation for us! I was barely twenty-one when I got married.[32]

Early in the relationship, an opportunity arose for Paul to show his mettle. Fran's former boyfriend from Fort Valley arrived on campus to play basketball against Paul's team. Other players and students were watching closely to see what would happen between the two young men. It did not appear to be a match-up that would favor Paul, and he says he succumbed to a moment of malice. "Everyone was buzzing about [it]. He was huge, six-three or four. He made about thirty points in the first half alone, and my friends were laughing because I was guarding him. He shot my eyes out! One of the only bad things I did was at one point, I pushed him over toward the bleachers; I should have gotten ejected from the game."[33]

Yet after his team was soundly beaten, Paul's instinct led him in a direction that surprised everyone—he went to talk with the fellow. "I told him, 'I know you used to know Fran well. Why don't you and she take some time to talk?' Everyone was real impressed with the way that reduced all the tension."[34] Stepping closer to a source of challenge or hostility, not to fight but to mediate, soon became one of Smith's special strengths.

In his final year at Talladega, Smith wrote a senior thesis that allowed his intellectual voice to be heard for the first time. The eighty-page document provides an early look at his ideas about God, faith, denominationalism, church practice, and doctrine. Titled "A Comparison of the Baptist and Congregationalist Denominations," the paper is articulate and thoughtful. It clearly reveals Smith's personal struggle with both his denominational affiliation and his choice to become a clergyman. In it, he asserts that "there is a great need for such a study as this, for the reason that [it] enables us to know why we are what we are."[35]

Despite all the support and training he received before he went to college, Smith describes himself on the first page of the thesis as having been uncertain about his future profession.

Before coming to college, I had no idea of becoming a minister. I wasn't too sure that I would come to college. At this state in life a young person is at the "brim of confusion," however I tried to unravel my confusion by coming to college.

Both my parents are Baptists, and so the rest of us in the family followed suit and became Baptists. Its [sic] interesting to know that out of seven members of our family, there are only three Baptists left.[36]

In the text, Smith reviews the history of the Baptist and Congregationalist denominations and identifies key differences between them, including their views on covenants, baptism, communion, the literal interpretation of the Bible, and whether God's Word is living or immutable. While recognizing positive aspects of Baptist beliefs and practices, Smith makes clear that he has journeyed away from the Baptist church of his family and feels closer to Congregationalism.

Among the distinctive characteristics of the Congregationalism that Smith cites approvingly are a concern for church unity versus a divided Protestantism, the fact that congregants are not asked to renounce the teachings of other churches, the tradition of allowing ministers from other denominations to serve as pastors in Congregational churches, and an emphasis on the liberty of the Christian person. He also writes that he is impressed by the Congregationalist focus on education and its critical role in founding colleges like Talladega.

At age twenty-two, Smith straightforwardly declares that he is not a literalist in his interpretation of the Bible—that he believes the Word of God is a living entity, and that he finds individual freedom and choice in matters of church doctrine to be of central importance. He asserts that the "narrowness" of Baptist ideas, such as on baptism in particular, "is one of my major reasons for rejecting the Baptists."[37] Rather than insisting on the necessity of full immersion as the Baptists do, Smith writes that he prefers the Congregationalists' freedom to choose between forms of baptism and their recognition of baptism performed in other denominations.[38]

Smith finds that Baptist and Congregationalist views of salvation through Jesus are quite in accord. But evincing the iconoclastic views and the prescience that Smith became known for, he writes, "I would question . . . references to 'heaven' where Jesus Christ is supposed to be now. I believe that Christ is somewhere in the universe, but to call this place heaven isn't exactly what I had in mind. I don't believe in a heaven or a hell in the sense that Heaven is the place for the good and Hell a place for the evil. I think that we as human beings make our heavens or hells here on earth."[39]

Perhaps most revealing is a viewpoint he articulates twice in his paper: "It makes no difference whether you're a Baptist, a Methodist, or a Congregationalist, we are all one under God. As long as God is the ultimate of any religion, I feel that this religion is good."[40] This kind of willingness to look beyond issues of sectarianism has animated his life ever since.

In concluding, Smith declares that his thesis has done its job: "As a result of this project, I know now why I am a Congregationalist, and not a Baptist, anymore. I am also aware of the fact that there is a great need for more people to look into the history of their denominations, to see if their group is doing God's will. This is important in our world today, if we are to ever become united."[41]

In May 1957, the Smith family gathered at Talladega to celebrate Paul's graduation with a BA in psychology and religion. Later, as a reward for his hard work, Leonard Smith gave his son $100 and the keys to the car. Paul had planned a celebratory road trip with his friend Richard English before beginning his studies at Hartford Seminary that fall. Though his new friend Andrew Young had suggested he participate in nonviolence training down south, Paul had made his plans and promised only that he would pray about it. In high spirits, he and English hit the highway, headed for Detroit.

Once there, though, Paul made a decision that would change his life. Shortly after arriving, a marquee outside a church caught his eye. It read: "Dr. Benjamin Elijah Mays—Everywhere I Turn, I Find Jesus." The chance to hear the president of Morehouse College and one of the most respected scholar-theologians of the day was irresistible to the young man. Smith attended the sermon and says it "penetrated my heart and soul."[42]

Afterward, he was on fire with determination to devote his life to God and service. He didn't need to joyride any longer. Smith turned back to South Bend to return the car and the remaining $75 to his father. It was Paul Smith's first truly adult decision, one that marked him indelibly. He says it was also the only time he ever saw his father cry. With that sweet send-off, Paul headed back to the South to begin his professional life.

CHAPTER 4

First Rites

In the spring of 1957, a Methodist church in Anniston, Alabama, contacted Talladega College looking for a temporary pastor. While not yet finished with his senior year, Smith did not see why his relative youth and inexperience should keep him from taking the job: "I was a student, but I was available, and I had something to say."[1] Every Sunday for four months, he boarded a regional bus in Talladega and traveled twenty-seven miles northeast up Route 21 to the church.

While the infamous, near-fatal attack outside Anniston on a bus full of Freedom Riders was still four years off,[2] getting on the segregated bus for an hour made Smith "not afraid, but nervous." As has so often been the case, though, he quickly acquired an advocate and protector. Another black minister who was riding the same bus each Sunday began to sit with him. "He looked out for me. We'd talk about what I was going to say at church that day. We were probably the only two Blacks on the bus. It cost 25¢ each way. The church paid that and gave me $10 [weekly]."[3]

Drawing on his friend's guidance and his own experience of preaching, Smith was able to meet the demands of that first professional job. He moved on quickly, however, to much weightier responsibilities. After his graduation, Smith was hired as a "summer supply" minister. This time, he was to serve at a Congregational church in Athens, Alabama, about ninety-five miles north of Birmingham. Smith was on a visit home to South Bend when he received word that a highly respected member of the Athens community had just died—Mr. Allen, the local mortician. Ending his visit early, Smith scrambled to catch a bus back to Alabama to assume his position as leader of the church community. He knew that, as the new pastor, he would be expected to lead the funerary rituals.

When he arrived in Athens, Smith and the man who came to pick him up were a bit surprised to see each other.

> There was a gay undertaker, embalmer, and hairdresser there named Jesse. He did everything. Everyone knew him and trusted him. . . .
>
> The bus was late. All they knew was that the minister was coming on the bus. Jesse was designated to pick me up. I got there in the middle of the night. And there was Jesse. He said, "You're mighty young—are you sure?" He was the decision-maker for the Black community in Athens. And he could sing![4]

Smith assured Jesse that he was the man they were waiting for, and they drove through the dark to Athens. As the new pastor, Smith discovered the next day that he had one important ally in the crisis. The deceased man's wife had gone to Talladega, "so she had confidence in me."[5] But the deacons of the church were skeptical when they met him. They grumbled, "That kid doesn't know how to do a funeral!"[6] Moving quickly to prove them wrong, Smith wrote up a bulletin for the service that created a structure for the ceremony. He enlisted the elders' aid in reading the Old Testament scripture. When it came time to commit the body to the ground—the part Smith was most unsure of—he had the old hands on his side, and they helped him conclude the rites. Thus, Smith started learning early how to lead others through the pressure, emotion, and politics of a small-town funeral. These skills would grow and deepen with time.

There were sharper lessons to come in Athens. While living with a host family, the Higginses, Smith became aware for the first time that on the radio in the South, Black people were spoken of using only their first names, never "Mr." or "Mrs." Being from the North and a city where that indignity, at least, was not the norm, Smith decided to take some action. He wrote to the station manager and soon received a letter in return. In it, Smith was told that he was in the South now, and the rules were different. He was to "remember his place," Smith said, and was told that they had "people who would take care of me if I didn't follow the rules."[7]

Despite the threat, Mr. Higgins did not tell Smith to back down. Instead, Higgins told the young man he was proud of him and then shared stories about how the older man and his family had "survived the cruelties of southern living and segregation."[8] Smith later realized that the support of such stalwart families had made a huge contribution to the political efforts of the day. They may never have marched in a protest, but they housed, fed, and encouraged the young firebrands in their midst. It was in fact the Higgins household that welcomed Smith when he was looking for a safe haven in the middle of the night on the way home from Selma in 1965.

Proving that his ministerial skills could earn him a living was critical in 1957, because Smith wanted to move forward in his courtship of Frances Pitts. At Christmas that year, he visited Fran's family in California and proposed to her. As Smith tells it, he was riding high when he arrived, fresh off his first airplane trip and carrying Granny's wedding ring in his pocket. He had finished his first semester at Hartford Theological Seminary and was on his way to a career in ministry. He enjoyed a wonderful visit with the family he expected to call in-laws and went back to the seminary feeling confident there was nothing to keep his plans from unfolding. However, in early February 1958, he received a letter.[9]

Fran's father was a warm but formidable intellectual who wrote to voice some strong objections to Fran and Paul marrying that year—or the next. Dr. Raymond J. Pitts Sr. had long before set himself a series of goals that he fulfilled on his way out of Fort Valley, Georgia, and the Deep South. He too was a member of Alpha Phi Alpha. While working and raising a family, Dr. Pitts became determined to earn his PhD in mathematics at the University of Michigan.[10] As Smith recalls, Pitts was told by one of the math professors when he arrived for classes, "We've never given a Black man a PhD in math. What makes you think we'll give you one?" And Pitts said, "You watch me!"[11] Over several years, he successfully completed the course of study. However, the degree was only awarded to him after the bigoted chair of the department died, many years later. Meanwhile, Pitts had moved his family to Pasadena, California, in 1956.

Dr. Pitts's three-page letter laid out his objections to Smith's marriage plans. He was cordial but serious: "I want to take up the matter of your and Fran's marriage at some length and suggest some changes in plans which I hope will be acceptable to you."[12] Dr. Pitts relayed the hopes he and his wife had that all their children would receive "the best education possible that would make of them the best Americans they could be."[13] He explained the family's move to California as motivated by that desire. "Frances has the chance to enter Pomona College, possibly on a scholarship. Pomona is a Liberal Arts College of the highest caliber and operated by the Congregational Church. Two years of study [after two years at Talladega] with the freedom from home responsibilities and with time to develop on her own initiative would make her the kind of person who could be a real asset as a minister's wife."[14]

Raymond Pitts was speaking from experience: "My girl too had my engagement ring and I could not even get back south for nearly two years."[15] But he believed Smith's hard work at the seminary toward his future goals would be sustaining through such a separation. He advised Smith to "strive to be the top man at the Seminary," and to use his time to study, travel, and make contacts that marriage would otherwise make difficult. But he was sympathetic: "The road to professional education is not an easy one. I would say that it is the most lonely road that a man can take, if he is serious about really doing something."[16]

With patience and logic, though, he explained all the advantages for both Paul and Fran if they both completed their education before they married. He described his own aims.

> I believed then that I could become one of the top flight mathematics teachers in this country; that from this could be made possible a good sound home and family life for my girl and the five children; that good sound education and travel would be the accepted way of life for us; that we would own a home, yes, and in this home each person would grow happily into the best possible person he could be; and above all that our family could be contributors to our American culture and not just consumers and victims of it as we are sometimes forced to be.[17]

The soundness of the argument and the gentleness of its delivery proved impossible to deny. In one of the few setbacks in Smith's adult life, the marriage was put on hold.

As predicted, the seminary provided the young man with absorbing challenges while he waited to move forward with Frances. The Hartford Theological Seminary in Connecticut was and is a progressive institution.[18] Associated with the United Church of Christ (UCC), it offers degrees and certificates in such fields as interfaith dialogue, Islamic chaplaincy, international peacemaking, transformational leadership, and spirituality. Its Christian-Muslim relations program has existed for a century. What was in Smith's day called the Kennedy School of Missions sent students all over the world to evangelize.[19] Foreign students also came to Hartford to study.

Smith chose the institution for those qualities, knowing too that his friend Andrew Young had graduated from Hartford a few years ahead of him. He went to Hartford anticipating the challenge of competing among the best, whomever they might be. As has happened over and over again in his life, Smith was breaking down racial barriers by simply enrolling there. "I was one of only three Black students. It was me, Ralph Logan Carson, and a Black woman [Julia McClain]. Guess who I was assigned to as a roommate? Ralph. The first day of class at orientation, they all looked at me and said, 'Where's Ralph? You have to meet him. He's going to be your roommate.'"[20]

Ralph was also blind. This might have been an obstacle for a less accepting person than Smith, but a mutually agreeable arrangement was soon organized. The school proposed that if Smith would read Ralph his lessons and help him get acclimated, he would be paid $50 a month. To the scholarship student who had worked his way through Talladega, "that was good money!" Soon, Ralph had nicknamed Smith "Mr. Smooth" and was attending basketball games to support his friend.

In 1957, everything about Hartford looked grand to the twenty-two-year-old. Smith felt that his world was expanding exponentially. The Hartford Seminary "was like heaven." Smith says, "Students from all over the world went to the Kennedy School and went from there to India and all over. . . . So I was not only going to a 95 percent white environment on this campus, but my orientation went way [beyond Hartford]." On a seminary trip further into New England, Smith said, "I remember being in a room with a fireplace. Fall was absolutely beautiful. I had never been in a hotel like that. . . . It was everything I had seen pictures of in books."[21]

Smith was impressed that the "big, white UCC churches" invited Hartford students to be on staff as student pastors, assistants, and youth group leaders. When Smith returned to Athens, Alabama, to work during the summer of 1958, they were amazed by how much he had learned in just one year.

While adept at being a racial pioneer, Smith kept an eye on how students of color were treated at Hartford. In his final year, Smith sent his parents a newspaper article listing the fieldwork assignments of about fifty Hartford students.[22] He himself had become a student assistant at Union Baptist, a large Black church downtown. For his parents, he underlined the names of the four other Black students, noting that only two of them were working in an "all Negro church."[23] He also underlined the name of his roommate, noting that he was white.

Fortunately for the historic record, Smith found ways to assuage the lone-
liness of his continued studies. Principal among them was keeping a diary.
Though it would be years before he would be given his Granny's diary, journaling became a lifelong form of reflection for him. Over sixty years, he has
produced more than eighty journals,[24] and he shows no sign of giving up
what he refers to as "my therapy."

Smith's earliest journal entry is dated March 21, 1957, during his senior
year at Talladega.[25] It consists of a rhyming love poem by someone else that
Smith copied into his notebook. His mind was surely on Frances, who accepted his Alpha Phi Alpha pin a few weeks later. Two poems by Smith follow, titled "The Lord Will Make a Way Somehow" and "Don't Quit." These
suggest the young man was giving himself a pep talk. In later entries, Smith's
topics include: "You Give Yourself Away," "No Faith," and "Love." There are
also aphorisms, including "A man should know himself, accept himself"
and "Don't make a career of religion just to change your own soul."[26]

On the inside cover of that first small maroon-and-black notebook,
Smith later inscribed his intentions: "*Existential Realizations*—in an attempt to capture the thoughts of my moods from time to time; an attempt
to acquaint myself better with myself. Most of us are moody from time
to time; it is my hope that I can understand myself, my reactions, and my
thoughts as I encounter myself through the various phases and aspects of
the world. Paul Smith 11/16/59."[27]

At the seminary, the notebooks were a place to work through sermon
ideas. One long passage, which focuses on how people discard their friends,
associates, even their church and God in pursuit of success, is labeled "Parts
of a Sermon 'Void if Detached.'" Other topics are listed on a page titled
"Sermon Points":

- Who has the choice to live life on his own terms? Compromises must be
  made. We have to live creatively in a frame of reference.
- Job: Even though he slay me, yet I will trust him.
- Life is a miracle, Love is a miracle.
- "God is there too in the desperation. I do not know why God should
  strike but God is what is stricken also: Life is what despairs in death and
  desperate is life still." J.B.[28]

From the beginning in his diaries, Smith is direct and honest about moments of inspiration and awe, feelings of anger and sadness, and his own
shortcomings. Recurrent themes include knowing one's self and knowing

God, confronting the fear of death, and race relations. In December 1959, for instance, after a white seminarian joins him at a service in a Black church, Smith records a view of race that has held firm through his life: "When you sincerely love God in your heart, and accept the love of God in Christ Jesus, you move from the realm of color into the realm of oneness; people become people[,] not kinds of."[29]

Smith's political beliefs also begin to come into view when he writes approvingly in June 1960: "[James] Lawson is accused of fomenting civil disobedience, but the Christian Church is grounded on 300 years of civil disobedience."[30] A few months later, he notes, "Many Negro leaders did not and have not believed that the student sit-ins have been right; therefore they have not responded to [them]. Perhaps it was the simplicity of the whole movement."[31]

In July 1961, Smith provides an early description of his approach to prayer and meditation.

> I create for myself an island of silence. I bring to my quiet time my concerns to examine them—to see them more clearly—and to know what God would have me do. My concern today is with the need for meaning, which is the condition of so many of us who come to the church. We need meaning to fill the empty places in our empty lives. I would therefore say to my church, say to me that which is significant so that I may have some directions as I seek to live with wholeness the brief days allotted to me.[32]

The last entry in the journal was written the day after Smith returned from the Selma encounter. He does not mention the spitting incident, asserting instead: "No man is an outsider in this world because we all belong here. In comment to being called 'outside' agitators in the racial strife in Selma, Alabama. Outside agitators are necessary to stir the consciences of the people."[33]

Another early journal was started in October 1959, Smith's last year at seminary.[34] The first entry is a furious outpouring to a God that seems uncaring about the struggles of Black people. Titled "A Psalm of Hatred," the passage was occasioned by the murders of Black men in three Mississippi towns: Money (where Emmett Till was killed in August 1955), Poplarville (where Mack Charles Parker was lynched in April 1959), and Clarksdale (where Booker T. Mixon was beaten and died of injuries officially blamed on a hit-and-run accident in October 1959). From the dating of the journal, it appears it was the news of Mixon's death that prompted Smith to write:

We call upon thee O God, as we lick the wounds from our recent defeats. Why is it O Lord, that thou cannot see us in all walks of life? Our black faces are smutty and filled with sweat from our battle. We remember too well our defeat at Money, Mississippi at your hands, the Great White Father; and yet you sent your wrath upon our brethren at Popularville [sic], ye on to Clarksdale, where the blood of the black man runs freely. Why O God has thou sent thy wrath upon our people? A people who lift their voices in deep, sensitive spirituals and songs to thee? Why hast thou sent down the angry ropes, the gnashing dogs and the evil demons, which whisk away our loved ones during the night? ... O God, we hate our persecutors, although you tell us to love; but thou knowest it is difficult for us to love when we can feel cold steel beating against our heads, blood running down our backs—our friends and loved ones being burned out of their homes. We hear convulsive sobs from our women and children as they run throughout our towns, burning and destroying. If thou lovest us as you say, why must we suffer so? Why does your wrath continue?

... Is there no balm in Gilead? Is there no peace in Mississippi? Hear us and answer![35]

The fact that he never again wrote of God as the "Great White Father" or accused God of being the source of people's misery suggests that these were the thoughts of a frightened and furious young man. More typically, Smith's early journal entries are thoughtful and measured.

Perhaps one of the tragedies of human society is that no public man is as good as his private self might have been. The interior life is the vital part of a man. Do we really know the interior of our lives? Obviously, yes, even though we fear the interior the most.

Calvin has said, "A man must know himself if he is to know God; and man must know God if he is to know himself." In Him we live and move and have our being.[36]

I look into my own life and wonder [about] my motivations and reasons for attending the flock. Is it because I have this need to be needed? Is it wrong to have such a need? ... The good news is that in all life, it begins and ends with God.[37]

In February 1960, Smith comments on what had long been an annual event in Protestant churches—"Race Relations Sunday."[38] Harkening back to his undergraduate thesis, he writes approvingly of Black and white ministers exchanging pulpits, giving all of them "a chance to be Christians for a change": "We have to stop fumbling along in the name of Christianity...."

All are our brothers or none is. Race Relations should be observed every day, not just at a special time of year. Our church doors should remain open to all, regardless of race, creed or color. God loves children and people, not races and colors."[39]

Paul Smith became "Rev. Mr." Smith upon completing his studies at the Hartford Seminary on May 23, 1960. The graduation program shows that his friends Ralph Logan Carson and Julia McClain graduated as well. Among the thirty-five others were eleven students from Connecticut, thirteen from other states, and one student each from Egypt, Syria, Lebanon, and the Philippines. At Hartford, Smith's understanding of people and of himself had undergone enormous growth.

By today's standards, Paul and Frances had seen very little of each other in their two-and-a-half-year engagement. While Paul was settling into his first semester in Connecticut, Fran had moved to California to spend her remaining college years closer to her family.

True to their vision, Fran's parents supported her desire to do a semester abroad. The trip was liberating; Fran says she first understood what freedom really felt like when she stepped off the plane in Copenhagen. She went on to graduate from Whittier College in California where she majored in psychology and sociology while securing her teaching credentials.

Having worked hard to obtain his professional credentials, Smith was thrilled to be following his heart at last. On June 12, 1960, a few weeks after they finished their studies, Paul and Fran married in Pasadena, California, surrounded by five hundred guests.

Smith carried the Hartford journal with him on the drive across the country with his parents. One entry mentions the awe-inspiring scenery they encountered. When his father commented, "All this was made by God," Smith calls him "a natural theologian in his own way [who] caught the glimpse of the eternal as it was revealed in the aesthetics of the countryside."[40] The observant son kept a meticulous record of the family's gas expenditures on the last page of the notebook.

On the day of the ceremony, Smith is still in an expansive mood, writing in his journal about marriage being "a wonderful estate to enter into, especially if the two people are in love and happy."[41] He notes that in a marriage with a foundation in Christian principles and in which the two people have "given completely of themselves," there is much to look forward to. He asserts that he "believes very strongly that ours has been such a marriage."[42]

Wedding of Frances Pitts and Paul Smith, Pasadena, California, 1960. Courtesy of the Smith Family.

Fran remembers only that she had never seen her betrothed with so short a haircut.[43]

In a journal note written on his fiftieth wedding anniversary,[44] Smith provides some details about the ceremony and the meaning he found in it decades later.

> 6/12/2010 Fifty years ago today I was in Pasadena, California to marry the person I love. Fran and I stood before her parents' Episcopal Priest on a beautiful afternoon and repeated our vows. My parents and Fran's parents stood happily by our side as we joyfully committed ourselves to each other. Kathy, Fran's sister and Bill, my younger brother were maid of honor and best man. I remember hundreds of people, black and white, happily sitting in the church in support of us. Classmates from Hartford Seminary surprised me by showing up for the ceremony. I had no idea they would attend. The two classmates were white students who had earlier graduated from seminary with me. Looking back I realize I was always destined to be involved in ministry that would include people from all racial and ethnic backgrounds. The fact of my being ordained in a denomination with only a handful of black people is just another sign of what would become my life's work.[45]

Later in their first summer together, though, Smith was struggling with the day-to-day reality of sharing his life. On August 5, 1960, he records an early installment in a lifelong rumination on how to handle anger:

> What is the best way to channel one's hostility? Where does one go when he gets angry? When should one forgive when there has been a misunderstanding? I have found in these two months of marriage that it is extremely difficult for two people with different backgrounds to work out their differences. It's even more difficult if there is a difference in the range and degree of experience along life's road. While these problems do exist, they will remain unless the two can work these differences out together.[46]

Without naming names, he muses about what to do if one person seems more secure than the other. He wonders whether one party should play the dominant role, making decisions knowing that unhappiness will result. Searching himself for fault and affirming his love for his wife, he concludes with a prayer.

> I am deeply troubled at this point because I don't quite know what the right thing to do happens to be. I think I know and this makes me feel that I'm being selfish. I do love my partner in marriage and will never stop loving her; however, the adjustment seems so pressing now. Can it be that our values

are mixed? Have I put too much emphasis upon things rather than on the essence that makes life[?] Oh God, help me in the midst of this crisis that together we might be brought to a clearer understanding of our roles and lives as we meet the cruelties and necessities of the day. [47]

With the union of Paul and Frances still strong after sixty years, it is clear they found a way to navigate through the difficulties of early marriage. After the wedding, they packed as many wedding gifts as they could into Paul's father's new Chevy for the drive back east. The partnership that would carry them into relationships with the most humble and the most powerful of people had finally begun.

CHAPTER 5

Urban Alliances

While disappointed that he was not asked to do his seminary fieldwork at one of the big white churches in Hartford, Smith found his own opportunity for interracial community building. The year before his marriage, Smith went to Buffalo, New York, for a summer internship at what became Salem United Church of Christ (hereafter Salem United).[1] There, the young pastor had to surmount a language barrier in addition to a racial one, but he plunged ahead: "When I got to Salem, 70% of the congregation spoke German. They didn't speak English. And they wanted me anyway . . . they heard me preach and they said, 'Uh, oh! We got one!'"[2]

The congregation liked Smith so much, they offered him a job to start immediately after his graduation from Hartford. They knew he might take a job elsewhere, but they were willing to wait for him. That was fortunate because, contrary to Smith's expectations, job offers were scarce the following year. After graduating in May 1960, the Baptists opened their arms to him again, and he again resisted their overtures. He knew he wanted an urban ministry and one where his seminary education would be valued. But despite the mounting evidence that he was skilled at crossing racial boundaries, he was still only being considered for certain positions: "It had to be a Black church. We were just not being called [by white churches]."[3]

A promising offer eventually came from an upscale Black United Church of Christ (UCC) congregation in Detroit. Smith responded quickly, acutely conscious that he was engaged and "didn't have a place to go, didn't have a job, didn't have a place to live!"[4] However, by the time the minister in Detroit called to extend his church's offer, Smith had already committed to Salem United. At a key turning point on his path, the young pastor chose

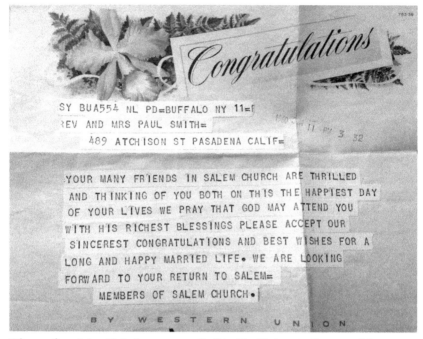

SY BUA554 NL PD=BUFFALO NY 11=

REV AND MRS PAUL SMITH=

   489 ATCHISON ST PASADENA CALIF=

YOUR MANY FRIENDS IN SALEM CHURCH ARE THRILLED
AND THINKING OF YOU BOTH ON THIS THE HAPPIEST DAY
OF YOUR LIVES WE PRAY THAT GOD MAY ATTEND YOU
WITH HIS RICHEST BLESSINGS PLEASE ACCEPT OUR
SINCEREST CONGRATULATIONS AND BEST WISHES FOR A
LONG AND HAPPY MARRIED LIFE. WE ARE LOOKING
FORWARD TO YOUR RETURN TO SALEM=
   MEMBERS OF SALEM CHURCH.

BY   WESTERN   UNION

Telegram from Salem United congregants, Buffalo, New York, 1960. Courtesy of the Smith Family.

to keep his word rather than chase after prestige: "The guy I was supposed to work with [in Buffalo], a white guy named Howard Fuller, [was] just a beautiful, beautiful human being. There was just no way. I said, 'You know that church is going to be so disappointed. That church has waited for me, knowing that I was between a rock and a hard place.' And not only did they offer me a job as assistant minister, they found an apartment for us."[5]

The telegram sent by Salem United just before Paul and Fran's wedding exemplifies the warmth and cordiality of Salem's outreach. In the end, the elite Black church got "no" for an answer, and the Smiths set their sights on Buffalo. The wisdom of Dr. Pitts's advice to finish their degrees before marrying became immediately apparent. With her degree finished and her impeccable teaching credentials from California, Fran quickly secured a job in Buffalo "making ten times more money than I was going to make as a minister," Smith says with a smile.[6]

Though it was in the Northeast, Buffalo had much in common with the South Bend of Smith's early years. German, Polish, Irish, and Italian immigrants had settled there during the first decades of the century, drawn by the promise of jobs in Buffalo's busy factories. By 1960, however, the city's heyday was over, and its population was beginning a long, slow decline.[7] Salem United was located on Sherman Street, on the east side of the city where Germans and Poles were concentrated.[8] African Americans who had come north looking for a new life lived nearby. The Smiths moved into the top floor of a two-family house that the church had rented for them and went straight to work.

Now that Smith had been "called" by a specific church, ordination and installation were to follow. The details of these ceremonies differ by denomination, but they are the most significant rites of passage in a young minister's career. Smith was ordained in the Congregationalist church with which Salem United had just merged. Celebrated in the context of a service, his ordination entailed his making a statement of his faith. Then by the laying on of hands, trusted leaders of the church formally recognized his new status in the congregation and wider church polity.

Smith's hiring made the paper,[9] and his supporters rallied to honor him. One of the pastors from St. John's in South Bend accompanied Smith's parents on the long road trip to Buffalo. Dr. John Bross journeyed all the way from Alabama to preach the ordination sermon. Two Black ministers in Buffalo with whom Smith had renewed ties participated in the service. Rev. William A. Hayes was a Congregational minister who had attended the same South Bend church and high school as Smith, and Rev. Porter W. Phillips Jr. was a Baptist minister whose family Smith knew.

The congregation at Salem United made good on the warmth they had extended to their young minister. Their interactions somehow worked despite their differences. Smith says they spoke very little English. Nonetheless, "they would take my hand. I prayed with them. They would talk with me even though I didn't understand what they were saying. But they were so interested and fascinated, that here was contact with an African American they were having toward the end of their lives."[10]

The author of an article published later by the *Presbyterian Survey* asked Smith how he was able to reach these parishioners.[11] The journalist wrote, "He tried to associate himself in the parishioners' minds with church traditions. By performing an annual candlelight service, for instance, he gained a degree of acceptance even though, he conjectured, the congregation may have been lulled by pleasant memories and 'may not have heard a single word I said.'"[12]

The article recounts that race only became a stumbling block when it came to Smith officiating at a funeral. "When one church leader died and the White pastor was out of town, Smith had to assume funeral duties.

Reluctantly, the family decided to allow the Black man to perform the ceremony, then the undertaker talked them out of it. A White minister was brought in."[13] "When the rest of the congregation heard about that," Smith told the reporter, "they made sure that everyone knew that sort of thing would not be condoned anymore. From that day, they made sure I'd be there for funerals."[14]

Smith's experience with one Salem parishioner in particular led him to a deep insight about the kind of work he had been called to do.

> I remember Christ Harlach. I saw him probably three weeks before he died. I can just hear his broken German with just a tinge of English, saying how much he appreciated my being there—that he could go home now to be with God. The circle was, for him, completed.[15]

Smith is emphatic when he tells this story.

> You can't have that experience in an all-white or all-Black church. You can't. You can't. I can see him now with tears in his eyes, knowing he was dying, and still he managed to say that. I knew I could not be settled on just a totally African American congregation. You can't have that kind of an experience in a single-race church. You just can't. You can't. The beauty is in the diversity.[16]

Bringing disparate people together into harmonious mutuality—creating what Dr. Martin Luther King Jr. called the "beloved community"—became Smith's life's work. In 1957, King described the ultimate goal of the movement that was gathering around him: "the end is reconciliation . . . redemption . . . the creation of the beloved community."[17] King drew on Gandhi to define such a community as grounded in a "love that can transform opposers into friends,"[18] a love so powerful, King said, it "might well be the salvation of our civilization."[19]

Dr. Smith has always been moved by this same spirit. He recognized early on the special sweetness that comes from finding respectful commonality with people unlike himself. Over the years, he has grown skilled at conflict resolution and mediation, bringing even adversaries into respectful working relationships with one another. His instinct has always been to connect across what appear to be barriers of difference.

At Salem United, Smith initially copastored with a white minister, Howard Fuller. Smith recalls, "He was really on it—a Renaissance man at Salem with these German parishioners. . . . He recruited me to work with him." While relations between senior and junior ministers can be fairly formal, Smith recalls, "Howard was the first real pastor other than my home minister who actually taught me what ministry was about. . . . Howard let me into the inner circle of ministers."[20]

There was also an outer circle, a local group that called itself the Ministerial Alliance (the Alliance). About a dozen clergy began to meet once a week in the spring of 1961 for fellowship and discussion about the social and political issues of the day. They were mostly young men, newly married and just starting out as professionals. Three of them were Black: Smith, Bill Hayes, and Porter Phillips. Smith recorded the minutes for an early meeting of the group in one of his journals. The notes show they had a chairman of the program committee, a president, and a constitution. Their concerns included a land development project, addressing segregation in area hospitals, and trying to combat the influence of organized crime in one part of the city.

> There was a little group of about twelve of us. We were kicking some butt! I mean, we were out there. A gangster owned everything, and we took him on. We were too young to be afraid. The government was so corrupt in Buffalo, the people took it over. Same as in Ferguson [Missouri].
> This gangster who controlled all of Buffalo—it was like Elliot Ness, really! And here we were, these young ministers making it tough for them.[21]

The gangster was Stefano Magaddino, a figure feared for decades in western New York.[22] Magaddino started out running a funeral home, began bootlegging during Prohibition, and later made his money through gambling, loansharking, and prostitution. A former FBI agent who led the Buffalo organized crime unit in those days said of Magaddino, "The don was a very powerful man, not only here but nationwide. . . . He was on the ruling commission of the mob."[23] Smith says now, "We were lucky we didn't get killed! But I think the gangster knew better. He knew we were insignificant, young innocent ministers trying to do the right thing."[24] Even so, Smith recalls that Rev. George Leak of Buffalo's African Methodist Episcopal Zion Church had to hire bodyguards after he ran the drug activity out of his neighborhood.

When the Alliance pulled straws in May 1961 to see who would represent them on a planned bus ride across the South, it was Leak who joined what came to be called the "Freedom Rides" organized by CORE. Leak narrowly escaped death when white segregationists, furious that the bus riders were testing the new federal mandate to desegregate interstate travel, attacked the Freedom Riders' broken-down Greyhound bus near Anniston, Alabama. The mob battered the bus with axes and pipes and eventually set it on fire. If there had not been an armed undercover government agent onboard who scared off the attackers, everyone in the bus would have died.[25]

George Leak's experience was surely part of what propelled Smith to seek out nonviolence training with Andrew Young that summer. After working for the National Council of Churches in New York for several years, Young himself had just returned to the South in 1961. There, he became a leader of the Citizenship School Program in Midway, Georgia, about thirty miles from Savannah, along with Septima Clark, Dorothy Cotton, and others.[26]

The week-long training sessions were held in a refurbished dormitory at the Dorchester Academy, an American Missionary Association school.[27] As Young later wrote, the program had a specific goal: "The basic idea at Dorchester was to establish voter registration using a few key people in 188 crucial counties that had black majorities across the Deep South but almost no black registered voters. Our hope was that the first people registered would in turn begin registration campaigns in their own counties."[28]

Participants were recruited from across the South. Young recalled recently, "We would charter a bus in Louisiana, and it would drive across Mississippi, Alabama, and Georgia, and bring people there on a Sunday afternoon. They'd get in Sunday night, we'd start Monday and we'd end up Saturday night and they'd start back."[29] The schedule included a big breakfast every day and morning classes including "practical civics," American and African American history, Gandhian nonviolent protest philosophy, and the basics of banking.[30] Everyone gathered in the evening for films and discussion. Each day ended with "prayers, singing, and testifying,"[31] and each week ended with a banquet dinner and a speaker (often Dr. King) before participants boarded the bus to go home.

Smith remembers Young's delight when he saw Smith getting off the bus to begin the training. Smith stayed with the Youngs rather than in the dorm and left determined to have a family just like the Youngs. And though he was not a rural southerner headed home to start a voter registration drive, Smith says the role-playing workshops and classes were life changing for him. He credits the training with helping him survive his encounter with violence in Selma. As Young remembers it, "What I saw in [Smith] was a new generation of ministers that were gonna have to carry on. Because . . . Dr. King was very frank. We just needed to find something worth living for, because we probably wouldn't live long doing what we were doing. He said we'll all be lucky if we see 40."[32]

Rev. Smith's energy and abilities quickly propelled him far beyond the burgeoning Salem United congregation. As he puts it, "I knew my gifts were more than just being a preacher, a minister. I had been exposed to more. I knew what possibilities were there."[33] He began to speak at other churches and appeared twice on television while living in Buffalo.

In 1963, the African American weekly magazine *JET* published several pages on Smith's success, highlighting his multiracial congregation and the fact that he was using jazz to reach his parishioners.[34] The young preacher said he did not see any conflict between "my religion and my interest in jazz." For him, it was a matter of using "my God-given talent to help spread the good news of the gospel."[35] One of four photos in the magazine captures Paul and Fran, well dressed and smiling on a couch with six-month-old Kathleen in Paul's arms. It was the era of the Kennedys' White House, and the attractive Smith family appeared to be in a Camelot of their own.

Smith was not content to rest in middle-class respectability, however. That same year, he took an additional post as industrial relations director for the Buffalo Urban League. He thereby joined a rising tide of activists and organizations mounting a huge push in the early 1960s to obtain fair employment opportunities for Black workers.[36] While the NAACP used the courts to try and secure justice, the Urban League's focus was on job training and placing Black candidates in corporate and industry jobs.[37]

A League official told a reporter that year about the need for the job Smith had been given.

> About 18 different organizations for civil rights, housing and jobs have popped up here (in Buffalo) during the last year. Many of them are handled by ministers, so we want to see if we can get a correlated program with them. I believe Rev. Mr. Smith is just the man to work with them.[38]

Smith has had connections with the Urban League ever since. Smith is a friend and adviser to the National Urban League's current president, Marc Morial. The mission of the organization remains essentially unchanged—to enable African Americans to achieve "their highest true social parity, economic self-reliance, power, and civil rights."[39] Smith says, "It all had to do with fact that I, as an African American kid, could not get a job in a white corporate firm."[40]

Smith was one of the early "brokers of inclusion," doing the legwork integral to opening American workplaces to people of color.[41] Being associated with the Urban League empowered Smith to push corporate managers to hire Black workers and improve company relations with people of color. He also worked to get contributions from white businesses for Urban League programs. He went on to work with the League in St. Louis, where he later listed in his journal four names under the heading "Jobs Secured."[42]

Through Smith's story, it is easy to see the spirit in which this work began. The tall, young, educated minister and family man making well-reasoned requests about job opportunities for others must have been hard to turn away. Smith was one of the many who articulated what can now be seen as simply "an earnest quest for decent jobs" on behalf of qualified candidates.[43]

Such efforts received a huge boost from the passage of the Civil Rights Act of 1964. Title VII made it illegal to discriminate "on the basis of race, color, religion, national origin or sex,"[44] and it was "the hardest-won section of that hard-won bill [passing] only after a historic 534-hour filibuster."[45] This legislation created a tidal wave of change in the worlds of business, government, and education that has not stopped to this day. The struggle for equal job opportunities for women, Latinos, Asian Americans, LGBTQ people, the elderly, and the disabled built upon the earlier fight for racial equality. Together, these efforts led to "a profound alteration ... in American workplaces over the last fifty years." Thanks to this "veritable revolution in thinking about race and gender and work,"[46] workplace equity is now seen as fair, necessary, and advantageous.

Working to change the system from within is not the approach advocated by more strident Black activists then or now, and Smith occasionally took some heat for his methods and beliefs. There came a day in Buffalo, for instance, when Black nationalist Malcolm X invited the whole Ministerial Alliance to attend his talk at a monthly gathering of local Muslims. Smith believes that Malcolm knew about the efforts of the Alliance to combat the criminal influences in Buffalo and approved of them.

However, when Smith arrived at the crowded hall on the appointed day, none of his colleagues were there. At first, Malcolm was cordial: "I [was] sitting next to him except when he went to the microphone to speak. I think he introduced me and thanked me for being 'brave to accept his invitation to be present that evening.'" Later on however, Smith says, "I got stomped on." The young minister's faith in collaboration across racial lines apparently did not impress perhaps the most vocal proponent of Black separatism at the time. Smith remembers, "He was addressing the 'evil, white, blue-eyed devils' and how they were controlling everything in America. He encouraged his followers to keep exposing the white devils for their treatment of Black people and keeping us in captivity. He spoke of himself as the one, along with his followers, to make sure the white devils would never enslave the Black Muslims."[47]

The rhetoric was harsh and directed at least in part toward people like Smith. Nonetheless, he is glad that he took the opportunity to hear Malcolm speak. "It was enlightening for me just to be in his presence and surrounded by such a devoted following of people."[48] The two did not meet again, since Malcolm X was assassinated two years later by members of the Nation of Islam, the Black nationalist group he had joined but later repudiated.

Smith's account of interacting with Malcolm X engendered much discussion at subsequent Alliance meetings. The young minister's willingness to meet others, including white people, on their own territory was beginning to set him apart. He says now, "It was the beginning of my understanding of ministry beyond my congregation and denomination."[49]

Smith established two lifelong professional and personal relationships in Buffalo that forever shaped his growth. One was with Rev. Marvin Chandler. Like Smith, Chandler had been born in Indiana and courted by the Baptist church after he finished his undergraduate degree. Chandler's great intelligence and warmth, however, drew the attention of mentors who encouraged him to pursue a graduate degree. Chandler was accepted into prestigious Colgate Rochester Divinity School where he studied from 1959 to 1963. The Smiths were already in Buffalo when Chandler moved his family there, intending to commute the seventy-five miles to Rochester for his studies.[50]

The two families quickly became close. Rev. Chandler's wife, Portia, says the two men were "like brothers, like two peas in a pod."[51] Both were dedicated, creative, high-energy people. Both had an interest in urban ministry and were comfortable with ecumenicalism. It was Chandler who began playing jazz services with Smith after discovering that Chandler was a gifted pianist.[52] Chandler recalls, "Paul and I felt each other's approach pretty well. We didn't try to analyze what was going on; we were just open to each other. His approach to religious experience is improvisational. And so is mine."[53]

Chandler fondly remembers the ministerial group he observed when he arrived: "it was an interracial and interfaith fellowship of confusion!" More seriously, he was impressed to find that "Howard's church was part of an alliance.... It was their urban interests that bound them together. It was a very mixed group racially."[54] Chandler notes that "Salem United was part of the denomination's experiment. They wanted to support that church toward integration.... It was in a changing neighborhood; the denomination was trying to reach out."[55]

The Chandlers soon joined the effort. Portia remembers, "Marvin, Paul, and Howard were three different types. They became close-knit. Howard was from a wealthy Boston family, very frugal."[56] She remembers having to pry more money out of him to pay for supplies for a summer program she assisted with. Together, Rev. Chandler says, the three pastors made Salem United "one of the first integrated churches in the city."[57]

Despite the fresh ideas in the air, there were many whose lives had not yet been touched by change in the mid-1960s. Frustration over still-unfulfilled promises began to erupt into violence. Urban conflagrations began flaring up all over the country in the mid-1960s. There were violent street confrontations in Harlem and Philadelphia in 1964, the Watts section of Los Angeles in August 1965, Chicago in 1966, and Newark and Detroit in 1967. Many of these events were sparked by confrontations between the urban poor and overzealous, heavy-handed police. Yet below the surface, the lack of jobs and ongoing employment discrimination fueled these fires.[58]

Rev. Chandler was among those called upon to try and defuse the tension. In 1964, he was asked to help calm three days of "race riots" in Rochester.[59] In addition to talking with people in the streets and neighborhoods, Chandler and others launched an effort to educate law enforcement officers. He is clear about how he viewed the root of the problem. "We talked to recruits in police academy class.... The whole problem is, it is taught as 'them and us.' When there are 4 or 5 Black kids on the corner, talking, they are not going to riot! It is part of the culture for them to gesture, and so on. It doesn't mean a doggone thing! [Police need to be] open to the possibility [that they are] misinterpreting ... cultural difference."[60]

Chandler's negotiation skills later carried him into the infamous confrontation between mostly Black inmates and white law enforcement officers at Attica Correctional Facility, located about halfway between Buffalo and Rochester in Upstate New York. In 1971, prisoners seized control of the prison and held it for four days as they negotiated for changes in what were truly barbaric conditions at the maximum security institution.[61] Chandler was one of the few people the prisoners trusted to act as their go-between with prison officials. In the end, Chandler was the last person to enter the prison to speak with the inmates before Governor Nelson Rockefeller ordered the state police to storm the facility. Rev. Chandler was on the premises when thirty-nine inmates and ten guards were killed in a matter of minutes. He says now, "At Attica Prison, I had to confront in a real way, my own fear, not just the possibility of death. To maintain my own position as a facilitator, I had to weave my way through that. My spirit, my soul, cried out. I don't have the right to curl up in a corner but [I have] to face the pain of fear and uncertainly even about my own self in those situations."[62]

Chandler says his work has involved the whole "complexity of the human situation. Beautiful, terrible, frightening." In his view, "the only way to really truly live is to be open to what life brings." And he says bluntly that he has learned, "If you want to fight for civil rights, you have to be ready to die."[63]

Another colleague with whom Smith had incredible synergy was the Rev. Carl Dudley. Dudley was pastor at the First Presbyterian Church of Buffalo from 1959 to 1962 and a member of the Ministerial Alliance.[64] Smith recalls they were "the agitators" in the group. Smith believes Dudley would have accompanied him to hear Malcolm X. However, by that time Dudley had taken a new job out of town.

In 1962, Dudley, who was white, was called to lead an all-Black church in downtown St. Louis. He had not been gone long before he contacted Smith, knowing Smith's abilities to build bridges across all kinds of social divides. Dudley proposed that Smith join him as copastor at Berea Presbyterian Church.

Leaving Buffalo meant disrupting the orderly life the Smiths had been building. While Fran recalls "that first job had a pretty decent salary," nothing was guaranteed in St. Louis. After marrying, Fran had expected that she would teach for a time and then have her first child before returning to work. She notes that this was not early feminism; it was practicality. Black wives and husbands both had to work to make enough money to support a family. Fran's mother had laid out the path for her. "The planning was [to have children] two years apart. It was a prescribed thing. My mother said you were supposed to do all this, being the oldest. You did what your parents said to do."[65]

Unexpected events had already interfered with the plan. Fran relates that her first pregnancy resulted in a miscarriage. She was told that she should wait some months before trying again. When Fran became pregnant again, her doctor insisted that she stop working immediately. Though it was in the middle of the school year, Fran complied. She points out that one could not teach school while pregnant in those days, so she didn't have much choice. Happily, the second pregnancy went well, and Kathleen, the first of the Smiths' three daughters, was born on September 7, 1962.

The timing of Rev. Dudley's offer was unfortunate in that the Smiths had just overcome considerable resistance to purchase a home. The neighbors in the segregated Williamsburg section of Buffalo had staged protests after hearing that a Black family was moving in. In a turn of events that had lifelong consequences for Smith, "the minister of the all-white Presbyterian church stepped up in our support. He and members of the congregation came over the day we moved in and welcomed us and were present to offset the protesting neighbors. That is when I decided to join the Presbyterian denomination."[66]

Smith took the fact that both Dudley and Berea were affiliated with the Presbyterian church as a further "clue" to God's plans for him. Following his heart and his spirit, Smith took the offer and put the Buffalo house back on the market. The idyllic family featured in *JET* magazine was moving on to new challenges. In St. Louis, the two dynamic ministers were about to show that interracial church leadership could bring to life a more radically inclusive church community.

CHAPTER 6

Prophets of Multiracial Christianity

In 1964, when Rev. Smith, his wife, and his daughter arrived in St. Louis from Buffalo, Rev. Carl Dudley had already been in the Mill Creek Valley section of the city's Central West End for two years, working to make a new mixed-income housing development into a racially integrated neighborhood. The community emerging there was like nothing anyone had seen before. Eventually encompassing 1,400 apartments and townhouses, LaClede Town was explicitly designed to bring a mix of people and residences together as a whole. As a former resident puts it, LaClede Town was "cool, hip, cheap and populated by people committed to making integration work."[1]

The development came to include a swimming pool, a Laundromat, a coffeehouse, and a pub. Artists contributed substantially to both LaClede Town's reputation and its street life. The resident Black Artists Group (BAG) became famous for its musical and theatrical performances.[2] A number of important jazz ensembles grew out of this rich context. There were poetry readings, dance concerts, and softball games. One historian asserts that LaClede Town was seen by many as "the heart of the city's counterculture."[3] Dudley's social justice and antiwar activism quickly "earned him national recognition and plaudits from the local black press."[4] Dudley met several times a year with King and the SCLC and was not surprised to learn later that the FBI had assembled a fat file on him and Berea.[5]

Rent in the new housing was set according to income. A concerted effort was made to house families in heterogeneous groups. People from different nations, cultural groups, economic strata, and religious communities lived, intentionally, side-by-side. As former resident Ellen Sweets wrote in 1997,

"It brought together a community of people—black, white, brown, Jews, Christians, Muslims, atheists, lawyers, architects, sanitation workers, actors, athletes, draft dodgers, hookers, social workers, welfare recipients, musicians, reporters, waiters, politicians, doctors."[6]

The Berea Presbyterian Church at 3010 Olive Street had had a strong Black congregation since its founding in 1898. Nonetheless, it barely escaped being flattened by bulldozers when everything else in the historic neighborhood was razed in 1959—the entire area had been declared a slum. Nearby, the massive and infamous Pruitt-Igoe public housing complex opened in 1954 only to be demolished twenty years later.[7] These efforts at "urban renewal" displaced thousands of residents, mostly people of color, without effective plans to resettle them. The resulting flows of urbanites into "the County," which is located outside the city proper, helped set the stage for later conflicts between police and residents in County towns like Ferguson, Missouri.

When the Smiths arrived, however, they joined a neighborhood on the upswing. Rev. Dudley's family had moved to a home across the street from Berea Church. Dudley was overseeing major renovations to the church building. These included reversing the orientation of the structure so that the front doors opened north toward Olive Street and the new development. A community room was added to the building that soon saw constant use. The Smiths settled into a small apartment nearby.

Rev. Smith's oldest daughter, Kathleen, was two when the family moved to St. Louis. She remembers Odessa, the elderly lady at the church who gave her and the Dudley children peppermints from her pockets.[8] She recalls hiding in the robes at her father's knees while he greeted parishioners on Sunday. She reveals that he was wearing his tennis whites under his robes so he could go directly to the court to play after the service. For her, Berea was "a family," a place defined by "community."[9]

The two ministers quickly became the spiritual heart of the neighborhood, according to Sweets. "Carl Dudley and Paul Smith, two Presbyterian ministers—one white, one black—transformed a historically black church with a dwindling congregation into an ethnically diverse institution that was often standing room only."[10]

One of many innovations at LaClede Town was the Circle Coffee Shop and Bookstore. This venue and its performance space became the artistic heart of the development. "The nearby Berea Presbyterian Church [administered] the Circle for the LaClede Town Management . . . and the Circle's tiny stage hosted readings, dance, improvisational theater and music from the likes of Hamiet Bluiett, Julius Hemphill and Oliver Lake—all with a strong focus on audience participation."[11]

For a time in the late 1960s and early 1970s, the community was considered a national model for successful urban renewal and integration. Carl's son Nathan Dudley notes that "it was unusual in that the people considered it their social life as well as their place of residence."[12]

Smith says, "It was experimental—interracial, interfaith, believers and nonbelievers, all together."[13] He emphasizes that the experience caused "a major, major shift in my thinking about what a church should be."[14] The church doors were open for all kinds of joint projects and activities, and events there drew people from other parts of St. Louis.[15] It was a middle-class congregation, with successful Black professionals from all over the city coming to worship.[16] Nathan Dudley cites the manager of the development, Jerry Berger, as describing Berea as "a dynamite church, one that's alive and unafraid."[17]

An energetic group of social scientists have been studying why multiracial Christian churches are still uncommon in this country. Even at the turn of the twenty-first century, less than 7 percent of American Christian churches were truly multiracial—that is, no one racial group accounts for more than 80 percent of the membership.[18] This has only begun to change in the last ten years.[19] The most successful multiracial churches have been found to allow separate cultures to exist within their membership *and* to create a new, unified church culture.[20] They have leadership that reflects the diversity of the congregation, and they foster extensive social interaction among church members. "Authentic" integration is their aim.[21] Characteristics that help a congregation move in this direction include having an inclusive worship style, creating intentional dialogue about racism, and being open to change.[22]

Belonging to a multiracial congregation changes people; it "is a powerful predictor of the racial diversity of a person's social relations."[23] On their own, Christian congregations tend to create and reinforce the very homogeneity they may hope to overcome.[24] Researchers who are themselves Christians have concluded that Christian churches *should be* multiracial and overtly "committed to dealing with one of the most important moral issues of this day—racism."[25] They have declared, "we need more people willing to be prophets of multiracial Christianity."[26] Most recently, Robert P. Jones of the Public Religion Research Institute makes the case *in White*

Too Long: The Legacy of White Supremacy in American Christianity that "white supremacy lives on today not just in explicitly and consciously held attitudes among white Christians; it has become deeply integrated into the DNA of white Christianity itself."[27] He suggests that white Christians consider the ways that "our complicity in this history, and our unwillingness to face it, have warped our own identities."[28]

In launching their interracial pastorate in 1964, Smith and Dudley were decades ahead of the curve. Serving a heterogeneous flock requires extra commitment; ministers must be "dedicated to continual learning, passionate about their mission, and experienced themselves in the daily negotiation of multiracial relationships."[29] All these qualities came naturally to Smith and Dudley and flourished through their partnership.

There were, of course, significant obstacles. The young pastors quickly became aware that there wasn't going to be enough money to pay both of them. Working the bureaucratic channels, a job as "director of race and religion" was created for Paul and paid for by the area Presbytery. As Smith remembers it, "they knew I could put people together of different races and religions." The job ultimately came to entail engaging members of different congregations, denominations, and faiths to join in civil rights activism.[30] "One of the signature programs we started involved white members of five suburban Presbyterian churches. . . . With the blessings of the St. Louis Presbytery and the five congregations, we invited a minimum of two white families to become full members of Berea Presbyterian Church. . . . Ferguson Presbyterian Church was one of the first congregations to send families to our program."[31] In 1965, when Smith and Dudley got off the plane in Selma to march with Dr. King, these were the churches whose ministers accompanied them.

Fortunately, collaborative leadership has come naturally to Smith from the beginning. Though Dudley was a few years older and more experienced than Smith, Smith says he never treated his new copastor as anything less than an equal. Dudley encouraged Smith take the lead on the Selma trip. This kind of professional and spiritual generosity resonated with Smith: "He celebrated my gifts like I celebrated his."[32] In contrast to some of his more autocratic colleagues, Smith has never hesitated to share power.

By joining Dudley at Berea Presbyterian and remaining in the denomination throughout his career, Rev. Smith's professional life has been shaped by a presbyterian model of church governance. This kind of church polity falls between the episcopal model, which concentrates power in the hands

REV. CARL S. DUDLEY   REV. PAUL SMITH

Our Heritage

Revs. Carl Dudley and Paul Smith, St. Louis, Missouri, 1965. Courtesy of the
Smith Family.

of a local bishop, and the congregational model, in which the local assembly
self-governs. Presbyterian churches split decision-making power between
a rotating group of elders elected from the congregation (the Session) and
an area council assembly made up of representatives from the local congregations (the Presbytery). The presbyteries in turn send representatives
to regional synods, and representatives from those bodies make up the na-
tional-level General Assembly.[33]

Lay leadership, then, is fundamental to Presbyterian church decision
making. Session members serve three-year terms and are "ordained" by
the laying on of hands, just like ministers. Ministers are called "teaching
elders," while elected lay leaders are referred to as "ruling elders." While
having a unique role vis-à-vis the congregation, a Presbyterian minister is
only advisory to the Session and is subject to the regulation and supervi-
sion of the Presbytery. Despite this, Smith emphasizes, "the congregation
doesn't have to *like* what you preach, but they can't tell you *what* to preach.
A Presbyterian minister's pulpit is free."[34]

In changing his denominational affiliation, Smith knew that he would
be one of what is still a small proportion of Presbyterian ministers who are
Black. Indeed, perhaps the best-known Black Presbyterian scholar, Rev. Dr.

Gayraud Wilmore, has commented dryly, "Anglo-Saxon Presbyterianism is about as close a cousin to the Black religious experience as 'Annie Laurie' by the Royal Bagpipes of Scotland is to 'Body and Soul' by Fats Domino."[35]

More seriously, Wilmore has explored the century-long history of Black Presbyterians holding "identity and integration in a creative tension" within the denomination.[36] In 1991, he wrote that the "ambivalence," the unity-within-diversity experience of Black Presbyterians, would prove instructive for the twenty-first-century church.[37] Though Rev. Smith has not been much involved with Black Presbyterians as a group, the influence he came to wield within the denomination illustrates the powerful potential of being a Black minister in a mostly white, mainline Christian church.

The congregation at Berea was ready to help Rev. Smith assume his new role. Early on, a parishioner asked Smith to stop by his house. The man, who worked as a chauffeur for a wealthy white executive, was known for his sharp appearance. Smith says, "Even when he was dying, he wore silk robes with his initials on them." Upon welcoming Smith to his home, the man presented Smith with a surprise from Rich's Department Store. "He said, 'I'm so glad you're here. You're young! I've made a purchase for you. I notice you don't have any white shirts. Presbyterians wear white shirts! I want you to be successful.' And he gave me four white shirts."[38]

Berea's congregation had long been politically active, and Dudley leaned hard to the left. In 1966, he and other ministers from St. Louis drove to Chicago regularly to study with activist Saul Alinsky, who was helping to organize and empower Black residents there.[39] At a time when controversy over the Vietnam War was becoming strident, Nathan Dudley remembers the suggestion that congregants invite the media to witness the burning of their draft cards in the sanctuary. When an elderly, longtime parishioner was asked what she thought of the plan, she said she thought that the sanctuary was "just the place for them to burn those cards."[40] While on the one hand running a summer day camp for kids, the church also provided meeting space for a local chapter of the Black Panthers.[41]

Smith remembers his first contact with a well-known Black St. Louis activist, Percy Green. The summer of 1964, the year Smith arrived, the city's Gateway Arch was being built, and Green wanted to launch protests over the lack of Black workers on the huge construction site. Green lived in LaClede Town and met with Dudley and Smith to enlist their help.[42] He explained that he would need them to bring food because he was going to shut the site down by climbing up and occupying the half-finished structure. When Green suggested that the Berea ministers join in, Smith says

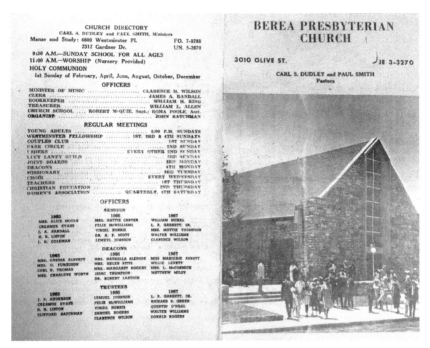

Worship service program, Berea Presbyterian Church, St. Louis, Missouri, 1965.
Courtesy of the Smith Family.

they told him, "We love you Percy but we aren't going to be climbing up on that arch!"[43] Falling to their deaths was not the kind of "direct action" either man had in mind. In the end, a white activist named Richard Daly joined Green 125 feet up, while compatriots met with the press below to demand that Black workers be hired on the public-funded project.[44]

A Berea worship service program from February 28, 1965 has survived among Smith's papers. Its cover photo captures Berea's grey stone façade with a crowd of well-dressed Black and white parishioners out front. Inside, the program shows that Revs. Dudley and Smith alternated in leading the service. It happens that on that day, Smith delivered "Void Where Detached," the sermon he had been working on since Hartford five or six years earlier.

Another innovation that emerged from the ministers' collaboration was bringing conversations about funerals and death into the open at their church. This was important because their multiracial congregation brought differing expectations to such events. At Easter in 1965, the young ministers together with Berea's lay leadership produced a mimeographed booklet on the subject that was distributed to parishioners. In it, they urged families to plan in advance for a loved one's death. They suggested never making funeral arrangements alone and cautioned people to keep their financial limitations in mind and remember "the simplicity of our faith."[45] Those with material goods were advised to have a will.

Expectations about funerary arrangements differed between Black and white parishioners. Many of the African Americans had grown up with the Black Baptist traditions Smith had known in South Bend. In those churches, the central focus of the funeral service was the open casket positioned in the front of the church near the pulpit. After the service was over, goodbyes were said directly to the deceased in the casket by mourners and preachers alike. Emotions tended to run high. After the funeral service, the casket was sometimes driven through the deceased person's neighborhood, "one more time." Cremation was not considered an option. Smith has heard many a Black Baptist minister exclaim, "You can't preach a funeral without a body!"[46] Meanwhile, some white Berea congregants preferred a closed casket or cremation and a memorial service.

At Berea, Dudley and Smith suggested there could be many ways to approach these issues. In the case of a funeral, they invented the tradition of covering the casket with a simple cloth that belonged to the church. That way, people could feel freer to choose a plain casket rather than an expensive one. The copastors also made clear that autopsies, organ donation, and donation of bodies for scientific study were "fully consistent with our Christian faith."[47]

The confluence of people, traditions, and personalities at Berea made the work difficult at times. Smith was paying close attention to the ways his flock interacted, as one journal entry shows.

> A few days ago a group of citizens in St. Louis came together to discuss ways of helping in the civil rights thrust. Only by the grace of God were these diverse people able to communicate and plan together. The backgrounds were so different, the interests so varied, that at one point they were eternally at one another's throat. After 48 hours we came together again and hopefully worked out our differences. . . . What happened to the group as we went our separate ways that day? Mad, hostile towards one another, accusations made! Someone, or something touched each individual, especially those who were grinding personal axes—and somehow caused us to see the significance of our purpose, which far outweighed any other concerns.[48]

A seasoned observer who lived in St. Louis at the time, Rev. Dr. Luther Smith Jr. (no relation), gives the Berea ministry high marks. Rev. Smith Jr.

was a minister and Thurman scholar whose family later attended Smith's church in Atlanta. He says:

> People were hopeful that this might represent something new for St. Louis.... Berea was so active as a church in community formation and bringing people together. There was a vitality and growth. They were Black and white clergy with an interracial congregation—it was very inspiring. It is difficult for me to remember another ministry that produced such excitement about the ways they thought about worship and outreach to the wider community.... Together they modeled the kind of crossing of the boundaries that we look for in the church.[49]

Dudley himself later wrote, "My idea of heaven is a reunion of these amazing people from our years in Berea Church."[50]

Despite the joyous successes of Berea and LaClede Town, the later 1960s were hard years. There is new weariness and recurrent anger in Smith's writing during this time. A journal entry dated April 20, 1967, reveals Smith's thoughts about how much community work remained to be done. "It seems programs are generally launched 'after' the fact, rather than 'before.' The programs come after people have taken all they can stand and turn to the streets to release their pent up frustrations. Soon this country will discover that people are indeed the country and unless we begin to deal with them as peoples,[51] we will continue to witness the bloodshed and wrath."[52]

In 1967—almost fifty years before the death of Michael Brown—Smith agonizes over the shooting death of a fourteen-year-old boy who was trying to rob a grocery store. He laments that the boy has died after a petty crime: "We (society) killed him. We caused his death because we are part of the system—we give consent and affirmation to it daily.... We should have provided a decent education. We should have given this boy an incentive.... What alternative does a Negro youngster have today? Death by the corner grocery or by a bullet in Vietnam?"[53]

Smith's anger reached terrible new heights in April 1968 when Rev. Dr. Martin Luther King Jr. was assassinated. With devastating suddenness, the man who had changed the country and who evoked both the ardent love and the virulent anger of so many Americans was gone. In the final entry in one early journal, written several weeks after the fact, Smith's fury spills over. "How do you respond to death? Do you cry? Do you shout? Do you rebel? Do you condemn? ... When Martin Luther King Jr. was assassinated on a balcony, I was literally bitter and my first words were 'damn the white people.' I look back over those first moments and will never forget the panic, the feelings of hostility, the darkness of the day—the phone calls to various people whom I have known. And then the long night which never seemed to end."[54]

Writing through his intense sorrow, Smith remembers their meeting at Talladega. With effort, he turns his thoughts to the future. "Where will it all end? I first met Martin [when] I was a bubbling senior at Talladega College and Martin came to our campus to speak. . . . Thank God he lived among us. . . . How long Lord, How long! Will we ever learn? Yet we are compelled now to turn the page and make Martin's dreams a reality."[55] With King's death, the passions and progress of the 1960s came to a crashing halt. Two months later, Senator Robert Kennedy was killed. Led by new firebrands like Stokely Carmichael, "Black Power" became the political refrain among many African Americans. This ideology did not countenance collaboration and negotiation between Black and white; rather, the Black community claimed control of its political and economic fortunes and declared that, if necessary, it would use violence to back up its demands. The days of white and Black working together to change society appeared to be over.

The biracial collaboration at Berea came to an end as well, albeit amicably. Rev. Smith remained an associate pastor at Berea until at least 1970, though he was simultaneously exploring new professional directions. In 1973, Rev. Dudley moved to Chicago to finish his doctorate and remained there to pursue an academic career.[56] Smith's connection with Berea remained strong; he was invited back in 1982 to speak at the eighty-fifth anniversary of the church's founding.

To the great consternation of those who had shared their lives there, LaClede Town—that shining new model of urban living—was itself demolished in 1995. After deteriorating through the 1980s and 1990s, the whole neighborhood came to be viewed as blighted once again and underwent another wave of destruction and rebuilding. In the end, the only thing left standing once again was Berea Church.

Today, the building has been repurposed as a conference center and stands empty most of the time. Nonetheless, irrepressible former LaClede Town residents have found each other online and have begun meeting periodically for reunions.[57] Their relationships are keeping the spirit of their beloved community alive.

CHAPTER 7

Black Employment, Black Theology, and Black Power

After the assassination of Dr. King, militant Black leaders unleashed their anger in blunt, uncompromising terms. A major articulation of the new political ideology was former SNCC leader James Forman's Black Manifesto of 1969 (the Manifesto).[1] Speaking for Detroit's National Black Economic Development Conference, Forman's document demanded "$500,000,000 from the white Christian churches and the Jewish synagogues. This total comes to $15 per nigger. . . . $15 dollars for every black brother and sister in the United States is only a beginning of the reparations due us as people who have been exploited and degraded, brutalized, killed and persecuted."[2] The statement specified that the money should be spent to develop a land bank and a Black university in the South, Black-owned publishing and TV outlets, a National Welfare Rights Organization, and a National Black Labor Strike and Defense Fund, among other projects. These claims were justified by the fact that "racist white America has exploited our resources, our minds, our bodies, our labor."[3] The Manifesto stated in no uncertain terms that "we are not opposed to force and we are not opposed to violence"[4] being used to back up the claims.

As part of a campaign to take their message directly to white religious institutions, Forman famously disrupted a service to read his text at Riverside Church in New York. This set off a fiery national conversation about white society making reparations to Black people for slavery and subsequent economic and political injustices. While some Christian groups including the Black Presbyterians took the Manifesto seriously, no collective response was ever mobilized.[5] Reparations only recently became the subject of renewed discussion when Ta-Nehisi Coates wrote a major piece for *The Atlantic* in 2014.[6] The issue was subsequently taken up in congressional hearings in June 2019.[7]

Smith, of course, knew about the Manifesto, but he was not roused by it. He contends that Forman's position was essentially "just give me some money and I will empower our people," rather than addressing inequality in deeper and more practical terms. He says, "At the time when it happened, 40 acres and a mule made sense. But [afterward] you're just back where you started from—not getting an education, not becoming a politician or a teacher. . . . You know, they never *got* the 40 acres and a mule. It was a ruse! We might still be plowing, hoping nothing happens to the mule! So I'm not a fan from a historical point of view."[8] Smith today has little patience for the subject of reparations in general. "You can't owe me unless you have my consent to owe me. I don't think a lot of black people gave their consent for what Dr. King called the promise of 'insufficient funds.' . . . How can you *atone* for the Holocaust? You can't *atone* for slavery!"[9]

Having learned at Selma that he could not fully tamp down the fury that might arise in him during direct political action, Smith carried the values of "the movement" into community activism and public service. In St. Louis, while copastoring at Berea, he took his place on the front lines of the battles for decent jobs and housing. From 1965 to 1967, Smith was president of Freedom of Residence (FOR), a fair housing initiative. The program at that time had four neighborhood sites where St. Louis residents could file complaints of housing discrimination, inflated rents, and/or substandard living conditions.[10] Smith documented those complaints, and FOR's legal staff pursued redress in the courts.

Smith later served as the first St. Louis director of Project Equality, an interfaith equal opportunity employment program created by the National Catholic Conference on Interracial Justice.[11] At the time, Smith says, there were only two such offices, one in St. Louis and one in Kansas City. Backed by the assertion that religious institutions had a moral responsibility to help address unfair employment practices, Project Equality had a broad impact; by 1966, it had enlisted the participation of ten thousand firms in twelve cities.[12]

Eventually, Smith was asked to help administer a $3 million Urban League antipoverty program.[13] In that role, he worked with William E. Douthit, the energetic and long-serving executive director of the St. Louis Urban League. In 1968, Douthit was reorganizing to "meet challenges and opportunities coming from the social and economic climate,"[14] and Smith lent his experience to the task.

From 1967 to 1971, Smith was also a paid consultant for the Office of Federal Contract Compliance. After the passage of the Civil Rights Act of 1964, companies doing business with the federal government were required to undergo reviews to assess their compliance with Title VII. As a contract relations specialist, Smith did investigatory research and wrote reports on his findings. He describes it as a heady position for an African American. Quite simply, he says, "everything that was closed to me, the government was hiring me to [open]."[15]

Smith was more diligent and enthusiastic about the job than many of the mostly white men he worked with. He is proud to say he actually gave some companies bad reviews, notably 3M in Minneapolis and McDonnell Douglas in St. Louis. He succeeded in getting their attention. In fact, he says, "They were pissed!" His bosses were flabbergasted. "People were saying, 'Rev. Smith is relentless! Get this guy off our backs!'"[16] Asked whether he enjoyed rattling people, Smith says mildly, "I didn't do it intentionally. I just did what I was trained to do. I didn't keep my light under a bushel."[17]

In addition to the new legislation, it was the willingness of the workers themselves to fight for their rights that was instrumental in creating this era of change.[18] By filing cases articulating the details of the inequalities they faced, workers helped to define what fair workplace opportunity should look like. They made sure that "new elements of representation, due process and public oversight" became operative in the corporate world.[19] Facilitating the process were people like Paul Smith, who played the role of "intermediaries who maneuvered between those seeking change and those resisting it."[20]

As vital as Title VII was (and is) to creating more equitable conditions of employment in this country, there were only weak systems of enforcement put in place to buttress the legislation. The Equal Employment Opportunity Commission (EEOC), a five-member bipartisan body appointed by the president, was set up in 1965 to hear claims about employment discrimination. Smith was among those who helped document complaints that were submitted to the EEOC for review and recommendations. The power of the commission to compel compliance was quickly compromised, however, when it became hopelessly backlogged with thousands of cases.[21] The scale of the problem was overwhelming. In 1972, Congress belatedly gave the EEOC the power to use litigation to back up its enforcement efforts, but by then corporate managers had learned that there was little risk in ignoring the new law. In subsequent years, funding and congressional support for Title VII dwindled.[22]

There were other factors that combined to hold back the wave of much-needed change. Just as the doors to employment began to open for Black candidates in the 1970s, "industrial restructuring wiped out most of those gains."[23] Automation and recession contributed to job losses in the huge textile, meatpacking, and auto industries.[24] The conservative political movement that took shape in the 1970s attacked the idea of affirmative action from the start.[25] Rather than redressing historic inequalities in employment opportunities, they contended that the new laws were going to establish a quota system that would disadvantage majority workers. They thereby "managed to turn an earnest request for decent jobs into a radical, even surly demand for a giveaway."[26] Efforts to obtain workplace equity have had to justify their existence ever since.

As educated, middle-class professionals, the Smiths had advantages that many of their peers did not. First, they had good jobs; Frances's teaching in particular brought in a larger and more regular paycheck than ministry. And as their family grew, they were able to secure housing in decent neighborhoods, even if it meant enduring hostility from their white neighbors. After they left LaClede Town they lived for a time in mostly white Moline Acres. There, they became lifelong friends with the Wilkenses, the only other Black family in the neighborhood. Lenny Wilkens was a professional basketball player who later rose to Hall of Fame status as both an NBA player and a coach. Wilkens remembers thinking that his family had already borne the brunt of the neighborhood's racial hostility when the Smiths moved in.[27] So he decided he wasn't going to make it too easy for the newcomers. When Paul walked down the block one day to introduce himself, Wilkens pretended he was too busy in his garage to notice him. Undaunted, Smith marched in to find him, and the two have been joking about it ever since.

The families became close as Wilkens and his wife Marilyn had a daughter and the Smiths welcomed Heather in 1965 and Krista in 1968. The men still riff on the fact that it was Paul, not Lenny, who accompanied Marilyn to the hospital for the birth of their second child. Lenny was out of town that day playing basketball for the St. Louis Hawks, so Marilyn enlisted Paul's help. Rather than giving his buddy credit for fulfilling this vital role,

Wilkens jokes that what *really* happened that day was that he showed Paul how to have *sons*.

Wilkens says that his friend has "that aura" that Wilkens found in Dr. King and in Nelson Mandela. He admires the fact that Smith "has great control of who he is. And a purpose.... He never loses sight of those things. He has helped a lot of people."[28] Wilkens asserts that Smith is one of "very few people that I think I'd put my life on the line for. And he would do the same for me."[29]

The family of five later moved again into the University City neighborhood where they lived until 1978. This community lies just north of Washington University. That institution, the city's pride and joy, is grandly sited at the top of a hill overlooking Forest Park. "U. City" was relatively integrated, being the home of many university people and Jewish families who were made to feel unwelcome in some other parts of St. Louis. Frances, who was an at-home mother with three small children in that period, remembers only a blur of family responsibilities.[30]

In stark contrast to the rise and fall of urban developments in the heart of the St. Louis, daughter Kathy says of well-groomed University City that "nothing here has changed."[31] The Smiths' house on Princeton Avenue is still the same dignified two-story brick structure she grew up in. In her youth, there was a pool in the backyard and a pool table in the basement. The house was the frequent site of parties enhanced by her mother's memorable cooking. The children safely rode their bikes on the quiet, curving streets. Kathy remembers that kids in the area all played together, whatever their backgrounds.

Since segregation had long rendered many of the city's social and recreational venues off limits to African Americans, they socialized mostly in their homes. Those who had the money built pools and tennis courts. As had been true for decades, people of color expected to share their homes with extended families, friends' families, and visitors. Among the mansions on Lindell Boulevard overlooking midcity Forest Park, there is a compound where Kathy and the children of a Black doctor played while their fathers competed on the family tennis court.

Through that physician, Smith quickly met and began to work with other doctors in town. Accompanying her father on visits to homes and hospitals, Kathy saw how valuable his presence was to the sick and the dying. Unlike more conservative ministers of color, Smith has long been sympathetic to the role that can be played by hospice and end-of-life planning to give patients a greater voice in the circumstances of their death. Smith says he differs in this approach from that of pastors whose exclusive focus on Jesus' power to cure and comfort precludes thinking about more immediate ways to support a fatally ill person and their family.

In 1971, a job opportunity for Smith facilitated an international sojourn for the whole family. A minister in Jamaica was taking a sabbatical, and Smith was asked to replace him. In addition to leading a congregation in downtown Kingston, Smith was hired to teach liberation theology at the nearby University of the West Indies Seminary. The Smiths and their three daughters moved to the seminary campus for the year.

The founder of Black liberation theology was Rev. Dr. James Cone, who taught at Union Theological Seminary in New York City for much of his career until his death in 2018. Dr. Cone was one of the sharpest critics of what he saw as a racist Christianity practiced by many whites in the United States since enslaved people were first brought here. His career was dedicated to developing an alternative approach to Christian theology that placed Black Americans in the theological center.

Cone's classic treatise, *Black Theology and Black Power*, was published in 1969.[32] In it, Cone builds on the work of theologian Paul Tillich and others to assert that Christian love must be accompanied by justice and power.[33] Cone explores the idea that the sole purpose of the church "is to be a visible manifestation of God's work in the affairs of men. . . . The Church of Christ is not bounded by standards of race, class, or occupation. . . . Rather the Church is God's suffering people."[34] Cone articulated an idea that was as yet unheard of in white theology—if Christ brought God's love to the oppressed, and Black people are oppressed due to their blackness, then "*Christ is black, baby*, with all of the features which are so detestable to white society" (emphasis in the original).[35] Taking these ideas yet further, Cone writes:

> It is the job of the church to become black with [Christ] and accept the shame which white society places on blacks. But the church knows that what is shame to the world is holiness to God. Black is holy, that is, it is a symbol of God's presence in history on behalf of the oppressed man. Where there is black, there is oppression; but blacks can be assured that where there is blackness, there is Christ who has taken on blackness so that what is evil in men's eyes might become good. Therefore Christ is black because he is oppressed and oppressed because he is black. And if the church is to join Christ by following his opening, it too must go where suffering is and become black also.[36]

The Smiths in Jamaica, West Indies, 1971. Courtesy of the Smith Family.

Cone suggests that to be free of hypocrisy, the church must be free of racism. Otherwise, the white church "makes racism a respectable attitude."[37] The potential transformation of the church, however, requires a major rethinking of white attitudes (his emphasis):

> The biblical doctrine of reconciliation can be made a reality only when white people are prepared to address black men as *black* men and not as some grease-painted form of white humanity....
>
> Reconciliation ... means that man can now be what he is—a creature made for fellowship with God. But that is only one side of reconciliation. To be reconciled with God involves reconciliation with the neighbor.... For black people it means that God has reconciled us to an acceptance of our blackness. If the death-resurrection of Christ means anything, it means that the blackness of black people is a creation of God himself. God came into the world in order that black people need not be ashamed of who they are. In Christ we not only know who we are, but who God is. This is the heart of the biblical message.[38]

It is not hard to imagine how radical these ideas sounded in the 1960s. For many, they might still seem radical today. When Rev. Smith arrived to teach the philosophy to Jamaican seminary students and parishioners, the Jamaican government was wary. He says, "The first month I taught in Jamaica, undercover people called the CID were in my classes every day. When my books came, they confiscated them. They had an undercover person in my class to be sure I wasn't coming there to destroy the country! They didn't know what liberation theology was."[39]

As usual, Rev. Smith immediately attracted attention for his preaching. He recalls that "there were maybe thirty people in this huge church, downtown in Kingston. Within a month or two, people were saying, 'You got to go hear da crazy minister at da church. He fascinating man!'"[40]

Smith's intuitiveness, magnanimity, and improvisation skills aroused people's attention. On Easter morning, he remembers intervening on behalf of a congregant who made others a bit uncomfortable. "You know in Christendom you can do communion with a common cup or the little individual cups. Easter Sunday morning, the place was packed. I never knew her name, but there was a little lady with a nice little hat. For some reason, there was always saliva coming out of her mouth."[41]

As Rev. Smith led the crowd through communion, they ran out of individual cups. "When I got to her row, I took the cup and gave it to her. Then because I could see what was going to happen, I took the cup right after her. After I had drunk from the cup, then everyone else took it after me. And then they said, 'Da crazy minister, he take da communion himself!' I just did it spontaneously. I knew instinctively the others wouldn't take communion after the lady with the saliva."[42]

Smith both delighted and unsettled people. While the seminary had specifically asked him to teach liberation theology, Rev. John Hoad, who had been appointed president of the seminary only a few years before, at one point pulled Smith aside to ask, "Could you just tone it down a bit?" Smith is still laughing about this today, exclaiming with gusto, "You can't tone down James Cone!"[43]

When Smith was asked to give the commencement address at graduation, he said, "'You need to hear from the man himself. James Cone is a friend.' . . . I called Cone and asked if he would come down to Jamaica to give the speech. He said, 'Are you kidding? I just got married. Of course I'll come to Jamaica!' Cone and his wife came, all expenses paid. . . . [At commencement, Cone] was up there being very smart, while the white faculty were huffing and puffing! They couldn't wait until he finished."[44]

Upon returning from Jamaica, Smith's professional path forward was not clearly defined. He preached more and more regularly at Second Presbyterian Church, located a few miles from Berea. For Second Presbyterian, hiring the gifted African American preacher was a step toward integrating the grand stone edifice begun in 1896.[45] For the Smiths, Second Presbyterian became their family church until they left St. Louis in 1978.

Dr. Kenneth and Mrs. Marge Smith (no relation) are longtime members of Second Presbyterian who have lived in the same central downtown neighborhood since the 1960s. They watched as Pruitt-Igoe and LaClede Town rose and fell. Over the decades since, they have been stalwarts among the lay leaders and clergy working to stem the resulting floods of people toward the suburbs. Early on, "there was a lot of hammering on the door saying we've got a lot of things going on that aren't right. And Paul was at the center of that with Carl Dudley."[46]

Eventually, they were among those who helped to entice Smith to join Second Church as a pastoral associate in 1975. "He preached and he worked with young people and taught classes. . . . The reason we recruited him was because of his record at Berea. We knew we could work together."[47] Dr. and Mrs. Smith describe the ways the reverend became part of their own congregation's efforts: "We were all talking the same language and doing common things together. . . . Carl Dudley—he crossed between the Black and the white community, and Paul crossed between the white and the Black community. So [with] those of us who had the social consciousness, we became a dedicated force."[48] These efforts led to the establishment of a tutoring program and a food pantry that are still active today.

A few years ago, Second Presbyterian called a new young minister who is biracial and a bridge builder. "As soon as [we] met this fellow Travis Winckler, he was acting like Paul. He's got tremendous potential. His wife is a Ph.D. Professor of Theology from University of St. Louis, so that's a pretty powerful team."[49] On Sunday, November 11, 2019, Rev. Smith returned to Second Presbyterian to preach a sermon called "Can We Talk?" and to lead a workshop on race with Rev. Winckler. Though they had just met, the two men effortlessly interwove their pastoral messages.

Rev. Smith's deft social touch and strong communication skills eventually led to solid job offers in the heart of the mostly white academic world. The 1970s were times of strident conflict on college campuses with students protesting the Vietnam War, asserting new identities, and demanding their rights. Smith bonded easily with both students and staff, offering them a sympathetic ear. His first appointment at elite Washington University in 1970 was as assistant to the vice chancellor.[50] After the family returned from Jamaica, he became director of housing and residential life, and in 1974, he was promoted to assistant vice chancellor with responsibility for both residential life and student affairs.[51] By the time he left St. Louis in 1978, Smith had risen to the rank of associate vice chancellor. In all these roles, of course, Smith was a racial pioneer breaking down barriers for other people of color.

Wash University also gave Smith his first opportunity to teach. Initially, he was hired to teach Black studies. Teaching has always come easily to this practiced and ebullient preacher. Smith has taught college classes part time in every city he has lived in since. His later courses included medical ethics and the works of Howard Thurman. His rapport is as powerful with students as it is with parishioners; people of all ages feel his concern, appreciate his experience, and respond to his message.

Smith still worked occasionally for the Presbytery during this period. For the American Bicentennial in 1976, Rev. Smith was asked to create a community event. Turning again to music as a unifying force, Smith formed a choir with kids from the mostly white churches near Eden Seminary where he was pursuing his PhD. He found a musician who composed jazz versions of classic Presbyterian hymns and asked him to work with the choir. The white children "had never had a jazz musician as a choir director before," Smith says, and there were some parents who were hesitant about allowing it. However, when the choir performed at the magnificent Webster Groves Presbyterian Church, it was such a success that the local TV station, KMOX, asked them to perform it again as part of their Sunday series.

That same year, Smith was given the opportunity to write about the history of the Black church for a Bicentennial issue of a local African American magazine, *Proud*.[52] The publication emerged out of a wave of "Black Nationalist–oriented" businesses in St. Louis in the later 1960s.[53] Smith's article follows the Black church from the days of slavery through the Civil War to the Great Migration and beyond. Much more directly than in his earlier life, he stresses the importance of Black theology as a source of empowerment for a disenfranchised people. He goes on to argue that "the black church by word and deed is committed to the liberation struggle. It understands that it must move for fundamental change in the society in which it lives."[54]

While staying close to his values, Smith was succeeding in professional realms far afield of ministry, and powerful observers in the African

GOLDEN ANNIVERSARY — Mr. and Mrs. Leonard Smith Sr. of 3703 Belle Vista will celebrate their 50th wedding anniversary with an open house from 2 to 5 p.m. next Sunday at the home of their son-in-law and daughter, Samual and Marlene Wright, 2250 Johnson. Smith and the former Josephine P. Johnson were married on Oct. 15, 1929, in South Bend and have lived here for 65 years. Their other children are Miss Joan Smith of Detroit, Leonard Smith Jr. of Niles, Rev. Paul Smith of Atlanta and William Smith of Los Angeles. There also are nine grandchildren. Their marriage vows will be renewed by their son, Rev. Paul Smith. The Smiths request that no gifts be given.

Leonard and Josephine Smith's fiftieth wedding anniversary announcement. Courtesy of the Smith Family.

American community were taking note. Early in the 1970s, Smith received word of his election to the most august Black men's association of them all, Sigma Pi Phi. Founded in 1904, "the Boulé," as it is known, is "the quintessential organization for professional black men . . . it is considered by many *the* elite men's club and its membership has included the most accomplished, excellent, and influential black men in every city for the last [112] years."[55]

One cannot seek out membership in this national society; a nominee is vetted in secret and voted in by his peers. Across the nation, members belong to local chapters that convene for a national conference every two years. When members cross paths in the working world, they are expected to offer each other professional and social support. Sigma Pi Phi brothers even perform special observances at each other's funerals. As impressive as the company may be, Dr. Smith does not hesitate to goad his fellow members into committing more of their resources to social service projects. He is frustrated by people who seem to want to rest on their laurels.

In 1977, while chairing an Equal Employment Opportunity Commission meeting in Kansas City, Missouri, Smith wrote a letter of thanks to his father. The text reveals some of his thoughts on life at age forty-two.

Dear Dad,

I am writing this letter to you from Kansas City, Mo.... My daughter Heather is with me. I have tried to take each of the girls on a trip with me so they can have time with me alone....

You see Dad, I have been thinking about the greater things of life. My life is so blessed, and I have been fortunate in my job and community possibilities that I began to think about where it all comes from. As I sit here in the hotel, with my daughter, I realize that it began with you. How much I am like you is still a mystery, but I know that very early in my life I caught your spirit. Very early in my life, I knew the meaning of hard work and achievement. You taught it to me and even more you showed me by example....

I am happy because I carry the spark of Leonard Smith, Sr. in me.... It helps me be a good husband as you have always been to mother. You have had ups and downs with her, and I have had the same ups and downs with Fran. But your love for mother has been an exceptional example for me.... I know how to be a father because you have always been a father to me....

Dad, you have also given me as a legacy, your wit, your warmth, your ability to know, understand and be comfortable with all people. I have never once seen you angered because you were black. I had a hard time remembering when I first became aware of my blackness. You taught us how to live and love all people—strange, that for a greater part of my life at 137 North Carlisle, I never knew prejudice or hatred. That spark is still in each of us thanks to you.

One more thing—those Sunday morning prayers and the periodic quizzes are never to be forgotten. Do you realize that was my beginning as a servant of the Master? I didn't know it at the time, but I'm sure you did....

Thank you Dad for giving me what you have. I will try to live up to all the fine and noble standards you have given, for they are reachable. I thank God for you for your strength and wisdom when days were dreary. I will strive to keep that spark always alive in me and I will pass it on to my children and they will pass it on to theirs.

Love your son, Paul[56]

Officiating at the funerals of family and close friends is expected of a minister, yet it exacts an emotional toll. When Leonard Smith Sr. died in 1983, son Paul helped lead his funeral. Having made a point of articulating his gratitude and love for his father, Smith was able to weather the storm. He wrote two months after the funeral: "I know I am grieving but it is not as I expected. I got through the funeral just fine even though I could not say all of the things I had written. . . . I am not sure if I would or could cry in front of mother or Marlene—interesting. What I feel now is peace and wonderment."[57]

In 1975, Smith helped lead the ceremonies honoring his dear grandmother, Odie Overby. Mrs. Overby's obituary notes that her grandson and a local minister presided jointly over the rites at Greater St. John Missionary Baptist Church. Though he was twenty years younger than the other minister, Smith proudly delivered the eulogy for his dear grandmother. Odie's tombstone lies next to that of her parents, Ferd and Nancy Wingo, in the tidy city cemetery not far from where her house stood on Birdsell Street.

CHAPTER 8

Undermining Everything That Separates

By the mid-1970s in St. Louis, Paul Smith had regained his balance. While conquering new audiences at Washington University, he began studying toward the doctorate that he completed at Eden Seminary in 1978. This was also the period in which his admiration for the Rev. Dr. Howard Thurman blossomed into a life-affirming personal relationship.

Smith first heard Dr. Thurman lecture at Hartford Seminary in 1958 and took every opportunity thereafter to hear the brilliant scholar speak. Thurman was famous for his enigmatic prose and the sonorous intensity of his speaking voice. He delivered lectures at over five hundred educational institutions over the course of his long, groundbreaking career.[1] Born in 1899 and the grandson of a woman who had been enslaved, Thurman fought to gain entry to elite Morehouse College and earned a doctorate from Rochester Theological Seminary, one of only a few Black students. He went on to a long career as a minister and professor at Oberlin College, Morehouse College, Spelman College, Howard University, and Boston University.[2]

It is not clear exactly when personal contact between Smith and Thurman began, but sometime around 1974, Berea parishioner Annalee Scott arranged for Smith to meet the man who had so inspired him. Scott was director of a proudly African American "Y" in downtown St. Louis called the Phyllis Wheatley Branch. Scott and her institution invited Dr. Thurman to speak in St. Louis each year. The celebrated minister/scholar had become close to Scott and her husband after they had shared their home with Thurman's daughter, Anne, while the young woman pursued an internship at the *St. Louis Post Dispatch*. As Smith remembers, "Annalee said, 'I would like you to meet Thurman since you talk so much about him in your sermons.' . . . So she arranged for me and Carl and about five other Black clergy in St. Louis to come have a private conversation with [him]."[3]

On their way to this long-awaited encounter, reality intervened. One of the Smiths' daughters became ill, delaying her parents' departure from their home. This heightened the drama of Smith's first meeting with Thurman.

> We were late coming to Annalee and Jim's apartment. We finally got over to that section of St. Louis and were climbing the stairs. As we get to the top, we hear Thurman speaking. We stop at the top of the stairs and look into the room, and he could see us.
>
> The best I can make out is that someone had asked him, "Who will carry on your work?" or something like that. Because Fran and I are standing in the vestibule, and there are about ten or twelve people listening, and without skipping a beat, he says, "Maybe that young man standing at the door with his wife." You can't make this stuff up! He said, "Young man, I'd like to get to know you better. Annalee thinks so much of you, so you *must* be something." So that's how our relationship began.[4]

Some found Dr. Thurman intimidating. James Cone writes that after accepting an invitation to visit Dr. Thurman in the early 1970s, he was unable to collect himself enough to have a substantive conversation with his fellow theologian.[5] Smith had no such hesitations. He identifies Thurman as the single individual with the greatest impact on his professional life, even more so than Andrew Young or Dr. King. Once his relationship with Dr. Thurman was established, Smith visited, corresponded, and collaborated with the peripatetic minister whenever he could.

Thurman intuitively understood Smith's work and enthusiastically articulated his support for it. He underwrote Smith's increasing midlife clarity about his mission in ministry, and the two began to work together directly hosting workshops and retreats. Neither had much use for formality, preferring to get in close to students, parishioners, and audiences. The only disappointment for Smith was that the relationship came to an end too quickly when Dr. Thurman died in 1981.

One particular project in Thurman's working life had a huge impact on Smith—the Church for the Fellowship of All Peoples in San Francisco. Fellowship Church was created during the wartime cultural turmoil of California in 1944. As Smith would later do with Carl Dudley at Berea, Thurman accepted an invitation to collaborate with a white Presbyterian minister, Rev. Dr. Alfred Fisk.[6] But rather than leading an existing congregation, Fisk proposed that he and Thurman cofound a wholly new, explicitly interracial church.

In a nation full of implicitly and explicitly segregated churches, the institution was truly innovative.[7] Dr. B. E. Mays wrote in 1983 that, in its time, Fellowship Church was "the only integrated congregation in both leadership and members in America."[8] The church drew the attention of powerful supporters like Eleanor Roosevelt and grew to include about 350 regular members and more than a thousand "members at large."[9] Thurman led the congregation as senior pastor for nine years, alternating with Rev. Fisk in the pulpit. Reflecting on this history, Smith says, "consciously or unconsciously [Fellowship Church] was my model for my congregations."[10]

Among Thurman's two dozen books, *Jesus and the Disinherited* may have contributed the most to American culture.[11] Dr. King is said to have had a copy of this book in his briefcase when he died. In this text, Thurman directly confronts what he saw as the fundamental failure of Christianity to address racial discrimination within the church. Famously, he evokes how "masses of men live with their backs constantly against the wall. They are the poor, the disinherited, the dispossessed. What does our religion say to them?"[12] Such questions had long troubled Thurman, but it was a man from a culture and religion completely outside his own who pushed him to sharpen his thinking on these issues. While part of a pioneering delegation of Black Americans invited to India in 1935, Thurman was asked penetrating questions by a Hindu scholar at a law school where he spoke. The man bluntly asked how Thurman could be committed to a faith that had been so destructive to Black people.[13]

A five-hour conversation ensued that led to public talks and ultimately culminated in the publication of *Jesus and the Disinherited* in 1949. Written in an accessible style despite its deep import, the study still yields fresh insights decades later. Just as it guided Rev. Smith and countless others through the confusion of the sixties, Thurman's wisdom remains instructive today.

Thurman's central point in the book is that when Jesus is understood as one of the disinherited himself, the full meaning of his message for all those who are subjugated becomes clear. Thurman emphasizes that Jesus was born into but ultimately severed from his ancient Jewish culture; he was poor; and he and most of his fellows were subjects, not citizens, of the Roman Empire in Palestine. Thurman argues that Jesus spoke as one who understood people suffering under oppression that threatened their very lives. The prophet's message was directed to people feeling the terrible insecurity of being subjected to violence, repression, and humiliation in their own land.

In terms that are sadly still salient today, Thurman describes the dilemma faced by people of color in 1940s America.

> The striking similarity between the social position of Jesus in Palestine and that of the vast majority of American Negroes is obvious to anyone who tarries long over the facts.... For the most part, Negroes assume that there are no basic citizenship rights, no fundamental protection, guaranteed to them by the state, because their status as citizens has never been clearly defined. There has been for them little protection from the dominant controllers of society and even less protection from the unrestrained elements within their own group.[14]

In his text, Thurman considers the corrosive effects of the fear, deception, and hate that result from living with such profound vulnerability. In addressing fear, he dissects the institutional methods whereby those without power are controlled. "The threat of violence within the framework of well-nigh limitless power is a weapon by which the weak are held in check. Artificial limitations are placed upon them, restricting freedom of movement, of employment, and of participation in the common life. These limitations are given formal or informal expression in general or specific policies of separateness or segregation. These policies tend to freeze the social status of the insecure."[15] The terror is compounded by the fact that the right to use violence is widely distributed among those in power. "The threat of violence may be implemented not only by constituted authority but also by anyone acting in behalf of the established order. Every member of the controllers' group is in a sense a special deputy authorized by the mores to enforce the pattern."[16]

Thurman points out the corrosive effects of responding to subjugation with deception. "The penalty of deception is to *become* a deception, with all sense of moral discrimination vitiated. A man who lies habitually becomes a lie, and it is increasingly impossible for him to know when he is lying and when he is not. In other words, the moral mercury of life is reduced to zero."[17] At that point, reclaiming one's inner life becomes even more difficult. Thurman says that, ultimately, Jesus' message is that honesty to God and to other people is one and the same: "the insistence of Jesus upon genuineness is absolute."[18]

Turning to hate, Thurman argues that it often arises out of relationships that are empty of genuine human feeling. His cardinal example is the "false fellowship" of the segregated South, where "there can be an abundance of sentimentality masquerading under the cloak of fellowship."[19] Thus in the section of the country where there is "the greatest contact between Negro and white there is the least real fellowship."[20] It is in the context of such fatally flawed relationships, he finds, that "the first step along the road of bitterness and hatred is assured." In terms that are even more true now than in the past, Thurman diagnoses "modern life" as being "so impersonal" that it is replete with circumstances that allow "the seeds of hatred to grow un-molested."[21] Both the strong and the weak can be infected by the ill will that comes from contact without real understanding of each other. If hatred becomes "a source of validation" for one's personality,[22] then the "illusion of righteousness is easy to create," and any kind of behavior toward the other can be justified. At that point, hatred can become "a device by which an individual seeks to protect himself against moral disintegration."[23]

Thurman suggests that people can instead follow Jesus' challenging counsel to love thine enemy. He emphasizes that this work requires mak-ing an active and honest effort. The powerful must relinquish the shield of their status, and the subjugated must give up their self-protective hostil-ity toward the powerful. "Love is possible only between two freed spirits. What one discovers in even a single experience in which barriers have been removed may become useful in building an over-all technique for loving one's enemy. There cannot be too great insistence on the point that we are here dealing with a discipline, a method, a technique, as over against some form of wishful thinking or simple desiring."[24]

Thurman decries the fact that this deep relationship between equals does not arise more often from common worship.

> It is in this connection that American Christianity has betrayed the religion of Jesus almost beyond redemption. Churches have been established for the underprivileged, for the weak, for the poor, on the theory that they prefer to be among themselves. . . . The result is that in the one place in which normal, free contacts might be most naturally established—in which the relations of the individual to his God should take priority over conditions of class, race, power, status, wealth, or the like—this place is one of the chief instruments for guaranteeing barriers.[25]

Ultimately, Thurman declares, "segregation is a complete ethical and moral evil. Whatever it may do for those who dwell on either side of the wall, one thing is certain: it poisons all normal contacts of those persons involved.

The first step toward love is a common sharing of a sense of mutual worth and value. This cannot be discovered in a vacuum."[26] Thurman argues that every individual must seek opportunities to cross the boundaries and learn about the other if hatred is to be uprooted. This process only happens "in the white heat of personal encounter. . . . No amount of good feeling for people in general, no amount of simple desiring, is an adequate substitute. It is an act of inner authority, well within the reach of everyone. . . . The ethical demand upon the more privileged and the underprivileged is the same."[27]

Theologian and scholar Dr. Luther Smith Jr. (no relation) published the first systematic consideration of Thurman's ideas in 1981. He has described Thurman's worldview and theology in terms that aptly describe Paul Smith as well.[28] Like his mentor, Smith is ecumenical in practice and in thought, easily making members of other faiths an integral part of his community. He has committed himself to racial integration rather than separation and has proven again and again that it is possible to build interracial and inter-cultural communities. In theological terms, both men emphasize the individual's experience of God more than the worship of Jesus as divine.[29] Their primary audience is the laity rather than other theologians and clerics. Like Thurman, Smith has never given up on the church and sees combating racism as the most urgent undeveloped aspect of Christianity's mission.[30]

Luther Smith's description of Howard Thurman as a prophet articulates the galvanizing effect of both men on those around them: "When others see how meaning flows through [his] life, something within their lives is aroused to discover their source for greater meaning and potential. [He] is not just an example but an inspirer; not just a leader but a maker of leaders; not the authority, but a revealer of authority."[31] Dr. Thurman has frequently been described as a mystic, and that term could easily apply to Dr. Smith as well. Smith and his mentor built their spiritual lives around self-reflection, contemplation, and divine inspiration, rather than doctrinal analysis. When they began to collaborate in the mid-1970s, the ministers were innovative in convening retreat-like seminars where like-minded people met to read, discuss, and meditate together.

Letters that passed between Smith and Thurman over the years reveal the texture of their relationship. In a missive written on the Howard Thurman Educational Trust's letterhead on January 29, 1975, Thurman asks for Smith's thoughts on a multiday workshop they had just completed.

Dear Paul Smith:

My first concern, dear brother, is that the Holy Spirit did not take any radical chances with you on the highway, because the traffic is not aware of the movement of the Spirit. When thoughts and feelings came upon you that could not be reduced to a manageable unit, I hope that Mrs. Smith was sufficiently rested to take the wheel.

You are a very exciting human being because of the way in which you honor thoughts and feelings that descend upon you with unerring vitality and specificity. I am sorry that we did not have a chance to visit but this will come later.

When you have a little margin of time will you set down in order, your reflections and suggestions for both our workshop experiences and future workshops?

Please give our love to Mrs. Smith and your young brood that keep their father on the straight and narrow.

Sincerely,
Howard Thurman[32]

In his reply dated February 12, Smith endorses the workshop's peaceful setting (near a fireplace, possibly in Thurman's San Francisco home), the small size of the group (no more than eight), and Thurman's assistant Joyce making a tape recording of the event. He asks about the possibility of giving each participant some private time with Thurman. Regarding Thurman's effect on others, Smith writes (his emphasis), "You are a very powerful presence and if one is not careful he may be overwhelmed. I got the sense that there were moments when we should have perhaps taken the time to hear everyone's response to *that particular moment* when the quietness prevailed and all present were on the same agenda. Perhaps the *silence*, (there were many) is enough but I guess I would have liked to 'check out' my thoughts against yours and the others present."[33] Smith suggests building in more time to absorb Thurman's impact: "I felt I had in a sense come to the Fountain. When my cup was full, I had no time to tarry. I needed time to rest—my intake was too much. By Friday afternoon, it began to run over. I would hope there was more time for reflection."[34] Smith concludes by describing the event's effects on him. "I would close by saying that my life was changed, refreshed and disturbed by this encounter. You have some idea because I am not frightened off by a group. When the spirit was in command you heard some of my cries. I have a better understanding of *me*; I feel closer to God and I am not ashamed of what I am in His presence. I have a better feeling for other human beings. I have not arrived, but I am on my journey."[35]

In one of his subsequent letters, Thurman praises Smith's spirit and celebrates their shared worldview (his emphasis): "Yours is a special calling and a very authentic mission. You *know* the meaningful contacts between people are more compelling than all the words, ideologies, prejudices and faiths that divide them; if such contacts are multiplied over a meaningful time interval they can undermine *everything* that separates."[36]

In choosing a dissertation topic for his Doctor of Ministry degree at Eden Theological Seminary in the mid-1970s, Smith found an opportunity to explore "everything that separates." Eden's campus, located in the St. Louis suburbs, consists of a quiet quadrangle of buildings graced by a majestic bell tower. Smith's dissertation was based on original research undertaken while he was working at Wash U., a few miles away.

Characteristically, Smith strode straight into the fray by choosing to study the relations between Black and Jewish students. Smith writes that his goal is to understand the students' "attitudes concerning each other and their relationships which are currently the source of tension and conflict in the general community of the university."[37] He later admits this was also a subject that had troubled him.

Smith starts his dissertation by citing Dr. Thurman and poet Langston Hughes as key influences on his life and work. He frames his research as a response to the Report of the National Advisory Commission on Civil Disorders, better known as the "Kerner Report," which was published in 1968. This document was the result of a bipartisan investigation into the causes of the riots that were ravaging the country in the mid-1960s.

The Kerner Report famously declared that the country was "moving toward two societies, one black, one white—separate and unequal."[38] Despite being so widely read that it became a best seller, the report's incisive findings about the crippling effects of "white racism" were rejected by Johnson and other lawmakers. If taken seriously, the document could have launched a national discussion fifty years ago about the causes of America's racial conflict. Regrettably, its recommendations were downplayed, denigrated, and ultimately dismissed.[39]

In his dissertation,[40] Smith's analysis begins with an overview of the ways he believes relations between Black and Jewish people deteriorated in the 1960s. He cites the conflict over school integration in Ocean Hill–Brownsville, New York and the rioting in Watts as two examples of increasing volatility in relations between these groups. He asserts that despite sharing a history of oppression and discrimination, the experiences of Blacks and Jews in America have differed in significant ways. Drawing on his experience working with fair housing activists at Freedom of Residence (FOR) in St. Louis,[41] he contends that Jews being property owners in urban neighborhoods inevitably pits them against Black people who live there.

In his chapter on the social history and theological perspective of Blacks and Jews, Smith eloquently articulates his view of the African American experience. Echoing James Cone, he writes that the Black experience has to do with moving from "Nobodiness" to "Somebodiness."[42] Since Black people do not have a specific common history to work from, he writes, they use stories, tales, sayings, songs, prayers, and sermons to find their common ground.[43] He says, "The Black experience is the coming together of the Black community to affirm the meaning and positive worth of Blackness to an insensitive White world." He cites Cone's *Black Theology and Black Power* as asserting that the Black experience "is self-determination and freedom whereby black people see themselves in a positive manner, with human dignity and worth."[44]

Smith is much less comfortable writing the section on Jewish identity. He asserts that Jews have had advantages in their positive self-image, their centuries-old culture, their color, and their greater psychological strength. He further states that the central concerns of Jewish people are their identity as Jews and their possession of Israel without interference from outside parties. He makes an effort to try and imagine a Jewish worldview. But he lapses into occasional stereotypes and does not seem to have any familiarity with the breadth of Jewish experience in this country or elsewhere.[45]

At the core of the thesis are the data Smith collected in interviews with forty college students: twenty Jewish, twenty Black. Though he uses fairly standard qualitative research methods, the design of the study would not stand up under scrutiny today. His sampling methods were weak. Smith handpicked the Black participants, and a Jewish student recruited the others. The resulting sample was badly skewed and too small to allow him to generalize from his findings. Smith did recognize his own "strong investment in the cause under investigation" and knew he should try and avoid bias.[46] Nevertheless, his data essentially confirmed the views he brought to the project. These were that Black and Jewish students had had very little real substantive interaction yet harbored negative attitudes toward each other nonetheless.[47]

Smith attempts to find a positive footing on which to end. He says that Black and Jewish people share the experience of estrangement from their homeland and their diasporic journeys. He urges identifying "a universal oneness which accentuates the positive worth of both" and a need to "search for a common ground that claims them as children of God."[48] He makes no mention of anything Blacks and Jews may share by virtue of being Americans and does not consider the possibility of any variation existing within these monolithic categories.

It becomes clear in a long addendum bound into the dissertation, however, that the most powerful part of this study occurred after the thesis was written. From the fall of 1977 through the spring of 1978, Smith undertook a course of independent study. Smith writes that his research had made him aware of prejudices toward Jews that he had had since he was a teenager and that he rediscovered in his administrative work at Wash U.[49] His awareness of this was sharpened when the rabbi he asked to read his thesis told him he thought it revealed anti-Jewish bias. In characteristic fashion, Smith sought out Rabbi Arnold Asher of Shaare Zedek Synagogue in University City to learn more. He writes, "Earlier I had learned that Arnie had read my thesis and in his opinion had judged it to be anti-Semitic. This was a new label for me and at first I was offended by his judgment. I later invited Arnie to lunch and we seemed to hit it off so I decided to ask him if he would teach me something about Jews. He agreed, with the understanding that I teach him something about Blacks."[50]

What resulted was a series of readings, discussions, and workshops that were designed to bring Smith's understanding of Black/Jewish relations into the real world. Rabbi Asher provided Smith with a reading list, and the men met once a week for discussions Smith admits were "challenging and often emotionally upsetting."

Though uncomfortable, this appears to have been the first real study of Jewish history and culture that Smith had ever undertaken. "It helped me to identify some of my biases, engage in meaningful dialogue without fear of offending while at the same time learning new information, and having the opportunity to ferret out kernels that could be used creatively in my ministry."[51]

As his education progressed, Smith began asking Rabbi Asher if he could engage the rabbi's congregation in conversation. Asher hesitated, informing Smith that some members of his synagogue had had negative experiences when Blacks like the Smiths had moved into their neighborhood. But Smith persisted, and eventually, an evening of discussion about his research findings was arranged. Both the reverend and the rabbi were concerned about how Smith would be received. They were relieved when "over 50 members showed up, greeted me with openness, and asked insightful questions and made salient comments. As we began the evening together, I knew almost immediately that my tradition and faith as a Christian pastor, as well as my ethnicity, had enough in common to enable dialogue and friendships to be established. Once again, my fears were allayed as well as theirs, because upon hearing my Black stories they found a kinship with some of their own."[52]

Even after his education had begun in earnest, Smith describes his visit to the synagogue as going "into the lion's den."[53] Nonetheless, Smith came to a profound realization "that what I had been doing and saying in my thesis and discussions with Arnie, was trying to out horror him with my stories. I imagine he was attempting the same but he did it more gracefully with less rhetoric than I."[54]

As became commonplace during his Brooklyn pastorate, Smith later invited the rabbi to speak at Second Presbyterian. Smith also initiated contact with the new assistant rabbi at Wash U. Their discussions led to plans for a course on Black-Jewish relations.[55] They then arranged a discussion session between Smith and three Black students with Jewish students at Hillel House.[56] On his way to this event, Smith realized he had not set foot inside the building in his eight years at the university. With typical humility and candor, he writes:

> First, I realized how jealous I was of the symbols of Jewishness and Judaism, which were very obvious. The building itself is beautiful, comfortable, spacious and a center of gathering for the Jews at the university. When compared to the quarters for Blacks, there is none. . . . What are our symbols I asked myself? All that really identifies us as Blacks is our color. Can it be that we need something more than color? Is there something other than color and if so, how is it perceived by others as well as ourselves? These questions were raised in my mind as I entered the room and remain largely unanswered even today.[57]

Nonetheless, at the end of the addendum, Rev. Smith confidently articulates the mission that continues to set him apart, even today: "I am most comfortable in situations that afford me opportunities to be a bridge between racial, political and religious groups. . . . Both as an administrator and pastor, my home is bridging the gap, initiating the points of contact, facilitating encounters and serving as an interpreter. Herein lies my ministry and the essence of my being."[58]

CHAPTER 9

Listening for the Sound of the Genuine

When offered the chance in 1978 to become Morehouse College's first-ever vice president reporting directly to the college's president Hugh Gloster, Smith felt destiny was at work. Landing that job meant that Rev. Smith now belonged in the company of his heroes. Howard Thurman had graduated from Morehouse at the top of his class in 1923 and later served as the director of religious life and a professor at the college.[1] The prodigious intellectual Dr. Benjamin Elijah Mays had led the institution during 1940–67. Mays's most famous student, Martin Luther King Jr., earned his undergraduate degree in sociology at Morehouse in 1948.[2] Morehouse remains the only college in America dedicated exclusively to serving African American men.

Smith's family was excited by the idea of moving to Atlanta where Maynard H. Jackson was serving as the first Black mayor of a southern city. Smith had his new doctorate in hand and some years of academic administration behind him. The society pages in the local newspaper picked up the happy story, describing a gala party at a fancy St. Louis home that brought together "Morehouse men" from all over town.[3] At the event, Washington University's Chancellor William H. Danforth praised Smith's contributions to university life during his eight years there.[4]

The chance to become part of the "Morehouse mystique" was a potent tonic for Smith. As he got settled, he discovered that Dr. Mays's furniture was in the office assigned to him. He was awed to find himself sitting behind Dr. Mays's desk and felt it was meant to be. His new boss, Dr. Hugh Gloster, had succeeded Dr. Mays as president in 1967 and had been leading Morehouse for about a decade when the Smiths arrived. As vice president, Smith had been hired to oversee academic matters on campus, so Gloster would have more time to devote to his other duties. Gloster had just that year launched a medical school at Morehouse and was in the midst of a huge and successful fund-raising campaign that necessitated extensive travel.[5]

One of the first visitors to the new vice president's office in August 1978 was a freshman who had wandered through the administration building to find Smith. C. Howie Hodges II would later become one of the super-achieving "surrogate sons" that Smith has embraced over the years. Hodges recounts that Smith knew his family before he was even born. Howie's Aunt Marie had been a Talladega classmate of Smith's, and his parents met the Smiths when they all were living in Buffalo, New York. Howie's father, Clemmon Hodges, had been a philosophy and religion major at Morehouse. He and Smith were Alpha Phi Alpha and later Sigma Pi Phi fraternity brothers. When the younger Hodges arrived on campus, his family advised him to get in touch with "Uncle Paul."

Hodges recalls going to find Smith's office in the administration building where the halls were bustling with new students and their parents. Smith gave him a warm welcome and soon suggested that the young man come by his office in the evening. Hopping into the humble green VW Beetle Smith had been given in lieu of salary at one point in St. Louis, the two drove to the Smiths' house in suburban College Park for dinner. In a practice that continues to this day, Howie drove and listened, while Smith rode and talked.[6]

Hodges testifies to the impact Smith had on students at Morehouse. Smith had joined the college as professor as well as vice president, and he immediately began teaching. His philosophy and religion course was an elective open to upperclassmen only. The man whose classes had caused such anxiety at the University of the West Indies was now in an environment that suited him perfectly—teaching gifted, dedicated students who were consciously striving to fulfill the dreams of those who had fought for Black empowerment. Hodges says the classroom on the first floor of James P. Brawley Hall was invariably packed. Its location on the Morehouse students' direct route to Spelman, the nearby women's college, was busy. That too ensured that Dr. Smith's crowded lecture hall gained a reputation.

Even though he was just a freshman, Hodges frequently attended class because he was driving Dr. Paul home afterward. He found the atmosphere electrifying; he took copious notes and was awed by the caliber of students in that room. Men like Jeh Johnson, Barack Obama's secretary of homeland security, and Robert Mallett, an international health-care executive, have indeed earned stellar reputations in the succeeding years. Even Dr. John Wilson, a recent president of Morehouse, was a student of Dr. Smith's in those days.[7]

The way that Smith wrapped Hodges into his family life was a huge comfort to the young man so far from his hometown in Buffalo. He says he escaped the dorms and spent most weekends at the Smiths' house that year. It was "a beautiful house, big, ranch-style—almost like a tri-level . . . [in a] beautiful, bucolic suburb, big tall trees, big yards. And that's where they lived—Paul, Fran, three girls and Sasha."[8] Sasha was a black Newfoundland dog, one of several that have been part of the Smith family over the years. Howie made himself useful by becoming the dog walker and house sitter when the Smiths were away. Hodges recalls that caring for Sasha in an air-conditioned house with a car in the driveway was not exactly a hardship for a college freshman.[9]

The Smiths' home was a tightly run ship, though. The daughters were growing up, and they had all inherited their parents' intelligence and good looks. As a father of three girls who was working at an all-men's campus, Smith was quick to make clear that his daughters should stay clear of Morehouse. And as far as sharing the College Park home on the weekends, "Pappa Paul," as Hodges now calls him, made the rules crystal clear. Smith proclaimed that when Howie stayed over, he would sleep in Smith's study where there was a pullout bed. That room was upstairs right next to the Smiths' own bedroom, a floor away from the girls' bedrooms downstairs. As Hodges remembers Smith saying, "I have got three daughters, and I don't want nothing to happen to them. And so I love you, but when you sleep, you're going to sleep in my office. . . . I'm keeping you close. I love you, but I'm going to keep you right up here!"[10]

Hodges says that being around Smith has challenged him to be his best. He recalls that on one occasion, Smith told him to come over for dinner, just as usual. When he arrived at the house, he found Dr. Howard Thurman was the guest for the evening. That night, Dr. Thurman leaned across the dinner table and said in the measured, basso voice he was famous for, "We share the same first name. Young man, what is the purpose of your life?" Hodges says his first thought was, "I've never seen so many beautiful gorgeous Black women in my entire life!" He then remembered the gut-wrenching D+ he had just received on his first college paper. Regaining his presence of mind, he mentioned neither thought. Instead he said, "I think I'd like to go into law. I want to serve. I want to give back. But I'm still trying to sort it out." All of that did in fact play out in the years ahead, and that evening, the plan seemed to satisfy the famous scholar.[11]

In November of that year, Smith invited Dr. Thurman to campus to give a public lecture and meet students. At the speaker's dinner, Smith's dream guest list became a reality. Assembled around the table at President Gloster's house were some of the best-respected academics and ministers in the country, including Howard Thurman and his wife Sue, Hugh Gloster, Benjamin Mays, and Martin Luther King Sr., a.k.a. "Daddy King." Smith says that he was the youngest person in the room, yet it was he who had brought the company together. The voluble Smith says that he mostly listened that night.

Even the more mundane aspects of his job were a pleasure for Smith. He relished the contact with students, and they responded quickly to his concern and attention. "I recognized them. I empowered them. Gave them a voice, a hearing. And I made sure that the . . . Resident Advisors took their jobs seriously. They were there to *help* the students!"[12] Hodges describes how well things were going. "He was very popular. The guys liked him, other faculty members liked him. Paul was interested in you, as an individual; [he was] approachable and didn't just look at the super gifted students."

Hodges says that "the relationships" were Rev. Smith's most powerful tools.[13] Upon arriving in Atlanta, Smith had quickly made friends and found tennis partners. His relationship with Ambassador Andrew Young was renewed now that the two were living in the same city. Atlanta's chief of police, George Napper, and Napper's chief of staff were soon playing tennis with Smith twice a week. Smith also got to know the public safety commissioner, Dr. Lee P. Brown.

This kind of networking had been natural to Smith since his college days, and it soon paid off for Morehouse students. The college occupies a densely packed group of buildings on busy streets in western Atlanta. As Smith remembers:

> They had built a new administration building named after Gloster, on the other side of the campus across a street with no streetlights. It was dangerous for students to cross the street there. Gloster tried to get a streetlight for that spot, but he wasn't successful. The next time I played tennis with the Chief, I said, "Can we get a streetlight?" He said, "Of course, I can do it." Within two weeks, we had a streetlight. Gloster had not been able to do it even with a graduate of his school [Maynard Jackson] as mayor.[14]

One can imagine that being upstaged by his new VP did not please President Gloster. "He hated that," Smith says of the streetlight incident. Despite—or perhaps because of—the fact that Smith was proving so highly effective as Gloster's No. 2 man, relations between the two began to deteriorate. Smith did not share the details of what was unfolding with his young protégé. Hodges says, "He doesn't want to crush your spirit or have things that he's going through dampen your enthusiasm for the school. So he kept a lot . . . to himself. But you could sense that there was less joy."[15]

Hodges says that even as an eighteen-year-old, he could see that Gloster and Smith were "like oil and water." From Smith's point of view, it was much worse than that. "I spent that year trying to stay alive because I thought I'd made a terrible mistake going to Morehouse. Gloster . . . was very difficult to work with. I didn't know that going in of course. Mays loved me. The President didn't. Gloster tried to undo whatever Mays had done there."[16]

The very day Smith went to tell Gloster he couldn't continue, he learned Gloster had just sent him a letter.

> I got fired and didn't even know it. I quit before I got the letter firing me. Instead of walking down the hall, Gloster sent a letter to the house. He thought I'd seen the letter when I went to talk to him, but I hadn't yet. I wanted to say this wasn't working out, but Gloster got very defensive. He said, "You are the biggest disappointment of my entire career as an administrator!" I said to myself, "I'm just going to get up and knock the shit outta him!" I'm not proud of that. But I didn't. I said, "I'm sorry you have that opinion but the bad news for you is, the entire faculty and students disagree with you." And I walked out.[17]

What Smith said was true. When the students learned he was leaving, they picketed Gloster's office and staged a sit-in to protest. They had responded wholeheartedly to Smith's warm personality and his tough love. Hodges sums it up: "Paul was beloved by the students, had the relationships in the community to get things done, quietly. Gloster got jealous, because he could see more and more that students leaned on Paul, less on [him]. If you met Gloster you would see, this was a man who needed to have his ego fed."[18]

Smith wrote frequently in his journals about his struggles at Morehouse. He was acutely disappointed that his job at a powerful Black institution working for a powerful Black boss had soured so quickly. It is possible that Smith's iconoclastic and independent nature was harder to control than he had anticipated.

However, he had no trouble at all joining forces with Dr. Thurman, who made regular visits to Atlanta. Smith invited Thurman to come to his classes and had students write to him; Thurman always wrote back. Halfway through his year at Morehouse, Smith recorded the excitement he felt when he got to meet with his mentor.

> 29 Jan. 1979
> Today, I spent a few moments with Dr. Howard Thurman who was en route (between flights) to San Francisco. What words of wisdom would be imparted? What more could we glean from this rare soul? When would the moment appear? I could hardly wait. I was very much in touch with my own feelings now, because I come alive when my sense of ME-NESS is near his.... When I have honed in upon his spirit, his words, his presence, I know the meaning of freedom.[19]

Smith had decorated his study in Atlanta with memorabilia related to Thurman and waited seventy-seven days between visits in 1978 and 1979 for the right moment to show Thurman the room. Smith was particularly proud of a banner that had been made for him emblazoned with what he felt were some of Thurman's most significant words: "Lord Center Me Down." The phrase evokes Quaker practice; Thurman had studied for a semester with Quaker Rufus Jones at Haverford College in 1929. Dr. Thurman later wrote, it was "a crucial experience, a watershed from which flowed much of the thought and endeavor to which I was to commit the rest of my working life."[20]

Smith patiently waited until the moment to show Thurman the room came of its own accord. He wrote after that visit finally materialized: "To have seen his eyes, to have witnessed his response—to see his excitement and to feel his joy upon seeing that banner, the pictures of the students, himself in a very special pose from the pulpit—what's 77 days when you have a moment like that one?"[21]

Smith freely shared his concerns and dilemmas with his mentor. In late August 1979, Smith records that he went to Thurman for advice and solace about his professional future.

> Today I spoke with "my guru" in California. I had three major agenda items. 1) Coretta King's visit; 2) my career choices . . . 3) consent to edit a book of meditations for me if his time permits . . . he wished to give deep thought to the career choices from the context of ME—where I was headed, the importance of this decision given the time in my life. . . . I feel something stirring

within me because my well has been low this past year. The long drought appears to be over and it has begun to rain again.[22]

With his administrative experience, education, and deft social skills, Smith might have pursued a college presidency himself. However, it was too soon to move the family again. So Smith applied for a job at Hillside Presbyterian Church, just outside Atlanta. Despite being in the midst of a decades-long decline in the popularity of liberal Protestant denominations,[23] Smith's next challenge would be revitalizing a dying, all-white church in suburban Decatur.

Hillside is an assemblage of low buildings built at the crown of a long, sloping piece of land. Founded in 1954, Hillside's membership of over six hundred in 1970 had steadily declined, and funds were running thin.[24] The Atlanta Presbytery sent advisers to talk with the congregation about their options.[25] The neighborhood was "in transition," which historically had meant whites were moving out because Blacks were moving in. This time, though, the white congregation wanted to stay and save their church by welcoming their new neighbors as fellow congregants. Smith soon became one of forty-four candidates being considered to lead the effort.

Only a few weeks later, the search committee was circulating a detailed letter recommending that the church call Dr. Smith. The team was effusive and quoted Smith's eloquent vision of their shared future.

> We wish we could transfer to you the very strong positive feelings we have for Paul, but this is a pleasure you will have to experience for yourself. . . . The following statement by Paul will give you some idea of the way he sees his role as a Minister and ours as a congregation:
>
> > "I believe the church is the one place in the universe where God's people may gather together to work on problems without fear. There, they will find God who [precedes] us in our concerns and who is able to address our fears. Here we are as one family; we are reduced to Oneness in God's house. No class, no race or clan shall be afraid here. Our task is to make the church that kind of place as we serve the Lord."[26]

Though it was not a routine part of the search process, the committee asked Smith to interact with the congregation informally to be sure they would be comfortable with him. A few weeks later, Smith made an unannounced visit to the congregation, then at a rural retreat center. Whatever problems the committee was anxious about did not materialize. In his journal, Smith wrote, "The Communion along the river, downstate Georgia—October 1979. . . . The setting was perfect, the occasion relaxed. . . . Topic of my meditation: The Sacramental Moment. The young people stayed near the water on the docks—they listened intently although giving the impression they were disinterested. . . . I knew if we could relate in this setting we would start on a new journey."[27]

Smith apparently reached his listeners that day; the full congregation later voted forty-nine for hiring Smith and ten against with one abstention.[28] Smith worked thereafter to develop relationships with those who had had doubts about him. He later wrote of a white parishioner's welcome and the way familiar rituals looked different the first day at his new pastorate.

> November 4, 1979 was my first Sunday in the pulpit. . . . 125 showed up; a large number of Blacks came that day. . . . B. Jones gave me a note I will always cherish, just minutes before the service began. He expressed his support and prayers for our work together—as well as that of his family. . . . The racial mixture on this first Sunday has remained for the last nine months. Communion took on a new meaning—even greater than breaking bread by the river—as brown hands broke bread, white hands received it. Now I understand how the table of our Lord is the dividing point; at the table, His table—we are all one.[29]

Members of the congregation said later that they felt that they had chosen the most qualified candidate, white or Black.[30]

Their offer to Smith was considered so unusual that the story made the *Atlanta Constitution* as well as newspapers as far away as Miami and Los Angeles.[31] The *Los Angeles Times* headline put it simply: "White Church in South Picks Black Pastor."[32] A Presbyterian journal revealed that Smith was one of only a few Black ministers in the denomination, and that being a Black minister called to lead an all-white church made the arrangement "unique among the more than four thousand congregations of the Presbyterian Church in the U.S."[33] In press interviews, Smith simply noted that he had done this several times before; he told the *Los Angeles Times* that he had "not one reservation racially" about accepting the job at Hillside.[34]

There were a few ripples in the water during the transition. Columbia High School down the road from Hillside had been embroiled in virulent confrontations between Black and white families since 1975 when court-ordered school integration began.[35] Through Andrew Young, Paul and Fran had been getting to know Dr. King's widow, Coretta, who lived in

Atlanta. Smith remembers that she had been asked by parents at Columbia High to act as a mediator in the dispute, so she was periodically in the neighborhood.

Mrs. King had seen the *Atlanta Constitution* article about Dr. Smith coming to Hillside and wanted to meet him. Her son Marty had been in his class at Morehouse. No doubt spontaneously, Smith asked her to come speak at his installation service, and the Presbytery approved the plan. This caused a stir, however, among some of the white teachers at Hillside who, Smith says, "felt betrayed" by his inviting her. He says, "Some thought her speaking was a power play, trying to force them to back down" in the fight against integration. People said, 'We've hired the wrong guy!'"[36]

Fortunately, when Mrs. King spoke during the service, she talked about what she was trying to achieve for both Black and white families at Columbia. She talked about her own kids and her involvement with the PTA. Smith remembers that she told the congregation they were brave for calling a Black pastor. She must have quieted the waters, because the friction between the congregation and their new pastor evaporated.

Smith says, "Coretta was a lovely woman, very strong."[37] But people didn't know how to behave around her. He remembers that when he and Fran invited her to dinner at their house, she walked in and said, "Where is everybody?" They learned that everywhere she was invited socially, a crowd showed up, eager to meet her in person. The Smiths told her they thought she might appreciate just being able to be herself, and she was indeed grateful. Rev. Smith remained in touch with her as a friend and adviser. He later suggested that she go visit Dr. Thurman in California and even worked with her secretary to book a flight. Smith remembers that when Mrs. King heard about it, she simply said, "When am I going?"[38]

After Smith's arrival and the newspaper coverage about it, Black membership at Hillside leapt to about 40 percent of the congregation.[39] At the time, Smith said, "I didn't come to this church with the intention of making it all Black. I wouldn't be upset if that happened, but it need not. We are a culturally plural congregation and have a ministry here that meets the needs of a wide cross-section of people."[40] Smith emphasizes that it was the church having Black *leadership*, not just Black membership, that made the difference. By June 1982, Hillside had over two hundred active members and a Black/white composition of about fifty-fifty.[41]

It was at Hillside that Rev. Smith's idiosyncratic approach to ministry began to fully flower. Recent research has identified five characteristic features of Black Protestant religious practice: an experience-based faith; seeing church life as essential for daily survival; appreciating the mystical and mysterious; expecting daily miracles; committing to the fight for social justice for all.[42] Despite his Presbyterianism, Smith instinctively incorporates them all. In addition, Smith's distinctive practice emphasizes sharing the pulpit, prioritizing racial balance in church affairs, and talking openly about political realities.

Hillside member and journalist Lisa Demer later profiled the church for a local newspaper, the *DeKalb News/Sun*. Her story praises the reverend for his "personableness, warmth and enthusiasm—plus his preaching abilities." She quotes Smith as saying, "I know who I am [and] I am not afraid to discover who I am not."[43] Bob Ussery, the first Black parishioner to become a member after Smith's arrival, said that Hillside's diversity and "outreach to bring a wholeness to the community" drew him to the church. At the time of the interview, Ussery was one of the first Black members of Hillside to serve on the Session.[44]

From her insider's perspective, Demer raised the issue of class as a factor shaping this new congregation. In her estimation, Smith's "quiet, creative approach in the pulpit, often focusing on national issues . . . attracts middle- and upper-middle-class people of both races." Smith himself spoke freely about integration at the level of class. Demer reported his assertion that "the caliber of Blacks attending Hillside would be just as uncomfortable with a jive-talking street Black as the whites would be with a potbellied redneck waving a Confederate flag. 'Lower classes could feel comfortable here because of who we are,' he says, 'but they wouldn't like the music and order of the service. They look for a livelier, more emotional and spontaneous program.'"[45]

Two parishioners worked especially closely with the reverend: Dr. Joanne Nurss, a white woman with a PhD in education, and Dr. Prince Rivers, a Black man with a doctorate in chemistry. The pairing of Black and white lay leadership has been another of Smith's methods for success. Nurss said that she and Rivers served as a sounding board for Rev. Smith. "The three of us did a lot of things together, a lot of planning. Paul would bounce ideas off us, [asking] 'What do you think?' . . . and we felt comfortable being honest with him. [We could say,] 'No, that's a crazy idea. It won't work!'"[46]

Before she passed away in 2016, Dr. Nurss talked about the class issue and being Clerk of Session during Smith's tenure at Hillside. "What Paul was able to do at Hillside was attract a large number of both Caucasians and African

Americans. . . . They were all middle class and well educated, in the same professions, so they had all this in common. [They] just were different races. In the ideal situation, you're going to have a church with a mix not just of races but socioeconomic status. But it is very hard to do it in that situation. Among other things, style of worship and so on is so different."[47]

The congregation quickly grew, but there was the perennial problem of how to help new and old parishioners get to know each other. An old technique was used to address the problem.

> We had a large group of people who got along very, very well. But we had people who had never socialized with people of the other race. So one of the first things that was [created] . . . was a program called Nurture Groups. We were divided up by area where we lived and the plan was that you would have a monthly meeting in your home. It could be a potluck, dessert, whatever. . . .
>
> You had people of course, African Americans, who had never been in a white home and whites who had never been in an African American home. What you discovered was, Oh your house is just like mine or nicer than mine, sometimes we would find out.[48]

Nurss was in a position to observe Smith's abilities as a fundraiser and financial manager, and she asserts that Smith exceeded everyone's expectations. When he arrived, Hillside had debts that were difficult to pay off with only about thirty regularly contributing members. The church did not even have enough money to pay Smith's full salary. The Presbytery urged Smith to be realistic about what he could accomplish.

> [Paul] inherited a church that was falling apart . . . the Presbytery was paying a chunk of his salary—the church had gotten a second mortgage on the property. . . . There was a plan that it would take five years before the Presbytery would stop paying part of his salary, and it [took only] three years. The second mortgage was paid off, the first mortgage was paid off, bing, bing, bing. And so his goal was to build up a multiracial congregation that was thriving . . . and leave behind a vibrant church. Which he did.[49]

Despite the progress that was made at Hillside, Smith was not always successful in bringing in the new parishioners he sought.[50] In 1982, nearby Agnes Scott College hired its first female president, Dr. Ruth Schmidt. Bringing her to Hillside would have been a real coup for Smith, yet a journal entry records that his overtures failed.

> My reaction to seeing the new president of Agnes Scott . . . at North Decatur Presbyterian Church . . . was anger. After all, I had written her in Massachusetts

long before she knew where Hillside ever was located. She only knew that it was in Decatur. I had invited her early on to visit; sent her an article from the Los Angeles Times. I followed up with a visit to the college. She came for a visit. I wrote another letter when I heard by the grapevine that she was thinking of joining N. Decatur. I wrote the letter in response to what I heard but not what I felt. Perhaps that was the mistake.[51]

Smith felt that Schmidt should take a risk for the cause of racial pluralism and was frustrated when she did not. He was also conscious of the loss of the resources she would have brought with her. "It is newsworthy for a Black to come to an all-white church; it is different and challenging. We do these kinds of things all the time. Why not expect the same from whites? . . . How will we ever become a self-sufficient church, truly racially plural, unless some whites . . . make a stand, make a statement (as George McMaster did) and join with us? It is clear to me how the white church continues to build itself. I am disappointed, but I am no longer as angry, now that I have written it down."[52]

Rev. George McMaster was a white Presbyterian minister who had been in retirement until he heard about Smith's call to Hillside through the Atlanta Presbytery. Believing in the prospects for a multiracial congregation, he joined Smith as copastor in 1981. Smith knew how powerful cross-racial church leadership could be and was happy to share his pulpit as Hillside's congregation grew.

Momentous things were also happening within the denomination in the early 1980s. After much deliberation, a great reconciliation of the northern and southern branches of the Presbyterian Church was enacted.[53] The two factions had divided in 1861 over the issue of slavery. In June 1983, the southern Presbyterian Church in the United States (PCUS) and the northern United Presbyterian Church in the U.S.A (PCUSA) met in Atlanta and formally rejoined to form the Presbyterian Church (U.S.A.).[54] The Smiths attended the event known as "the Reunion" with thousands of others and were no doubt among those for whom it resonated most deeply.[55] The reverend wrote in his journal afterward: "Today it happened. After 123 years we [PCUS/PCUSA]became one. The music in the World Congress Center at the moment of the vote was a sacramental moment. Cheers, clapping, watching, rejoicing and the new church was off to a start. As I marched alongside of my wife I realized this was a very special moment in history in the life of our church. I thank God for the opportunity to be part of it. Even though there was no PA system we were able to hear Andy Young, Mayor of Atlanta."[56]

Smith had been asked to participate in the celebration by introducing newly elected Mayor Young to the huge crowd. Smith reveals a slightly bruised ego when he looks back on these events a few months later.

> It seems as though success is always just out of my reach. Of course that all depends on what I mean by success. . . . As 8,000 people marched . . . in celebration of the reunion I felt my heart beating with joy as we watched the steps of City Hall. The day was perfect and the people were happy. . . . I ran ahead to make sure everything was in place; particularly the mayor who is known to be elsewhere at times like this. And then it happened. The mayor was there and the staff was there. I was waiting for the opportunity to present the mayor. However the public address system was not there. It never arrived. There were too many people in the streets and surrounding City Hall that the truck could not get near enough to set up its equipment. I did introduce Andy with a bullhorn. [It was significant] in yet another sense—for this is how we spoke to the marchers during the civil rights movement days.[57]

In another journal entry from that period, Rev. Smith records a much less public but deeply meaningful event that "confirms the validity in my mind of the racially incorporated church."[58] Smith writes of attending the funeral for the father of a Hillside parishioner in Hoschton, Georgia, a small, all-white town about forty-five miles north of Atlanta. Smith's history in the Deep South had made him hyperaware of how his arrival, unannounced, to join the family of the bereaved might be received. Several members of Hillside's congregation accompanied him.

> The undertaker's helper, in a black suit, mud on his black shoes, and his belly hanging over his belt, was standing at the door of the church when we drove up. He looked as we parked the car and was there to open the door for us when we were about to enter. He was cordial, a bit startled but did not seem to mind, since we seemed to know where we were going. A Black man, two white women, and one Black woman, made history as we entered the church. The door creaked as did the floors as we entered directing the eyes of all present toward us. . . . The family arrived shortly after and we were all asked to stand as they filed into the church. Those who had not seen us before could see us now but most eyes were fixed on the bronze casket.[59]

As the family was leaving the church, the man from Hillside saw Paul and the others and came to greet them. "I reached for his hand, but he reached for me and put his arms around me in a warm and moving embrace. With tears in his eyes he said, 'Paul you will never know how much this means to us to have you here; just knowing that you cared enough means so much.' It was a sacramental moment. The kind that can only come in a racially incorporated church. . . . Now I am convinced that it is critical to have the church truly plural for that is the only way to authenticate the gospels."[60]

Smith tested this philosophy by bringing white parishioners from Hillside to the historic downtown Atlanta church where both Martin Luther King Sr. and Martin Luther King Jr. had been pastors. Lecturing on *Jesus and the Disinherited* at Ebenezer Baptist Church, Smith felt it was "clear that Blacks and Whites can indeed have an opportunity to dialogue and interact in a setting which is totally Black." He was happy to find that by creating such opportunities, "race, class, economics can be discussed without fear of intimidation."[61]

In addition to teaching at Morehouse Medical School and the Candler School of Theology at Emory, Smith taught classes at Columbia Seminary, located a few miles down the road from Hillside Church. One of his students in a class on Howard Thurman was Mike Trautman. Trautman says Columbia students were unlikely to be reading works like *Jesus and the Disinherited* in anyone else's class.

> It was a pivotal class for me. He was able to introduce Thurman's work, to share his personal experience of Thurman. [It gave us an] eye-opening sense of who Thurman was.[62]
>
> [It was an] all-white seminary—we were not going to read non-Presbyterians. Thurman was a unique soul. I . . . would have [studied] James Cone, liberation theology, because I was very much interested in those alternative ways. But I never would have had Thurman without Paul.[63]

During his first year in the Deep South, Trautman remembers feeling uncomfortable that there was no discussion around the seminary of the "Child Murders," some twenty-five unsolved killings of Black children that terrified Atlanta between 1979 and 1982.[64] When a suspect was arrested in 1982 and sent to prison, Rev. Smith was in fact asked to speak about it, albeit at an all-white church in Montgomery, Alabama, 160 miles away. In his usual way, Smith turned the invitation on its ear by bringing along a colleague from the Presbytery, white minister Marvin Simmers. Together, they delivered what they called a "dialogue sermon"—a public, cross-racial conversation with a unified message—that even murderers are children of God who deserve compassion. That event made the paper too.[65]

Trautman had grown up in a multiracial family and neighborhood in Bridgeport, Connecticut's biggest city. He felt out of place in Georgia but soon found kindred spirits. "Columbia was pretty much all white at that time. There were two African American students, Elbert Darden, another guy that Paul adopted, and Will Coleman. [We] all became friends. We all felt—I didn't grow up with the southern Presbyterian Church and so it was [a] really strange place. . . . So we all kind of hung together. And Paul became the person who mentored us and cared for us and got us through that experience."[66]

Some of that "care" was rough-and-tumble and delivered on the tennis court. Trautman admits the good minister had some competitive fires that may not have been seen anywhere else.

> Paul liked running Elbert and me all around the tennis court. It was the only place where you'd see Paul brag. Elbert was . . . a hell of an athlete. . . . But he caught on much faster than I did. He would say, "Mike, he's selling you wolf cookies!" It's an urban term—he's trying to get into your head and intimidate you. "Don't let him do that to you!"[67]
>
> [Smith] would talk stuff to us all the time. [The tennis court was] one of the places he had fun with it. I wonder how that worked its way out as a younger man. He had such an integration, a sense of who he was, where he came from, where he felt called to be and do in life.[68]

Trautman and his wife had visited Hillside in 1979 after relocating to Decatur. He recalls that they pulled up in the Hillside parking lot one Sunday morning, hoping to explore a church in their new neighborhood. They had no way of knowing what kind of difficulties the church was going through. He laughs, remembering the welcome they received. "People rushed out to greet us so enthusiastically that it actually spooked us!" Hillside became the Trautmans' home church nonetheless.

Smith guided Trautman through his seminary fieldwork at Hillside in the summers of 1980 and 1981. Smith's easy, egalitarian style meant that the young man had much broader opportunities than was customary.

> He gave me the freedom to experiment. Took me on calls with him, and I got to preach. I went with him on visits to people, new members. . . . He has an amazing gift of attracting people. People gravitate toward him because of his personality and depth.
>
> He helped me experience what it would be like to be a minister. I realized I had a lot to learn! The people skills, especially hanging in there with people who may not like a decision you've made. You have to learn how to handle folks who might be difficult for the life of the church.

Hillside was a pretty progressive church for those days.... Paul attracted a lot of socially mobile people, people with experience and power. He's never threatened by someone who in one walk of life may have wielded power. It took me a long time to appreciate what I learned from him.[69]

Rev. Trautman remembers a conversation in particular that profoundly affected him. It may also reveal a fundamental doctrinal aspect of Smith's belief. One day as Rev. Smith dropped him off at the seminary, Trautman asked a question he had been mulling over from theology class.

[The] question was—What would faith look like to you if they found Jesus's bones? Paul said, "That really doesn't matter to me." That was a huge shift of paradigm. I was a history major! But it changed my whole perspective. Paul said, "Wherever Jesus is, if I end up there, I'll be alright with that." To me, it captured Jesus's story and concerns.... That was the base of being, the sound of the genuine.

That response has gotten more and more powerful for me as I've gotten older, as I see more and more people's own understanding of their faith. It has allowed me to be less judgmental of others.... I'm now the age Paul was when I [first] knew him. That [perspective] has taken more and more root. It has made me a better human being.... He taught me—pay attention to other people's journeys.[70]

One fortunate outcome of the move to Atlanta was that Smith was present for a significant event late in Howard Thurman's career. In 1980, Howard Thurman delivered a celebrated speech titled "Listening for the Sound of the Genuine" to the women graduating from Spelman.[71] It was a sort of homecoming for Thurman, who had preached every week in the same church while teaching at Spelman early in his career. The text has been widely reprinted. At least some of what Thurman meant by "the sound of the genuine" is captured in this excerpt (his emphasis).

There is in every person something that waits and listens for the sound of the genuine in herself.... Nobody like you has ever been born and no one like you will ever be born again—you are the only one....

I wonder if you can get still enough—not quiet enough—still enough, to hear rumblings up from your unique and essential idiom, the sound of the genuine in you....

Now there is something in everybody that waits and listens for the sound of the genuine in other people. *I must wait and listen for the sound of the genuine in you.* I must wait. For if I cannot hear it, then in my scheme of things, you are not ever present....

Paul Smith (left), Howard Thurman (second from right), and others, Spelman College, Atlanta, Georgia, 1980. Photo by Jo Moore Stewart.

> Now if I hear the sound of the genuine in me and if you hear the sound of the genuine in you [then] the wall that separates and divides will disappear, and we will become one because the sound of the genuine makes the same music.[72]

In *The Luminous Darkness: The Anatomy of Segregation and the Ground of Hope*, first published in 1965, Thurman explores the deeper meaning of "the genuine":

> Always it is a human being who hungers, who is sick, who is ignorant, who suffers. And he cannot be touched in any way that counts unless the word gets through to him that he is being experienced as a human being by the persons for whom he is the object of good works. . . . When I identify with a man, I become one with him and in him I see myself. . . . This is the true meaning of . . . listening for the sound of the genuine in another. Such an experience cannot become a dogma—it has to remain experiential all the way . . . it requires exposure, sustained exposure.[73]

Thurman writes with devastating simplicity about how one of the cardinal sins of segregation is that it deprives people of the opportunity to experience one another in this deep way.[74] Rev. Smith has always been tuned in to the genuine, in himself and in others. Mike Trautman has said of him, "I think 'the sound of the genuine' is how he'd describe God."[75]

Starting in March 1980, Smith deepened his knowledge of this incisive theologian's work by leading what became a monthly study group called the "Howard Thurman Ethical and Enrichment Circle." The purpose of this formally constituted body was to "perpetuate the memory and teachings of Dr. Howard Thurman."[76] It had several dozen members, including some from the Hillside congregation and honorary members such as Dr. Benjamin E. Mays and Rev. Martin Luther King Sr. Coleading with Smith was Dr. George Thomas of Shaw Temple AME Zion Church and the Interdenominational Theological Center in Atlanta.

In May 1980 the group hosted Dr. Thurman himself. After the sage died in April the following year, the Circle held a celebration of the theologian's life annually in addition to their regular gatherings. Their meetings made use of more than 100 recordings of Thurman's speeches and meditations. One of their main activities was fund-raising to help build a Reading and Listening Room dedicated to Thurman in the Woodruff Library at the Atlanta University Center. Ardent members of the Circle made a scrapbook for Dr. Smith in 1986 after he announced he was leaving Atlanta. Included are twelve handwritten letters of thanks describing his impact on them.[77]

Despite all his training and preparation, Rev. Smith was still stunned when he received word that Dr. Thurman had died. His pages-long journal entry that day reveals his anger, soul-searching, and search for meaning. Eventually, Smith accepts the solace offered by his wife and the inspiration of Dr. Thurman's own philosophy.

> 4/10/81 The news came today that Howard Thurman had died. It is a fact that I cannot deny. Even though Luther [Smith Jr.] and I spoke nearly 3 hours today about Thurman and the future (not knowing that he had died), the fact is—he is dead. Nothing can be done about it. It is so final and complete. Somehow, I knew I was being prepared for SOMETHING. First, the incredible news that the President [Reagan] and three others had been shot; then the news that Jim Whitaker had suddenly died of a heart attack—we had been with each other just a few hours before. Then the news that my father would need an operation on his heart for another time; and the frantic call from my sister in Detroit that my/our mother was depressed because of the phone call from our brother William. . . . Death appeared to be all around me, giving me clues that it was hovering around. . . .
>
> The news came while Luther and I had been having conversations about Thurman—his thought, his life and where we might go from here. . . . He is gone; that laugh which utilized every ounce of himself has been silenced. . . .

That ability to dramatize the words of the Bible—and the words of life itself, is no longer to be heard again. . . .

It is further significant that Fran gently told me the news that Howard had died. The love of my life had meandered out to the driveway . . . and then she told me—"Wait a minute they have been trying to reach you all day." In one breath she gave me the news and in the same moment I could feel her arms of comfort around me. A moment I will never forget and a reminder that those arms would enfold me again and again for moments such as this. . . .

The truth of the matter is that he continues to live on the hearts and minds of many[;] that he left so many thoughtful words and challenges [is] not an accident. That he continuously challenges each of us to find that spark in ourselves is truly beautiful.[78]

CHAPTER 10

Building a Beloved Community, 1986–2006

As the fourteenth senior minister at the First Presbyterian Church of Brooklyn (FPC), Rev. Smith garnered all the resources he needed to bring a genuine, beloved community to life.[1] Over two decades from 1986 to 2006, he and several hundred willing collaborators turned a traditional white-majority church into a growing, changing, working model of multicultural engagement.

In answering the call to First Presbyterian, Smith also made history as the church's first minister of color in almost two centuries.[2] Founded in 1822 and occupying its current home since 1847, First Church is a massive brownstone edifice on Henry Street in one of New York City's oldest neighborhoods. Its imposing façade peaks with a bell tower 120 feet high.

A few blocks away, fine buildings and gardens line the Brooklyn Heights "Promenade," an elevated walkway overlooking New York Harbor and the skyline of Lower Manhattan. At the north end of the neighborhood, down a steep slope, is the Fulton Ferry landing that Walt Whitman exalted in his poem "Crossing Brooklyn Ferry." There, parks now border the surging East River across from the historic South Street Seaport. Dominating the landing is one of the two huge stone footings that support the iconic and graceful Brooklyn Bridge.

Inside, First Church is plush and warm with generous proportions, ornate woodwork, and Tiffany stained-glass windows. The pulpit is situated high above the cushioned, carved-wood pews, facing a large balcony that can seat the overflow Sunday worshippers. A large pipe organ rises behind the pulpit.

First Presbyterian Church, 124 Henry St., Brooklyn, New York. Photo by the author.

Attached to the sanctuary is a large two-story brick building that houses a nursery school on the ground floor. A wide corner staircase leads one flight up to the expansive Elliott Room, named after a long-serving pastor. There, amid thick carpet, easy chairs, and portraits of previous pastors, the congregation holds its social events. Off a landing halfway up the stairs is the pastor's study, a meditative haven with dark woodwork, tall windows, and a working fireplace. The church complex includes a four-story manse next door to the main building that is equally grand.

The strength of Rev. Smith's preaching in St. Louis led to his appointment at First Church. In early 1985 William Edwards 2d, the only Black member of the First Church Pastor Nominating Committee (PNC), submitted Smith's name for candidacy. During his student days in St. Louis, Edwards had heard Rev. Smith speak at Berea. He later told the *New York Times* that Smith was "one of the most dynamic ministers in all St. Louis."[3]

After reading newspaper articles about Smith's work in Atlanta, the PNC contacted him about the job in New York. While Hillside had considered more than forty candidates when Smith was hired, the search committee in New York was reviewing more than a hundred resumes.[4]

In October 1985, while accompanying his youngest daughter, Krista, to look at colleges, Paul agreed to stop in Brooklyn to meet the search committee. He and Krista were hosted by parishioner Carroll Dickson, who lived a few blocks from the church. Smith delivered a sermon and recorded his thoughts in one of his journals.

> I preached—Was received greatly; warmly. The setting was warm and open. The committee was favorably impressed. We returned to Carroll's living room.... I knew and felt I would be asked to come as their pastor. I felt a bit strange in that moment because I realized I was going to leave Hillside. The thought had not crossed my mind until this afternoon. I would have to wait— they would have to wait; but the sacramental moment had come. When that moment comes each of us must ask—what will we do with it?[5]

Afterward, the committee unanimously decided to recommend Smith to the rest of the congregation. Pressed by the committee for a commitment, Smith promised that he would take the job if it were offered. But upon returning home, he was informed that he had made a key mistake—Fran had not been part of the decision. Despite the fact that he knew she would be thrilled to move to New York, Fran wanted to see the place before they committed themselves. A trip to Brooklyn for Fran was soon arranged. Smith says that after a full tour of First Church, she made it clear that she wanted the kitchen in the manse renovated to her specifications. After the search committee agreed to her requests, she told them, "He can come."[6]

In mid-January, Smith preached at First Presbyterian to a congregation that would vote afterward on hiring him. He wrote in his journal while he waited to speak. "Hard not to focus on myself.... The vote of the congregation follows—A strange system—both congregation and preacher on the spot.... I wonder what the people are feeling? The names of previous ministers are etched on the walls! What must they be thinking now as they see this black man of God being nominated to the pulpit? I wonder what Mrs. Elliot really thinks as she remembers the 32 years her husband served here as the beloved pastor."[7] Afterward, the congregation made sure the Smiths were comfortable while they deliberated.

> 1:26 pm. We sit together at the study desk; the fire is crackling in the fireplace. Fran and I are served a buffet lunch with a bottle of red wine.... The congregational meeting has been called to order by John McNabb.... I experience

Fran in this moment, in a new and exciting way. Clearly, she is as happy as I am about our future here together. Clearly she has played a significant role in whatever decision is now being decided. She has affirmed me, the PNC, this congregation and this committee—this community. . . . Never has her presence been more important than now. So we wait together—in a joyful, celebrative mood (we feel the only vote can be yes) arranging in our minds the furniture in the study—what pictures will go where—what books there! Thinking ahead and feeling blessed. We kiss—a warm and tender kiss which says thank you for being who you are; thank you for 25 years of wonderful loving and caring. "We deserve this one," she kept saying. I agree.[8]

Smith wrote later about the outcome of the vote:

Carroll Dickson comes into the room. How will we ever forget the excitement in his eyes; the glow on his face; the care and patience with which he says, "Paul you are our pastor and they want you in the room." Slowly he climbs the stairs—his breathing is heavy/short. He has recently been to the hospital; his 80 years is beginning to catch up with him. And yet, there could be nothing to stop him from being the bearer of the good news of my call to the pastorate.

I remember Fran—excitement all over her face as we entered the Elliott room to the applause and singing of the doxology. People were smiling, I was crying and others began to cry. . . . In that sacramental moment we became one voice; one congregation.[9]

This time, the news of Smith's hiring was published in the *New York Times*. The paper reported that while the parishioners' first vote, by paper ballot, was sixty-seven to twenty-three in support of Smith, a second oral vote was unanimously in favor.[10] The journalist described the scene:

The new pastor, who will move to Brooklyn in June, wiped away tears as he and his wife, Frances, were ushered into the room to a standing ovation. In a choked voice, he said, "I can assure you that this is one of the few times I will be without words."

He went on, his voice clearing: "This is the high point of my professional career. I pledge to you that together we will climb new mountains. I also pledge that we will have a lot of fun together."[11]

Interviewed about the challenge of leading a mostly white congregation, Smith said, "I'm confident I can deal with it. It's a nontraditional thing and that's good for the church."[12] Smith said he hoped to be "[a] catalyst, a visionary, a dreamer, to prod the interest of this church and community." He challenged the congregation to become "a voice in the wilderness." He said innovation had been the secret of his success at Hillside, where the membership had grown to three hundred.[13]

In February 1986, Smith moved to Brooklyn ahead of Frances and the rest of the family. He soon discovered that there were still nine holdouts who had doubts about his skills. Wanting to make a connection with these people, he convinced the search committee to break the rules and tell him who they were. One was a pillar of the church who had voted not to hire Smith, while his wife had voted yes. The reverend remembers finding an opportunity to connect with the man on a visit to the man's wife in the hospital.

> Connie rises up in her bed to greet me. Jim says not one word, not hello, nothing. Connie and I were talking; she was saying she was looking forward to my being her pastor. Then she says she's getting a little tired.
>
> She says, "Jim, Dr. Smith doesn't know how to get around N.Y. Why don't you help him get to the subway?" . . .
>
> Jim has to walk out of the hospital with me and he obviously doesn't want to. We get down from the 8th floor in [the] elevator, and he still says nothing. We get four or five steps outside and there is a torrential downpour. We have to go back in. Then Jim says, "What the hell. We're going to take a cab." He says a few things in the cab. We get to the manse first; he lived one block over. I said—"My wife's not here, yours in hospital and it's dinnertime. Why don't we go get a drink and some dinner?" Jim said, "What the hell" and he became my strongest advocate.[14]

Smith visited each of the others who were resistant, saying he "wanted to know a little about them and they about me." Other opportunities arose that allowed them to see more of who he was. "Jim . . . comes to see his daughter on Grandparents Day and finds Andy Young sitting there in the church. Andy told him, 'I practically raised that boy!' about me. So it was validation. Andrew Young didn't just come to preach; he really knew me. From that point on, it was like, 'Don't you ever say anything about Dr. Smith! . . . It was a hell of a ride, a hell of a run.'"[15]

In the end, all nine continued to attend First Church. Alexander Bennett, a longtime parishioner at First Church, told the *Times* that hiring Smith was "the most historic event since the time of [nineteenth-century abolitionist pastor Samuel Hanson] Cox."[16] Englishman Bennett quickly became an enthusiastic supporter of Smith's initiatives. Initially, he acted as a bridge between the new pastor and existing congregation members. In time, he became one of Smith's closest friends at First Church; Smith mentions him frequently in subsequent journal entries.

Dr. Smith had other hurdles to cross, however. At that time, the Presbytery of New York City was composed of some 115 congregations. The Presbytery has critical veto power; it has to meet with the candidate and approve the appointment before a new minister can answer the call of a particular church. In Smith's case, "there were some arrogant guys on the Presbytery who had been turned down for First Church. They asked me ridiculous questions. I looked at them and said, 'What does this have to do with being the pastor of this church?' They said, 'We simply want to know what you think.' I said, 'What I think has nothing to do with what I can do if I become the minister here.'" Others asked more substantive questions about Smith's leadership of Hillside Church in Atlanta.

After the interview, Smith says, "you leave, they vote, and you come back in to a round of applause."[17] Or at least, that's how it went for him. Despite a lifelong exasperation with well-meaning yet slow-moving bureaucracies, Smith was later elected to a year's service leading the New York Presbytery as Moderator.[18] Historically, a Black Presbyterian having supervisory power over denominational practice was very unusual.[19] However, Smith quickly developed a reputation among his New York peers for resolving conflict with straight talk, equanimity, and practical optimism.

After successfully navigating through his initial contacts with the Presbytery, Smith was ready to be officially installed as senior minister. The Presbytery authorizes, organizes, and pays for a minister's installation. Once again, Smith had surprises up his sleeve.

> There was total disbelief when I told them Ambassador Andrew Young was going to speak for my installation.
> First Church was packed, even that big balcony. Must have been 50–60 years since anyone had used it. The church was packed, cameras, press—those old white guys were so impressed! They were saying, "Oh my gosh, who is this guy??" . . . They knew I was something different. To their credit, every one of those steeple pastors was very supportive. They were very generous to me. And I helped them.[20]

The local *Heights Press* reported that over seven hundred people, including a city councilman, representatives from the mayor's and borough president's offices, and newsman Gil Noble, attended the installation service at 3:00 p.m. on September 21, 1986.[21] Andrew Young gave the sermon. The program reveals that Drs. Nurss and Rivers from Hillside Church helped lead the service.[22] Elder Carroll Dickson delivered the gospel lesson. There was organ and choral music, an Old Testament lesson by the president of

New York Theological Seminary, and an epistle lesson by Rev. Choong Sik Ahn from the Korean Presbyterian Church of Brooklyn (which at that time was sharing the church facility).[23]

First Church elders, representatives from the Presbytery, Presbyterian parish ministers, and other local clergy made up the group that led the actual installation ritual. This culminated with leaders placing their hands on the new pastor's shoulders as they asked him to pledge that he would serve faithfully according to the precepts of the church. After he had done so, the congregation pledged to provide for his welfare, to stand by him in times of difficulty, and to honor his authority. Then all joined in prayer.

The Presbytery Moderator then said, "Paul, you are now minister of the word for this congregation. Whatever you do, in [word] or deed, do everything in the name of the Lord Jesus, giving thanks to God the Father through him. Amen. Welcome to this ministry."[24] The *Heights Press* reported that Smith said that he believed he was "called by God to serve the church in Brooklyn Heights."[25]

Smith did manage to put a personal twist on the installation proceedings by bringing his mother from South Bend to attend the service and by organizing a series of seminars to be held the day before. The seminar topics were all close to Smith's heart. For the mid-1980s, the agenda was fairly progressive: Presbyterians and pluralism; music as a faith-enhancing experience; the AIDS crisis; medicine and ethics; the peace movement; the church's position on Nicaragua; and issues surrounding death and dying. These were subjects he went on to address in sermons, workshops, and political activism with his new congregation.

Smith stated after his installation that his intention "was to develop a truly interracial and intercultural church in the Heights."[26] By all accounts, he was remarkably successful. As Andrew Young articulates it: "I was always very impressed with that church. Throughout Paul's ministry, I've never known him to have anything but a multiracial, multicultural congregation. I think he's probably one of the few preachers that can say that. Even his pastorates here in Atlanta were very well integrated before he went to Brooklyn."[27]

Over the course of two decades, the active membership at First Church went from about 60 to between 350 and 400.[28] Instinctively, Smith incorporated many of the elements identified by sociological researchers as leading to strong multicultural churches.[29] For instance, First Church had a strong

Then Atlanta
mayor Andrew
Young at
Rev. Smith's
installation
service, First
Presbyterian
Church, 1986.
Courtesy of the
Smith Family.

mission statement that asserted that inclusiveness was a primary goal. The congregation welcomed, in an increasingly conscious way, the perspectives of people from myriad communities: Black, white, interracial, international, intercultural, interfaith, LGBT, believer, and nonbeliever. Slowly, Smith developed an amalgam of worship styles to serve this diverse group. This helped to create a self-consciously integrated community that celebrated both its variety and its harmony. These values held firm even after Smith's retirement in 2006.

Part of what made Rev. Smith so successful was his openness to seekers of all faiths and his ability to make immediate and deep spiritual connections with people.[30] One member of the congregation, a white middle-aged therapist, had been looking for a church dedicated to creating a more racially and culturally integrated society. She also wanted a church she and her Jewish husband could feel comfortable attending together. The first time she went to First Church, she says, "Paul, of course, greeted me warmly. I told him that I was five months pregnant, and he was very congratulatory, was very sweet. The following Sunday I went back. I am sitting towards the back, and during the Prayers for the People, he said, looking straight at me, asked for prayers 'for those among us who aren't born yet.' He just looked right at me, and I just thought, wow—that's somebody who is paying attention. I felt like he just gathered me in."[31]

Another white professional woman who became a devoted First Church member says she too had a powerful experience the first time she encountered Smith. "I walked in and Paul was preaching. I sat in the back. He got all lathered up, saying, 'When your back is against the wall, when nothing else works, when you feel alone, etc., etc., etc. [and then finally he said], God hears you.' And I just burst into tears. So I started going to [Smith's] church."[32]

Dr. Sam Murumba, a Ugandan law professor who joined First Church in 1991 with his family, was seeking a dynamic, politically active church after relocating from Australia.[33] His family's last church had been nondenominational, but they were attracted by Rev. Smith's history in the civil rights movement. They also appreciated the warm welcome they received from Dorothy Gill, an elderly African American woman and lifelong Brooklynite who was a fixture in the congregation. Gill embodied the ethos of the church: "She was the mother of everybody. Everybody. It didn't matter [who you were]. Dorothy would go up and say, 'I love you.'"[34]

Another professional couple visited First Church at Easter in 1991 to hear Handel and were moved to find themselves sitting next to Arthur Ashe and his wife. That very first Sunday, Rev. Smith learned they were from the Midwest and told them, "You gotta come next week, okay? We're planning an all-church retreat and you have to come on that." They quickly found themselves in charge of planning the event. Both ended up serving for many years on the Session and in other key lay leadership positions.[35]

Parishioners quickly learned that Smith would draw them into all kinds of roles they had not envisioned for themselves. Smith's pastoral style was freewheeling, enveloping, and enthusiastic. Dr. Murumba, for example, found himself asked to contribute to the service with little to no advance notice. "Paul had a way of involving everybody. . . . He's very spontaneous. We'd start the service and then do the passing of the peace. Then he might walk by and say, 'Sam, can you do the pastoral prayer today?' . . . With Paul, there was no rigid form."[36]

Many members of the congregation were impressed with the ways Smith used his history and contacts to bring political consciousness into discussion at First Church. One former parishioner's current church in Atlanta had an erudite minister, but the political awareness was missing: "What's going on around you, and what your response should be as a Christian person, we don't talk about. Of course, some people think you shouldn't mix politics and religion. Especially in the South. But Paul would always talk about what was going on—and relate it to the Gospel."[37]

Another strong and distinctive personality at First Church was a white woman named Dorothy Turmail. She had joined First Church long before Smith's arrival. Among the many things she contributed to the First Church community were huge cloth banners she designed and sewed. One emblazoned with "The Coat of Many Colors" was what brought the law professor's wife into First Church for her initial visit. Another banner hung outside over the front doors of the church simply proclaimed, "Struggle and Celebration."

A few years into his tenure in Brooklyn, Smith wrote in his journal about his strategy.

> FPC serves two very different groups of people. First, there is our actual membership who generally show up on Sunday or attend meetings which are important to the life and mission of FPC. I can always count upon this group, because for the most part, they have given much of themselves to the mission. ... They are always there making their thoughts known.
>
> The second congregation represents the community with its varied interests. During the Persian Gulf "crisis" ... we focused the church's attention on a Christian/biblical moral and ethical response. On Christmas Eve, 1990, I made my first pulpit statement regarding the escalation of military machinery, manpower and personnel. That service gathered together some 300 people mostly from the community. On Jan. 17th, I put together an ecumenical prayer vigil which brought together over 700 (mostly from the community). This event was followed by a forum with Rep. Steve Solarz, Major Owens, Rev. Goldie Sherrill and Rabbi Brickner, co-sponsored by Brooklyn SANE.[38]

Brooklyn Heights has been a haven for the wealthy since the nineteenth century, and Smith eventually inhabited its most sanctified precincts. He chuckles remembering that part of the deal to hire him included having his membership dues for the local private racquet club paid in perpetuity. He is still a member of "The Casino," which was built in 1904 with indoor tennis and squash courts, a gym, and a restaurant. With the same courageous enthusiasm he brought to swimming in the segregated pool in South Bend,

Smith immediately became one of the few people of color who frequented the club.

Tennis inevitably brought Smith together with Mayor David Dinkins, the only Black mayor in New York City's history. Dinkins was an avid player and is still a fan; it was through his efforts that the U.S. Tennis Center in Queens became the biggest tennis venue in the world. Smith met Dinkins around 1990, early in Dinkins's term as mayor. As Smith tells it, one day he found himself playing doubles against investment banker Ronald Gault and the new mayor, complete with security detail. Smith and his partner stunned the high-profile team. "We kicked their butts! They couldn't believe it. Some preacher comes in here and beats us! [Dinkins] said, 'We should get to know each other.' I said my son-in-law is from Trenton. David knew the son-in-law's parents. He said, 'Stop by the office and see me.' I said, 'City Hall?!' He said to one of his people, 'This is Paul. Make it happen.' So I went to his office."[39]

After that, Smith and Dinkins played against each other often. Dinkins visited First Church many times, and the two became close. Smith played master of ceremonies at a book party at Macy's Herald Square celebrating the publication of Dinkins's autobiography in February 2014. VIP guests included Dr. Roscoe Brown, one of the Tuskegee Airmen, a group of African American pilots who performed valiantly during World War II. As is typical of the banter between Smith and the former mayor, Dinkins took the microphone to say of his tennis opponent, "The pastor cheats! He goes to the back of the court between games and prays! So what do you think the outcome will be?!" The former mayor said later, "That's the beauty of tennis. You don't get mad—you try to get even!"[40] More seriously, Dinkins says, "If [Paul] says jump, I say, how high? I consider him a very good friend. He's just a likeable guy who had the ability to walk with kings." And as a preacher, Dinkins says, "he always had the audience in his hand."[41]

Tennis also fostered much less predictable friendships. Smith met Charles Clayman, a New York lawyer who lived down the block from the manse, at the tennis club. Clayman notes dryly, "He was a young Black guy who grew up in the Midwest, went to a historic Black school and became a minister; I was [a] Jewish kid from Quincy, Mass who went to Harvard and became a lawyer. We just had everything in common!"[42]

Meeting to play tennis and eat breakfast once a week at the Clark Street Diner, Clayman says he and Smith "became very close." Clayman says he found in Smith someone who was always open to learning and interested in other points of view: "There is a confidence, but no arrogance."[43] Over time, Clayman became Smith's "de facto general counsel." "I know a lot about politics. I'm a criminal defense lawyer, been 47 years in NYC, general counsel to a guy that was deputy mayor. [Paul] would listen. Sometimes followed my advice, sometimes wouldn't. It was meant for him to get a perspective from someone who only had his interests at heart. No agenda."[44]

Over the years, Paul and Fran grew close to Clayman's family. Smith brought his special sensitivity to Clayman's son's wedding in Michigan. Clayman recalls: "I have a wonderful daughter in-law.... She was very nervous, before the wedding.... She walked up to the podium and Paul noticed how nervous she was, and he leaned over and kissed her on the cheek. It was the most beautiful thing I've ever seen in my life. So that's who he is."[45] In 2018, the Smiths traveled to Paris so that the reverend could preside over the renewal of Clayman's own marriage vows.

Reviewing their many years together, Clayman says his relationship with Smith has unusual qualities. "Paul is unlike most other people. There's something incredibly unique—it's not that it's holy. There's something unique about his presence. There are some people, when you're in their presence, it makes you feel better. With Paul, it is all the time.... It is one of the most important things in my life, having a friend like that. It is something I never in the world would have imagined. And I have thousands of friends! That's what I do. But nobody like him."[46]

Clayman recounts how events tended to unfold at First Church. His friend Charles Joseph Hynes was the special prosecutor who successfully argued the case against white teens whose racist hostility led to the death of a Black man in Howard Beach, Queens, in 1986.[47] When Clayman introduced Hynes to Smith some months later, Smith invited the prosecutor to speak at First Church. "There was a nice crowd. Joe's one of these great Irish lawyers who can talk pretty well. And then Paul got up and spoke. And it was just phenomenal. It was a little of the southern Black minister, a lot of passion, it was poetry—it was beautiful. And Joe is a good lawyer and I know Joe well, but they were on different planets.... I would never have wanted to speak on the same program as Paul. He's just miraculous."[48] In the end, Clayman says a number of people from the tennis club liked Smith so much they joined his church.

Rev. Smith was soon introduced by First Church members to the Rembrandt Club, "perhaps the most anachronistic of a handful of generations-old private clubs in Brooklyn Heights."[49] Limited to a hundred men—corporate leaders, lawyers, and the like—the group meets five times a year to hear a speaker and share a meal. Black tie is required. Meetings have been held in members' well-appointed Heights homes since 1880.

When Smith was proposed as a prospective member, there was some discreet vetting. Smith says, "They were checking me out as the first Black member—is he worthy? Can he speak the King's English? They would never say that of course." Smith's friends were looking out for him: "They were the ones who would say, in essence, 'you need to apologize' if anyone had said something racist." But that never happened. Smith says, "There were some people there I never talked to, who never spoke to me. But I'm used to that."[50] The fact that Smith already belonged to the most exclusive African American men's fraternity, Sigma Pi Phi, must have reassured Rembrandt members of his qualifications.

Being part of elite groups like the Rembrandt Club was appropriate for someone leading First Church. Smith learned a great deal by participating, and it opened other doors for him. He was soon asked to serve on the boards of a number of institutions including the Brooklyn Academy of Music, Long Island University, and Long Island College Hospital. After he began teaching classes at Union Theological and New York seminaries, he was asked to join the boards of Manhattan institutions as well.

Perhaps furthest afield for him was serving on the board of the National Abortion Rights Action League (NARAL).[51] Smith attended monthly meetings of NARAL for more than ten years and became a confidant of the group's longtime director, Kate Michelman. He raised their issues at meetings of the Urban League and NAACP and encouraged NARAL to extend itself to those organizations to forge connections with African American women. His congregation supported this work, accompanying him when he joined a huge march on Washington, D.C., in 1989 to defend abortion rights.[52] Smith says that First Church became the place to gather when he and others participated in political marches.

Smith has maintained his contact with church families he knew decades ago. A daughter of Marge and Ken Smith from St. Louis is currently a member at First Church. After moving to New York a few years after Smith assumed the pastorate, Carl Dudley's son Nathan joined the congregation. Dudley has a unique perspective on the man who baptized him and watched him grow up. He remembers being amazed as a child that Smith could walk around the church and preach without notes.[53] After reconnecting with

Smith, Dudley asked him to co-officiate at his interfaith wedding in 2000 to Stephanie Jones, a performance artist and Buddhist. Dudley, who has become a leader at First Church, says of his old family friend, "The church was incredibly open under Paul. . . . He accomplished a great deal at First Church. The Session took a huge leap of faith hiring him. And it was also a leap of faith for him to take that church. . . . [It] was a re-creation racially of the Thurman-esque church in San Francisco. . . . Spiritually, building-a-community-wise, it was obviously a success. It was like a dream of an integrated world."[54]

Now a father with interracial children and the founder of a charter school in New York, Dudley is incisive about what the goal of a church should be (his emphasis). "Integration as a word in the political sphere has disappeared, but it didn't die at First Church. Now 'diversity' is the word. But it is not enough to just get happy in our diversity. The question is [not just] are you diverse, [but] are you *anti-racist*?"[55]

Another longtime parishioner, Jim Johnson, is a Harvard-educated African American lawyer who has known Smith since 1995. He initially visited First Church after reading about Rev. Smith in Arthur Ashe's memoir. He explains further why just looking for "diversity" is not enough.

> Paul's church . . . was home for me in a way that other places had not been. It was not diverse in the way that a lot of places are . . . in the sense of the diversity of a crayon box—a lot of color but all wax inside? Instead [Smith] created space in which those who believed could commune with those who had questions. And those who had questions would not feel uncomfortable. . . . At a time when anti-Muslim sentiment was high, and it is even worse now, he had imams delivering messages and cantors giving Old Testament scripture.[56]

Johnson has given a good deal of thought to what made Smith's ministry so successful. He highlights the uninhibited warmth of the congregation and its iconoclastic tone. "Paul blew up the hierarchy. . . . The power of Paul's ministry is that he doesn't worry about the law. He gets to the practices. . . . We touch each other [at First Church] . . . we hug! There's five to ten minutes in which people will go around the congregation and everyone touches everyone else . . . in a very robust way, in a safe way, [even] complete strangers."[57]

Rev. Fred Davie is another African American Presbyterian who has known Smith since the early 1990s. Currently executive vice president at Union Theological Seminary in Manhattan, Davie served as a parish associate at First Church for some years, acting in an unpaid support role to the senior minister. Davie was so well known and respected that he was asked to consider applying for the senior pastor position when Smith retired. Davie thought seriously about it but feels that administration, not parish ministry, is what he is called to do.[58]

Davie says that Smith is, at once, "a colleague, mentor, friend. He has a commitment to multicultural worship. He is intentional about it. It's about social justice and community change."[59] From his vantage point as fellow clergy, Davie says of Smith, "Paul is deeply spiritual and reflective himself. He taps into God's presence, accessing the Divine out of a wellspring he's able to share with others. There is intentionality when he breaks down barriers. He has had an extraordinarily successful ministry in Brooklyn."[60]

In contrast to ministers who don't often let others speak from their pulpit, Davie says, "Paul never grasped for power. He loved to delegate, to bring in people."[61] And unlike his own calling, Davie says, "Paul in his heart, soul, and bones is a parish minister. He loves the liturgy and the ritual. He seeks a profound engagement in people's lives."[62]

Davie attests to the fact that at First Church, the choir, the Session, and the congregation were all self-consciously inclusive. He reveals that he and another parish associate, Lee Hancock, were among those who pushed Smith to make his ministry explicitly welcoming to gay and lesbian people. One of the few criticisms voiced by former members of First Church was that Smith came a bit late to recognizing that the LGBTQ community's quest for rights and justice was just the most recent front in the same battle Smith had been engaged in for decades. Smith later led a Sunday service at which he, Hancock, Davie, and another parish associate all gave sermons on gender and sexuality.

One lay leader believes that it was the heartbreaking loss of Smith's youngest brother to AIDS in 1990 that helped mobilize Smith's thinking on the issue. William had become estranged from the family in the 1980s, and it is possible he acquired the new and fatal scourge, HIV, through same-sex contact. Whatever the cause of the disease, it was brother Paul who supported him through the wasting and painful death caused by AIDS. Paul also was the one who broke the news to their mother when Willie died.

Dr. Smith subsequently became outspoken about the need to include LGBTQ people in Presbyterian congregations, despite the fact that the denomination's Book of Order explicitly prohibited it. When told that prospective congregants had to be asked about their sexuality and denied membership if they were gay, Smith voiced his objections to the highest levels of the Presbyterian hierarchy. "I said to the national committee . . . I'll ask them first if they like peas or beans. . . . And if they say peas and not beans, I'll use that as a reason to not accept them! That's how stupid what you're asking us to do is. And I am not going to do it. Come and get me."[63] Eventually, First Presbyterian became a publicly dissenting church within the denomination for supporting the rights of LGBTQ people. In 2015, the national Presbyterian Church (U.S.A.) as a whole voted to recognize gay and lesbian marriage.[64]

As young families joined the church and the membership grew, Smith's weekly routine grew busy with the rituals of a thriving congregation. Parishioners loved the way he walked new babies around the church to introduce them to the congregational family. He was known for saying, "the birth of a baby is life's answer to death."[65] Smith's most comprehensive journal written while at First Church is filled with notes to and about babies he has baptized, couples he has married, and funerals he has performed.[66] Over roughly six years between January 2000 and October 2006, Smith recorded details about sixty-nine baptisms, thirty-five weddings, and twenty funerals. If each of these rituals is an occasion when individuals and their families are literally touched by the church through the minister, it becomes clear how deeply and how often a clergyman like Smith gets to channel God's love and compassion to his flock.

Marcia Smith (no relation), a lawyer who served as Clerk of Session for most of Smith's tenure at First Church, describes his methods.

> People came because they were looking for faith, for a church home. It was still organized religion. It had some structure. But we had a lot of interfaith couples. A lot didn't even know what Presbyterianism was. They came because they liked the music and Paul and the message—we're all in this together. He made it safe to question the fact that Black people don't like to talk to white people and white people don't like to talk to Black people . . . now Latino and Asian people are part of the conversation too.[67]

However, working with Smith had its challenges, she says. "If you wanted to work with Paul, you had to be flexible and go with him in the service."[68] She and the two Dorothys were among those who also kept the paperwork flowing between First Church and the Presbytery.[69] Paying attention to those kinds of details is not Smith's strong suit. Like Joanne Nurss and Prince Rivers at Hillside in Atlanta, they provided the structure that supported Smith's spiritual spontaneity.

Over the years, the congregation heard from a crowd of nationally known figures including Tom Foley (who was Speaker of the House in the late eighties), other congressional leaders, David Dinkins, Brooklyn politicians, Rev. Jesse Jackson, Marc Morial of the Urban League, and renowned law professor Derrick Bell. Some decided to stay. Smith grew fond of Barack Obama's later Attorney General Loretta Lynch when she attended First Church. He is happy to note that at one time, "there were eleven Harvard Law School graduates and their professor—Derrick Bell—attending First Church. That was just magic."[70] Smith became close to lawyer Barry Ford and his wife Lisa Mensah who went on to become undersecretary of agriculture in the Obama administration. At the same time, Smith notes, "we had those not in lofty positions as well—a NYC bus driver. I still hear from her."[71]

While many of these parishioners were people of color, Marcia Smith says that the reverend also sought to make connections with upper- and middle-class white people "who weren't going to be taught about race [anywhere else].... He was about educating the people who were in power" in order to create change.[72]

Around the time of Smith's retirement, Janet Dewart Bell, the wife of revered law professor Derrick Bell and a scholar in her own right, spoke formally at church about her view of Smith's accomplishments.[73]

> I am and have been grateful to this church for being the inclusive and caring community that it is, for being a model of diversity.... This church is an integral part of my life. I come to First Church to share God. This church and Paul have helped give me the courage to bear witness and tell my testimony.... This is a wonderful and beloved community, where we have the freedom to be ourselves. We can be committed and joyful. We can even "disobey" Paul's and Beth's occasional dictates to "please remain in your pews during the passing of the peace."[74]

Dr. Bell mentions the stories about Smith's grandmother, Odie Wingo, that were well-known to regulars at FPC. "I debated with myself the title of today's talk: I almost called it 'From His Grandmother's Porch.' We all know how his grandmother brooded over him and helped him make his journey to responsible adulthood."[75]

Dr. Bell says of Smith, "Dr. Paul has been our direct link with the legacy and inspiration of Rev. Dr. Martin Luther King, a participant in the Selma March and other 'sacramental moments.' Paul was there—side by side with

Dr. King and Rev. Andy Young."[76] She quotes another church elder who said: "Real diversity is hard work. It's not easy to get all our egos, set beliefs, and defenses in one place and surrender to a higher authority. Paul has been the inspiration, but we must remain true to the mission. It doesn't just happen." Bell summed up her remarks about Smith with these words: "Joy. Love. Faith. Commitment. Compassion. Deep water lessons."[77]

Many who were active First Church members agree that key themes in Smith's ministry were diversity and inclusion, the theology and writings of Howard Thurman, and the political struggle for justice. Added to these was the example Smith set for introspection. Professor Murumba says, "Paul was multidimensional. We had a wonderful pastor in Australia. . . . But he did not really have this inward thing that Paul has. I've never seen that much. Church leaders are more used to talking; there's very little reflection. [Smith's] Eastern methods, the quietness, the meditation—that was quite distinctive. The commitment to that is also quite strong with Paul."[78]

Smith insisted that the church elders on the Session should be consciously multiracial. He changed the chemistry of the group with his methods. Murumba remembers, "When I first got on Session, I thought we'd do admin business. But we met in Paul's office, and he said, 'I want to go around and you tell me about your most moving experiences.' He did the same on Session retreat. We'd do that all day. There'd be reflective meditative moments and then he paired us with somebody else. I was paired with Dottie T. It was a wonderful moment."[79]

As things began to change at First Church, one parishioner remembers Rev. Smith saying during a service: "Look around you—this is what heaven should look like!"[80] Andrew Young later said he was impressed that "two of the most effective people in government [at that time] were members of Smith's church . . . Lisa Mensah and Loretta Lynch. For a church to produce two members of a president's cabinet and subcabinet is quite significant."[81]

In 1991, Rev. Smith wrote in his journal: "Music is an antidote to bitterness."[82] Since his days as a young pastor using jazz to attract newcomers to his church in Buffalo, Smith has wielded music as an elemental unifying tool. However, music is also a fundamental part of denominational practice, and it can be a stumbling block for a heterogeneous congregation. As Smith's daughter Krista put it while discussing her family's choice to attend a Presbyterian church in Summit, New Jersey: "I wanted the traditions I grew up with because that was such a part of my upbringing. . . . I wanted my kids to learn the [hymns] I learned growing up. The hymns are different in other churches."[83]

Aware of the way that familiar music grounds a congregation, Rev. Smith did not move quickly to change the music at First Presbyterian. From the time of Smith's arrival in 1986 into the 1990s, there were about eight people in the choir plus four paid soloists. The hymns were chosen from the standard Presbyterian hymnal. There was a choir director and an organist. On several of the church retreats Smith initiated, gospel music was sung and discussed, and Smith hoped that the music director might be inspired to move in the direction of a more diverse style. However, nothing changed until the impetus came from the congregation itself.

First, a group of parishioners decided they wanted to start a gospel choir. Eventually, two choirs formed: one traditional, one gospel. To Smith's chagrin, they settled into two essentially racially divided groups (though there was one woman who proudly called herself the "token white" in the gospel choir). Dr. Murumba, whose wife and daughter sang in the choir, recounts, "Paul said, 'I can't have two choirs. They have to merge.' Well, the gospel choir people didn't want to merge! In fact one or two left the church. Paul said, 'We can't have it any other way. We can't have two separate choirs divided by race.' That was around 1993–94. Then they merged choirs."[84] Murumba points out that Smith has his limits. "Diversity was a very big thing for Paul. He was willing to go with the flow, but on that one, he was extremely rigid."[85]

At the time, Smith was on the board of trustees at the Brooklyn Academy of Music (BAM), the internationally known arts center a few miles away in downtown Brooklyn. In the year 2000, BAM had just initiated the "Sounds of Praise" gospel brunches intended to bring the powerful church music of Brooklyn to a wider arts audience.[86] It was in this context of renewed celebration of the art form that Smith began to push for more gospel music at FPC.

Soon a new choir director was added to the mix. Amy Neuner joined First Church with her husband around 2000 after they moved to New York from Wisconsin. Both are classically trained musicians. The Neuners wandered into First Church to look at the Tiffany windows and were immediately drawn by the music and by Rev. Paul's sermon. Ron Metcalf, a prodigious musician with ties to Broadway, had just been hired informally to bring a gospel flavor to the music, and he was playing piano that day. Neuner says she knew nothing about gospel but found it completely captivating. After they joined the church, her husband Chris volunteered to play the bass for services, and Neuner began to assist Metcalf in organizing the music for the choir.

Embracing the move toward a more ecumenical sound, Metcalf hired a drummer and two gospel soloists. However, Metcalf soon moved on to other venues, leaving Amy Neuner attempting to fill his shoes. "Paul said, 'Ron told me that he trusts he can leave everything in your hands.' Paul has such a genuine, loving, supportive nature. He was telling me, 'You can do this.' I didn't know gospel music. . . . Paul said, 'I trust you and you're going to learn.' He was so genuine and loving. He said, 'It is okay. We'll learn and keep on going.'" [87]

Neuner hit her stride after a colleague at the Long Island school where she was teaching music gave her a boost. Neuner declares, "The African American hymnbook absolutely changed my life and the entire scope of my ministry at FPC.[88] It was the key that unlocked the mystery of all the songs that were sung in Black churches that I had been to."[89] What Neuner learned from the hymnbook turned out to be essential to her success in developing new music and arrangements for the choir. "For the first time, I could see the whole picture right in front of me. The notation made sense to me. It was the missing link. I had very, very little experience with improvisation, chord symbols, etc. The hymnal allowed me as a classically trained musician to sit down, play, and learn and experience hundreds of new pieces and in turn be able to teach them to our choir and congregation."[90]

Neuner was so adept at this, she became FPC's minister of music. Over time, the choir has come to incorporate everything from spirituals to contemporary rock and even secular music. Neuner explains how Smith's philosophy helped shape the choir's goal of reaching everyone in the congregation. "We all have our own prejudices and things that really move us. Paul was always so intentional. The only reason this works is because we were not afraid to talk about this. He would say, 'When we do communion today, it can't all be white guys. We have to do communion as we are actually represented' . . . everyone knows when they come, there's going to be something for them. . . . Paul was really into allowing people to be ministered to in many different ways."[91]

Eventually, a kind of shorthand developed between Smith and the musicians that made the music a spontaneous and integrated part of the mood of the service. As Neuner relates:

Everything became much more improvisational. It was like, "If I ever start talking about Grandmother's porch ...." [There was music he wanted to start up.] He would be building to it. It was more a Black style of worship. It is not really seen in Presbyterian churches....

Paul had a couple of songs I'd consider his signature songs. "I Don't Feel Noways Tired"—when things were getting really deep and intense, we sang that song a lot. Sometimes he'd start singing something else like "The Lord Is My Light and My Salvation." Paul would always sing, "Whom shall I fear, the Lord is the strength, whom shall I fear?" They are both gospel but old traditional hymn-type gospel. They are out of the African American hymnbook.[92]

Sam Murumba says of Neuner: "She became the interim and got so good. She has an amazing talent for bringing people together. In fact, Paul was right. Amy was really a pastoral figure. So the choir became like a mini-church. You'd go in Saturday morning and find them praying together. They help each other in all kinds of ways."[93]

It was in the process of choosing and rehearsing new music that the deepest community building took place. As Neuner relates:

We had amazing conversations at choir rehearsals—some of the deepest conversations about race and what some of the songs meant to different people.

[Once, someone asked] us to do "Dem Bones" based on the scripture readings of the day. Jim Johnson raised his hand and said, "I can't participate in this arrangement. It is because of the choir who originally performed the song and what it meant in its time and place." And what that meant to him as a Black man. We had a thirty-minute conversation about what these spirituals mean, how they can't all be lumped into one category. Those are some real conversations![94]

An FPC parishioner outside the choir testifies to its power as well. Describing what made First Church special, she exclaimed, "The music! That was the thing that brought people together unbelievably. I miss that so much. I would feel God through that music. A lot of African American spirituals and things like that—people moving and talking. It was electric. I left church high. I leave church now, and I ain't high. I do not feel like, 'Wow, God is great!' I did at First Church."[95]

The choir developed a special relationship with Professor Derrick Bell, who attended the church with his wife Janet. Bell was a celebrated law professor who first made a name for himself as a young lawyer working for Thurgood Marshall at the NAACP Legal Defense Fund in the 1960s.[96] Bell's uncompromising sense of justice led him to several highly principled decisions including leaving a tenured position at Harvard Law School to protest the institution's unwillingness to tenure female professors of color. In 1992, Bell joined the law faculty at New York University and thereafter became a regular member of First Church. One former FPC elder remembers making a connection with him the very first time she went to FPC to hear gospel music—it turned out Dr. Bell too was a devotee of the music.[97] Eventually, a number of Bell's Harvard students became regular attendees.

At some point in the early 2000s, Dr. Bell invited the choir to join him at the annual Race in American Society lecture that he sponsored for freshmen at NYU Law. Celebrated for its diversity and spirit, the choir appeared at the event annually, even after Bell's death in 2011. Their connection with Bell was so strong that when the congregation heard one Sunday that Dr. Bell was in his final hours at a Manhattan hospital, the choir spontaneously took action. One singer relates, "Amy Neuner rounded us up, and we left the service to go to the hospital. We went to visit Derrick's room and sang to him around in his bed. Paul was there and I was literally leaning on Paul. It was really one of the special moments of my life. It was really extraordinary. [Bell] ended up living another couple of days. We filled up that hospital room; there were about twelve to fifteen people."[98]

As Dr. Bell's pastor, Rev. Smith opened and closed the memorial service that honored Bell after his death in late 2011. Distinguished speakers at the Riverside Church event included Professor Charles Ogletree Jr. of Harvard; John Sexton, then president of NYU; and Gloria Steinem.[99] The FPC choir and their soloist Bertilla Baker sang Smith's favorites "Order My Steps" and "No Ways Tired" along with two other pieces. The glorious diversity of the singers and their heartfelt delivery of African American song was noted by several speakers. Smith's musical ministry had taken on a powerful life of its own.

Smith got a big laugh from the audience of hundreds when he began his final blessing, saying he had retired from First Church "not because of age, not because of health but because Derrick Bell stole my choir!" He then led a vivid meditation on letting Dr. Bell go: "Feel him soaring up beyond the clouds! Feel his dynamic presence as he greets the angels of his life. And the God of his life greets him and says: 'Well done! Well done thy good and faithful servant! Inherit the kingdom I have prepared for you.'"[100]

The powerful connections forged between members of the FPC choir have continued even after Smith's retirement. One singer says, "I stayed because they were my family. And the choir—that was a community within the community. . . . Members of the congregation also stepped up and took on important leadership roles. But Paul had set it up that way. He was never the kind of leader who wanted to have the power all for himself. He 'nurtured a lay leadership.' Not everyone would do that."[101]

Smith was comfortable allowing lay leaders to carry the energy of the church into many outreach programs. There is an active group organized by a lay leader that has been visiting and assisting a sister church in Cuba for many years. The current neighborhood food pantry where people can get a free bag of groceries developed out of an earlier ministry called the "Two Penny Lunch." Professor Murumba and his family were among those who cooked food and served it on Saturdays to homeless people housed in the St. George Hotel around the corner.

Smith's instinctive ecumenicalism burgeoned in the cultural crucible of New York City. In 1987, when a parishioner whose foundation wanted to give an award to the Dalai Lama asked if the event could be held at First Church, Smith opened the doors of the church to him.[102] Smith remembers that Henry Street was blocked to traffic, monks lined the sidewalks, and a neighborhood crowd gathered to watch. Over the years, Buddhists, Sufis, rabbis, and leaders of other Christian denominations were invited to the church to speak, hold workshops, or conduct joint events with the First Church community.

Neighborhood interfaith ties have always been a natural part of Smith's all-embracing pastorates. Murumba relates, "Under Paul, we've had lovely dialogues and conversations with a lot of religious institutions in this neighborhood. Congregation Mt. Sinai. Now Brooklyn Heights Synagogue linked with us. Muslims on Atlantic Ave."[103]

In February 2000, FPC's adult education program launched a series of workshops titled "Bridges: Embracing World Spiritual Traditions." A local newspaper noted that First Church's effort "was different from many presentations given locally in recent years in that the approach was meant to be personal rather than academic."[104] Sue Carlson, who helped to create the series, told a reporter that the speakers had to be "devout in his or her own faith tradition." The first speaker, Tariq Quadir, spoke about basic practices and beliefs in Islam, emphasizing the Muslim view that Jews and Christians are "their cousins."[105]

Smith initiated contacts with several neighborhood synagogues including Congregation Mt. Sinai nearby on Cadman Plaza. Rabbi Joseph

Potasnik of that synagogue appeared with Smith on radio and TV religious programming.[106] Their congregations regularly exchanged choirs. Smith eventually instituted an annual Passover seder at FPC. Evidence of the warm relations in the neighborhood came, for example, in 1999 when First Church received a contribution check from a local Jewish couple. They wrote of FPC in an accompanying note: "This multicultural house of worship embodies the best traditions of our Borough."[107]

Interfaith ties became especially important in 2001 after 9/11. Brooklyn Heights is so close to Lower Manhattan that the cloud of dust and smoke from the falling World Trade Center towers blew across the East River and smothered the neighborhood. Amy Neuner had just taken the job as music director when the terrorist attack occurred, and she recalls Smith's response. "He called and said, 'Come to the church.' I said, 'What is our plan? What are we going to do?' He said, 'We don't need a plan—just show up and [the] spirit will guide us.'"[108]

After the collapse of the towers, neighborhood residents gathered on the Promenade, watching the fires burn at Ground Zero and sharing their stories and their shock. Within a day or two, Smith and Potasnik were both there when a group of Muslims assembled for a solidarity march with non-Muslims who wanted to support them. Smith says he noticed that the Muslims needed to communicate even more than the clergy, and he passed his megaphone over to them. Many such moments of generosity helped to soothe the sorrow of the succeeding days.

As the years passed, Rev. Smith and First Church began to use retreats of varying scale to further build and strengthen the congregation. In addition to daylong Session retreats, family weekends were organized around the national celebration of Martin Luther King Jr.'s birthday. Parishioners and their children lived together in a rented house outside the city, organizing their activities and meals communally. It was particularly effective for the children, who "bonded like you wouldn't believe. They had no preconceived notions."[109] Older children took responsibility for the younger ones, freeing parents to engage with each other. One participant said that the weekend was so powerful in uniting the community, she wondered what would have happened if there had been ten more years of such events.[110]

One of the most powerful retreat settings they used was Ghost Ranch in Abiquiú, New Mexico, a property then owned by the Presbyterian Church. The luminous high desert terrain is so spectacular that it inspired artist

Georgia O'Keefe's most celebrated work. Use of Ghost Ranch was by invitation only and rotated among the Presbyterian leadership. Starting in 1991, First Church visited the site for about ten years running. Smith invited friends and parishioners from all his pastorates to commune with each other and the wild landscape of the Southwest.

Artist Sue Carlson participated in three of the Ghost Ranch retreats. She recalls that Paul's outreach knew no bounds.

> There was tremendous energy there. There was a strong Native American presence. The light there is so beautiful. There are some places on the planet like Greece where the light is so beautiful, people naturally start to believe in spiritual things. . . . It had that kind of very unusual light.
>
> So people who were involved in Paul's ministry would meet there—people from St. Louis, Buffalo, Atlanta, Brooklyn. We all got to meet each other. I met Marvin Chandler and Carl Dudley and his wife; at one point Andy Young came. Congregation members from all of those churches came too. It was beautiful. The energy was really great. If you loved Paul, it was all Paul Smith, all the time![111]

Incorporating many smaller workshops over a week or two, the overall retreat was called "Under the Tent." Smith relates that on one of his early trips, he began to think of how to bring groups there to do spiritual work together. He thought of a revival meeting as a model and imagined a tent under which the healing work could be done. The next year, a real circus tent was obtained and set up on site. The rule was that under the tent was a sacred space where anything could be said or asked. With important guests participating, the course started to attract people far beyond First Church. As Smith saw it, "We were trying to learn. You were free to say things then that couldn't get spoken. Under the tent was the sacred space. . . . Other people wanted to be under the tent. Ambassador Young was sitting under the tent! You had to sign up in advance. . . . They had to cut off registration for my course."[112]

Carlson says that the central themes of the retreats were Howard Thurman's writing and inclusivity. But there was more. "It was mostly about the spectacular place and how we were all together. We'd go on walks at night in the desert. He would take people with a flashlight. He had this huge ten-foot rock he called his prayer rock. It had a flat top and he could bring people to sit together on the rock."[113]

Smith started a new journal on the occasion of his first journey to Ghost Ranch. He wrote on his first morning there:

There is something quite extraordinary about waking up to the view of the mountains. I have had a similar feeling when I have awakened to [a] view of the ocean or any body of water. The Creator! Ah! That is who the Creator is. Creation is Creator and Creator is Creation. It can hardly be missed when in the presence of a body of water or majestic mountains. . . . Just walking from my room to Cottonwood was so uplifting. It was as though the mountains and the quietness were waiting for me. I am energized in the moment I step on the path. . . . I respond by saying, "Thank you Lord."[114]

On that trip, Smith writes of reading a biography of Langston Hughes, conducting workshops with Presbyterian colleagues, hearing that Thurgood Marshall had retired, and recounting his road trip with Fran after their wedding in California. The scenery continually moves him, especially a place called Echo Canyon.

Hearing my voice/echo from this canyon is beyond description. Only feelings can be expressed. I spoke out these words to this marvelous canyon. Peace, love, grace, celebrate, joy—wow. . . . When I hear[d] my voice coming back to me I thought I was hearing God speaking to me. . . . Awesome, powerful, moving and deeply spiritual. There is strength and energy all around. As I look up to the top of the rim my eyes fill with tears. The spirit of the Lord is in this place. That's it! You must be an apostle of sensitiveness to understand fully understand this power. Right now I feel I am on holy ground. . . . Lord, let me bask in this beauty and power. Keep me looking upwards.[115]

As in other journals, Smith writes of his love for Frances and his gratitude for what was at that point thirty-one years of marriage. One day he takes Fran with him to Echo Canyon so she can experience it herself.

There was great anticipation in my heart as we slowly walked up the trail to the base of the great canyon. She had not seen Lion Rock on her previous visit so we had an opportunity to see this creation and artistry of the wind. Over two hundred million years have gone by and the wind has created this masterpiece. . . . We kissed and held each other for a few moments in thanksgiving of our time together. She spoke aloud the word "peace" and heard her voice echoing back. Yes, there was something of great value being there with my Fran. As we came down from the canyon we both agreed there was energy spewing forth from this canyon. We are now recipients of that energy. Thank you Lord.[116]

These retreats gave rise to some of the most transcendent moments of Smith's ministry. One year early on, he and Fred Davie won a grant from

Marvin Chandler and Paul Smith playing jazz, Brooklyn, New York, late 1980s.
Courtesy of the Smith Family.

the Ford Foundation to develop their retreat concept. The money allowed
them to rent equipment like a good piano for Marvin Chandler when he
joined them in New Mexico. On many occasions, Revs. Chandler and Smith
shared their collaborative worship service style to great effect.

> Paul and I felt each other's approach pretty well. We didn't try to analyze what
> was going on; we were just open to each other. His approach to religious ex-
> perience is improvisational. And so is mine.
>
> One time at Ghost Ranch, he started a meditation and I started playing be-
> hind him. And it really was a very spiritual experience for everybody there. It
> was an intense moment in my life. An extraordinary moment of spirituality.[117]

Chandler visited First Church several times over the years to perform his
distinctive brand of musical sermons and give guidance to the music program. Revs. Chandler and Smith have an almost uncanny sense of connection that has not waned over the years. When asked what is special about
Smith's day-to-day work as a minister, Chandler says:

> Paul makes love real. At the same time he is not a sap. He's very worldly in his
> perception of what I think of as the dual character of life; the tragi-comedy
> of life....

Paul is a conduit person. He is always the receptacle for something that is moving.[118]

It is only this long-term, very intuitive friend who can suggest something of the toll the work takes on Smith. "My own spirit reaches out to Paul because I feel a kindred acuity about the aspects of life we cannot really explain that are just as real as the material and physical. . . . I know him well enough to know that his heart aches a lot because of what he experiences. He looks for and longs for a sense of comradeship, for fellow seekers."[119]

Chandler concludes: "Paul is one of the most gifted people I've ever met in my long lifetime (and it has been long!). He's intellectually sharp, spiritually sensitive. He has a great gift of empathy for human beings. He has a wonderful sense of humor, laughs easily. And he cries easily. That is a great strength in a man."[120]

CHAPTER 11

Speaking Truth to Power

Becoming the minister of a historic Brooklyn church meant Smith was stepping onto a crowded stage full of outsized personalities. He took on this challenge during a particularly volatile period in New York City's history. Though still little understood at the time, HIV/AIDS began devastating the city's gay community in the 1980s. In a decade already rife with crime, crack cocaine would greatly intensify the city's problems with drug addiction and drug-related violence. And the kinds of racially motivated killings and public controversies Smith had mostly viewed from afar began occurring on his very doorstep.

One famous case that polarized the city in the mid-1980s was that of the "Subway Vigilante," Bernhard Goetz. Goetz shot four African American men he said were trying to rob him on the train. Despite the fact that one of his victims was paralyzed for life and that Goetz's violence was later shown to be premeditated, he received almost no prison time.[1] Two years later, a mob of young white men in Howard Beach, Queens, chased Black men whose car had broken down in their neighborhood. One of the hapless strangers was hit by a car and killed in the process, and another was badly beaten. The resulting community outrage and international press coverage "transformed predominantly white Howard Beach into a metonym for racial hatred."[2]

Another media frenzy arose in 1987 when Black teenager Tawana Brawley accused four white men of raping her and leaving her covered with racial slurs and feces by the side of the road. After months of incendiary press coverage, a grand jury concluded that the fifteen-year-old had invented the story, apparently to explain having run away from home for several days.[3]

Then in 1989, five Black teenagers were convicted of raping and almost killing a woman who was jogging in Central Park. The defendants in the "Central Park Jogger" case received serious prison time, yet then private citizen Donald Trump famously took out an $85,000 ad in the *New York Times*, arguing that the death penalty should be reinstated. It is fortunate that it was not; after years in prison, the boys were exonerated when another man confessed to the crime.[4]

Perhaps most devastating for Brooklyn was the violence in the Crown Heights neighborhood in 1991 after a Jewish man following a motorcade hit two Black children on the sidewalk, killing one and seriously injuring the other. That night, a Jewish visitor to the city, Yankel Rosenbaum, was stabbed to death, and the subsequent three days of rioting shook Brooklyn to its core.[5]

A regular participant in the media controversy surrounding these cases was Brooklynite, Baptist minister, and African American activist Rev. Al Sharpton. Dr. Smith is not close to Sharpton but has worked with him over the years to improve opportunities and secure justice for African Americans. The two were introduced by Andy Cooper, a Brooklyn-based civil rights activist and journalist. In 1984 Cooper founded the *City Sun*, a weekly newspaper that covered African American news. Smith says Cooper insisted on introducing him to Sharpton after he heard that Smith was publicly repudiating Rev. Al's overly zealous role as spokesman in the Tawana Brawley case. Over the years Smith and Sharpton have had different approaches to public controversy—Sharpton taking the spotlight to defend people he thought had been wronged and Smith commenting only when the facts were known.[6]

Smith has also distinguished himself from some of the other well-known ministers in Brooklyn by remaining easily accessible to parishioners and the public. He is not impressed by the adulation won by megachurch ministers. His preference is still to downplay his status and accomplishments unless there is a good reason to assert them. He has never flaunted his contacts or traveled with an entourage. For much of his career, others have spread the word about what Smith is capable of, and he prides himself on never having asked for the power or money that have nonetheless been conferred upon him.

Rev. Smith's approach has been to move toward sources of conflict *before* they boil over. In a way that seems especially farsighted now, Smith worked from early on at First Church to make connections with the local

84th Precinct of the New York City Police Department (NYPD). It started when parishioner Dorothy Gill suggested Smith should be introduced at the precinct. Shortly thereafter, Smith began leading a prayer as the officers when out for their morning watch. He began brainstorming about a regular event honoring the work of police officers in the neighborhood. It turned out that he already knew the man he needed to talk with.

> When I got to the Heights, I knew there were issues between the police and community. I thought maybe I should offer to do some diversity training for the precinct. Get to know them, have a service where we honor them. . . .
>
> It just so happened that the new police commissioner had been the chief in Atlanta—Lee Brown. . . . He said, "What do you want to do?" I said, "Just get to know each other." . . . Within twenty-four hours, a police car pulls up with the precinct [captain] saying, "My commissioner said I should meet you." He was a nice guy. I told him what I wanted to do. . . .
>
> Every February we had a service for the officers and their families. They were all in their uniforms. We gave thanks for the officers and families.[7]

Smith developed a workshop-style diversity training program that was required for newly graduated recruits. Not all of them were happy about it.

> One of the cops in the workshop said, "What the hell?? I'm a good guy. Why should I have to do this training?" I got into a real heated debate with him. . . . He was belligerent. They did not know he was the kind of guy who could be like that. [His colleagues] had not seen that side of him. So it was a perfect example of what we were trying to deal with.
>
> There are some things that are basics. We need to recognize differences. When you are policing a certain area of Brooklyn, there are certain kinds of people there, and you have to have respect for them. Don't just make assumptions. You need to get to know them. And then I say, "How do you feel about what I just said?"[8]

Having good relations with the police department was mutually beneficial. Sometimes it meant that Smith had an opportunity to be a peacemaker in the community.

> One time there was a demonstration near the courthouse in Brooklyn. There were a couple of thousand people. There was a massive police presence. It was getting a bit tense. The precinct captain called me and asked me to come take a look at this. I knew immediately there were too many police officers. I said, "Do you need that many people? You'll get applause if you take a hundred

of these officers and leave." He said, "I can't do that!" I said, "Why?" He said, "Well, I guess I can." And he did it. And the tension went down just like that.

A couple of months later . . . a [police officer] committed suicide. His wife had been at one of our services. She was a staunch Catholic, but she said Rev. Smith is doing the ceremony [for her husband].[9]

Sometimes Smith was able to get special access to help a parishioner.

In another case, one of our Hispanic kids was falsely accused of a crime and put in jail. . . . His mother called me and said, "He's in a holding cell." I said, "It is not this precinct," but she said, "Please come." Because I had a relationship with the 84th, the people at the other precinct let me go back to the cell with Dorothy Gill. The precinct captain knew I was working with the 84th. They wouldn't even let his mother in there to see him, but they let Dorothy Gill and me. If you have that kind of relationship with people, you can do almost anything.[10]

Smith's work with law enforcement received national recognition when he was invited to the White House in the mid-1990s to talk about President Bill Clinton's new crime bill.[11] Smith shared his successes with the 84th Precinct, which were essentially the kind of police reform measures that are being discussed again today. Yet there was no chance that his practical methods of creating ties between local residents and police might have influenced the writing of the bill; just a few months after he returned from Washington, the massive and now infamous Violent Crime Control and Law Enforcement Act of 1994 became law.[12] Responding to the violence and fear caused by the rise of crack cocaine use, the legislation enabled the government to wage a monumental "war on drugs" that has proven ineffective at best and hugely destructive to communities of color at worst."[13] The bill contained a huge array of "tough on crime" measures including the definition of sixty new death penalty offenses, new federal offenses related to gang activity, and a "three-strikes" provision that essentially mandated life imprisonment for many repeat offenders.[14]

The disproportionate effects of this legislation on young Black men and communities of color have since been severely criticized. Former ACLU lawyer and Stanford professor Michelle Alexander argues in her very influential book *The New Jim Crow* that the mass incarceration resulting from these has consigned people to a condition so delimiting it should be recognized as a "racial undercaste."[15] Alexander argues that like slavery and

Jim Crow, this "new system of social control" ensures that several million people who are either incarcerated or have criminal records are "relegated to the margins of mainstream society . . . where discrimination in employment, housing and access to education [is] perfectly legal" and where their right to vote can be permanently denied.[16] Alexander's book has had a huge impact, helping to spur the current criminal justice reform movement.

Over the years, Rev. Smith has carried his special brand of compassion to people who are incarcerated. In Atlanta, he was encouraged by a friend, Rev. Ed Davis, to develop a death row ministry. For over a year, Smith visited condemned men on a weekly basis in the Georgia State Prison in Jackson. Several of the men were executed during his work there. Later, he taught in the New York Theological Seminary program at the Sing Sing Maximum Security Correctional Facility in Ossining, New York.

While he was trained to handle whatever situation might arise in these prisons, he says he never felt physically threatened by the men he met with there. He remembers that they rarely asked him for prayers, but they confessed to him and were grateful for his visits. He even had occasion to visit Black Panthers founder Bobby Seale while Seale was serving a four-year prison sentence in San Francisco. At Sing Sing, he got permission to bring in a boom box, because he wanted the men to hear music. He says they later formed a choir.

Smith's contacts within the NYPD proved vital after the terrorist attack on the World Trade Center on September 11, 2001. Thich Nhat Hanh, the Vietnamese Buddhist monk and peace activist, came to New York City and wanted to go to Ground Zero. The Buddhist knew Andrew Young because Hanh had been in communication with Rev. Dr. Martin Luther King Jr. about the Vietnam War. Hanh contacted Young who suggested that perhaps Smith could help them get access to the site, which was off limits to the public. Smith contacted the 84th Precinct and was provided with a police escort to Ground Zero. A policeman there recognized them and allowed them to enter. "Thich Nhat Hanh wanted to climb 'the pile' and Andy [Young] went with him. Fred [Davie] and I and the other monks stayed behind. . . . The onlookers who were being kept away from the site went quiet when they saw the whole group arrive. Everyone recognized Andy. Andy later said it was one of the most profound things he had ever done."[17]

Despite his professional stature and the network of powerful friends he developed in New York City, Smith has been rudely reminded—more than once—that none of that confers immunity against the racial prejudice that people of color can encounter anywhere, at any moment, in our country. One weekday morning in March 1999, Smith went into a Gristedes grocery store less than a half-block from the manse, dressed down in sweatpants and a baseball cap. He had been diagnosed with Type II diabetes in the 1990s, and he visited the drugstore there regularly to fill his insulin prescription. At that point, he had lived in Brooklyn Heights for almost thirteen years.[18]

Smith paid for the insulin and put it in his pocket. Then, on his way out of the store, a white security guard stopped him and accused him of stealing. He asked what Smith had in his pocket; he replied, "None of your business." The guard said, "I saw you take something from the store." Smith says, "I thought he was kidding. I said, 'I'm Dr. Smith. I live right down there.' He said, 'That doesn't mean anything to me.' So I said, 'What's the issue here?'"[19]

Smith tried to reason with the guard, but the guard prevented him from leaving the store until the manager of the pharmacy was called to determine if he had paid for the insulin. By that time, Smith was furious. He said to the man, "'I sure hope to hell you have a good attorney. You have just profiled the wrong person.' I said, 'I'm going to have to have [a] public [apology]. Otherwise, I will make sure nobody comes into this store.' . . . The next morning the owner's on the phone with me [saying], 'What can we do?' I didn't want them to just settle with me. I wanted them to know how egregious it was."[20]

As news of the insult circulated among First Church parishioners, community members, and other clergy in the neighborhood, outrage quickly gathered steam. In his sermon that Sunday, Smith talked about what had happened, saying if it happened to him, it could probably happen to a lot of them too. After the service, he and about a hundred parishioners walked together to the store. They blocked the entrance in protest, demanding a public apology for Rev. Smith. Their plan was to organize a boycott of the store if they did not get a response. Eventually, the store manager came out and made the apology, saying he had done so privately to Rev. Smith the night of the incident. The vice president in charge of security for Gristedes told the *Daily News*, "It was a misunderstanding. It was embarrassing to the management of Gristedes and to the reverend. [Gristedes] apologized and agreed to work together so that nothing like this will happen again."[21]

The protest and the boycott were called off, and the security company said it would institute sensitivity training for its employees. Yet it was not lost on anyone who knows Smith that the very man who had been publicly called a thief might have been hired the next day to train others on how to avoid such egregious mistakes.

When Smith asked the Session at his church how many people had had an experience like his at the Brooklyn grocery store, every Black person in the racially mixed group raised their hands. Being Black in America means being treated with suspicion in a way that does not affect most white people in daily life. Routinely, the benefit of the doubt is not extended to people of color. Routinely, they are treated with mistrust rather than respect. Routinely, they are guilty until proven innocent. The fact that this is not true for most white people, most of the time, is part of what is called "white privilege."

Smith is still honing his techniques for addressing these issues. He recently said this work involves

> employees getting to know each other.... Creating a safe space where people can talk. Exercises that indicate where and why you have bias—for example, asking everyone to raise their hands if they grew up in an all-white community. It helps people see why they have the views they have, to reveal them.
>
> I am now adding a meditative component—a quiet session so that when we get to tough places we become conscious of what caused us to go there.
>
> I ask them, what is unconscious about bias? ... How does it play a part in companies they select to work with them? Are they using African Americans and other minorities or just going with their "circle of certainty"—people like themselves? This may be unconscious.... You unpack [the biases] and then look at whether they are driving the company. If they are, that's a problem.
>
> You have to have awareness of diversity and inclusion issues in your business DNA. [It has] to be part of the process on a daily basis—making it conscious.[22]

Smith has frequently been asked to sit at the management side of the table, a position that can lead to criticism from employees and onlookers. Yet Smith is known for his integrity. As another Presbyterian minister puts it, "the life he lives ... matches the words he preaches."[23] Smith points out that he always speaks his mind, no matter who may be paying him. He makes clear that corporations have come to *him*, and he has given them the straight talk they asked for. He bristles when asked if he could ever be compromised by this.

> I just spoke truth to power. There was never any thought that I couldn't do what I wanted. I would just say, "Why don't you hire African Americans? Why don't you hire women for these jobs?"

What differentiates me from those other ministers is that I'm a reconciler. A good listener, good negotiator. And it comes out of my faith tradition. I didn't go to business school! It comes from Thurman. Thurman brought diverse people together. . . .

If you are committed to justice, you have to be sitting at the table. Oppressor and oppressed must come together. You can ask, how does scripture inform us about the situation we are in? Excluding a group like gays and lesbians—how do you cure that? You come to the table.

There's a difference between influence and power. Influence is evocative; power is coercive.[24]

Smith tells a story about resolving a labor dispute for a nationally known retailer to illustrate his point.

At First Church, someone gave my name to the head of a union. He came to the manse at about 7:00 at night. I told him to call [his counterpart in management] and ask him to come here and have breakfast. He said, "What makes you think he'll come?" I said, "What makes you think he won't?"

They came to my house [that night]. . . . I put logs on in the fireplace. I said, "You don't know me. I don't know why I am here either except that the spirit moved me to do this." We sat there for over 2 hours and the CEO cancelled his flight out of town. . . . They walked out shaking hands. The [CEO] said, "There is more to say but I want Dr. Paul in the room."[25]

As a consultant and mediator, Smith has carried the civil rights banner proudly into the corporate world. Since the later 1980s, Smith's intervention has been felt directly and indirectly all over the country. He was particularly influential as a diversity consultant for Macy's Inc. Macy's operates hundreds of stores across the country and employs around 130,000 workers.[26] The firm has an especially high profile in New York City. Standing twenty stories high, the flagship store has anchored 34th Street in Manhattan since 1902. Macy's sponsors both the famous Thanksgiving Day parade with its gigantic balloons and the gargantuan New York City fireworks display on the Fourth of July. This is a company that takes its public image and its relationship with the community seriously.

Smith worked most closely with Edward Goldberg, who joined the company in the mid-1970s and retired in 2015 as Macy's senior vice president for external affairs. Goldberg remembers that Smith began consulting for the company in 1987–88, when New York City's "race relations were at an all-time low."[27] Goldberg had been directed by management to see if Rev. Smith could be of help to the company. When Goldberg met Smith at

First Church in Brooklyn, he says they "instantly" had a rapport. Goldberg quickly became convinced that hiring Smith as his adviser made excellent business sense.[28] He said, "It became apparent to me that either you get involved and develop your relationships with communities or at some point in time, you will lose the respect and loyalty of the consumer."[29]

Rev. Smith was put to use in creative ways, depending on the problem being addressed.

> I recall that we had a serious issue in our Delaware store where there had been some customer complaints about store associates in which insensitive remarks or lack of service was mentioned.
>
>   I asked Paul to become involved and in a short time he visited the store posing as a customer, and after several days of careful study he developed a plan to meet with all of our employees in groups over a period of days in order to discuss and teach. Needless to say Paul won over the store associates and the complaints in that arena went way down. For several years after, the employees would always ask for Paul.[30]

With stores all over the country, Goldberg knew that they needed to look at how the company's policies affected communities of all kinds—both urban and suburban. Smith, he felt, had the right connections and experience to help with this situation. "He was very actively engaged in the Brooklyn community, but Paul also has a national and international posture," Goldberg said. "He knows people all over the world. Paul is a member of the Boulé.... I knew from the very beginning that [Paul] had his finger on the pulse of things that were happening community-wise, particularly African American community-wise, throughout the country."[31]

Goldberg and Smith settled into a pattern of speaking every other week or so to discuss policy developments and/or current events. They often met at one of the restaurants in the 34th Street store. Smith introduced Goldberg to key people in his huge network of leaders in the Urban League, the HBCUs, government, and law enforcement. Following Smith's lead, Goldberg developed friendships with the publishers of journals like the *Amsterdam News*, the *Carib News*, the *Christian Times*, and *El Diario/La Prensa*.[32] Goldberg's success in creating these relationships affirmed for Smith that when people sit at the same table, they learn to respect each other. Goldberg regularly attended the annual conferences of Rev. Al Sharpton's National Action Network and Rev. Jesse Jackson's Rainbow Push Coalition. Over the years, Goldberg and his wife socialized frequently with the Smiths. Eventually, they came to know each other's children and grandchildren.

After he discovered that Goldberg had been trained as a cantor in the Jewish faith, Smith began inviting him to participate in services at First Church. "I would go to Paul's church a couple of times a year on a Sunday, and I would give the readings from the Old Testament," Goldberg said. "Since I was trained in liturgy and music, I would sing some of the Old Testament for the congregation. So it was not only our relationship but also the relationship with Paul's congregation. Paul would tease me every once in a while and say, 'You know I'm not going to let you come anymore. They are asking for you more than they are me!'"[33]

The benefits of the relationship flowed both ways. In 1998, Goldberg presented the Brooklyn congregation with a check for $15,000 from Macy's to use as the church board and lay leadership saw fit.[34] After Goldberg became a trustee at Smith's alma mater, Talladega College, Smith says that Macy's funded the refurbishment of the famous *Amistad Murals* on campus and supported their exhibition in eight art galleries around the country between 2012 and 2016.[35]

Rev. Smith's contributions proved especially important when Macy's and other large retailers were accused of racially profiling shoppers. In 2004–5 and then again in 2013–14, Macy's was sued by individuals who felt their rights were violated after they were unjustly detained and accused of shoplifting. On both occasions, the New York State attorney general's office investigated the complaints and secured agreements with Macy's to forestall future episodes. The *New York Times* has reported that Macy's twice paid around $600,000 to settle such lawsuits.[36]

Goldberg asserts that the mistakes were not due to company policies. In fact, all employees, including those in security, agree in writing to abide by all of Macy's policies regarding proper procedures for interacting with the public. Goldberg says the company has a zero-tolerance policy when it comes to breaching these best practice standards. But with more than 100,000 employees across the country, Goldberg says, a few are bound to make mistakes.

In the case of the flagship store in particular, the sheer volume of people moving through the building on a daily basis is enormous. Twenty million people visit the store each year, and business worth hundreds of millions of dollars is transacted there. Over 4,400 people work in the building every day, and the number rises to 6,500 during holiday periods. Goldberg says, "You have to put it into perspective. The 34th Street store is in fact a little city. It occupies more than two million square feet of space. Each year, we deal with an incredible amount of people. Some are truly nefarious people. Some come there looking to steal."[37]

According to a New York State statute known as the "shopkeeper's privilege," people caught shoplifting can be made to pay the cost of the item if it is not in condition to be resold, as well as a penalty of up to five times the cost of the item.[38] These arrangements can be settled at the store without a trial, and afterward the person may be free to go. But the New York City police can also be summoned, especially in the case of a repeat offender or when a person appears dangerous. Under those circumstances, some arrangements must be made for holding the individual until law enforcement arrives.

Goldberg states that, in his day, company policy simply called for a store to have a holding room with a table, chair, and a lockable door. However, in some cases, security personnel appear to have created more intimidating places to hold people suspected of crimes. The *New York Times* revealed in 2005 that "dozens of security officers patrol the Herald Square store . . . where people suspected of shoplifting are fingerprinted and detained, often behind metal bars in a holding cell."[39] The reporter found that in all, "more than twelve thousand people passed through detention rooms in 105 Macy's stores" in 2002, including 1,900 at the flagship store.[40]

Smith found even the rare use of in-house detention chilling. He was asked to investigate conditions at the 34th Street store and to write a report on his findings. He did so and made it clear that the jail-like nature of the space where accused shoplifters were held disturbed him deeply. While he was not in a position to insist that the holding rooms be dismantled, Smith felt his report was taken seriously. He later helped to formulate the "Customers' Bill of Rights" that is posted in all of Macy's stores.[41] Goldberg says it has become a mainstay in the industry.

In one Midwestern Macy's store, Smith trained managers and other staff to deal appropriately with Muslim customers. Despite some resistance, they spent four full days in the reverend's workshops. He also helped the company navigate the local waters when Macy's acquired the iconic Marshall Field's store in Chicago. Marshall Field's had been a fixture in downtown Chicago for over a century and was part of the city's lore. Smith and another Macy's representative were asked to run focus groups to learn how customers were reacting to the rebranding. What they uncovered posed a formidable challenge. Smith remembers:

> There were sixty thousand signatures objecting to Marshall Field's becoming Macy's! They were saying, "We are going to be turning in our credit cards." . . . Four days later, Ed [Goldberg] comes. I said, "You have some pissed off people!" We had to find a way to bring them back.

Edward Goldberg and Paul Smith, Macy's 34th Street, New York, New York, 2018.
Photo by the author.

We [assembled] easily fifty top community leaders at the dinner table at
Macy's flagship store in Chicago. . . . [Ed got up to speak,] saying, "We made
a huge mistake. We didn't take into account the history the community has
with Marshall Field's." Ed said, "Now that I know what I know, we made a
mistake." And that completely defused the anger. . . . Then we had a good meal
and started talking to each other. With sixty thousand signatures! It changed
on a dime. He defused it, because he was honest.[42]

Despite their successes over many years of working together, Smith has
not been called to advise the company since Goldberg's retirement. After
Goldberg's unexpected illness and death in February 2020, the reverend
mourned the loss of yet another dear friend and collaborator.

Smith's blend of straight talk and problem-solving skills have also made him a bridge builder at Honda Motors. In the mid-1990s, African American leaders had made it clear to the growing Japanese firm that they didn't have sufficient numbers of African American auto dealers in their network. Rev. Jesse Jackson threatened the company with a boycott if they did not make some changes. Executives at Honda realized they needed to pay attention to critical diversity issues.

Jeffrey Smith (no relation) was one of the Honda America managers given responsibility for this change. In 1998, he became project manager for a new venture in the South. The firm had identified a location where they wanted to build a new automobile manufacturing plant. The site was in Lincoln, Alabama, seven miles from Talladega College. As they began to develop their plans, someone suggested Paul Smith could help facilitate the process. Jeffrey Smith recalls that he had interviewed many "diversity consultants," without much success: "Everyone I spoke with told me that money was the answer."[43]

Within ten minutes of meeting with Rev. Smith in New York, Jeffrey Smith says he knew he had found the man they needed to build community in Alabama: "Paul did not talk about money being the key to success. He talked about Honda's need to be genuine, intentional, strategic and authentic." Dr. Smith went on to serve as "a tough critic, an inspiring catalyst, and a moral conscience" for the company.[44]

Jeffrey Smith knew that paying attention to culture was going to be essential to the success of the Alabama facility. "We were pioneers. . . . It was [a] $140 million investment, 1,500 associates [employees], 120,000 vehicles. The company was thinking about the business reality of that; some of us were thinking about the *cultural* aspect of that. Going from mostly white Ohio—moving to well below the Mason-Dixon line, to an area that had been the epicenter of the civil rights movement—I felt before we turned a single piece of ground over to build that plant, we had to understand where we were going."[45]

The two Smiths soon traveled to Alabama together. The population in Lincoln in 1990 was approximately three thousand. When the group stopped their car at a small roadside shop to get a cold drink, the reverend mentioned that he never would have gone inside a store like that while he was in college, because he couldn't be sure that he would come out again. The Honda exec found this personal history deeply moving.

Drawing on his extensive network, Rev. Smith set up meetings between Honda executives and the mayor of Birmingham, the NAACP, the Southern Christian Leadership Conference in Anniston, the president and board of Talladega, the head of the Birmingham Civil Rights Museum, and the publisher of the *Birmingham Times*. The goal was for Honda's Japanese employees to learn about the history, politics, and way of life in that part of the country.[46]

Smith knew the whole project could be seriously undermined if Honda did not gain the support of elected state leadership. He had the Honda representatives meet with members of the caucus of Black Alabama legislators. He ensured that Honda representatives contacted the two Black churches in Lincoln. He insisted that local people get the training they needed to compete for jobs at the factory.

Later, when Japanese employees moved to Alabama to get the new plant running, Smith was asked to help them make the transition. His first step was to show them parts of the documentary series *Eyes on the Prize*. Next he called on Marguerite Archie-Hudson, a former classmate, who was then president of Talladega. She met with executives from Honda to explain the history of the college and its success in producing high-achieving graduates. The college was subsequently commissioned to develop a sensitivity training program that became mandatory for every Honda executive who was going to work in Alabama.

Honda's position, Jeffrey Smith says, is that "the population inside the plant should look like the population outside the plant." They knew their operations would be scrutinized to see whether they achieved what they had promised. He relates that "we had leaders in the African American communities like the National Association of Minority Auto Dealers who said, 'We're going to watch you.' And I said, 'We are going to *report* to you how we're doing.' And that's what we did."[47]

Rev. Smith also carried out sensitivity training sessions for Honda in other parts of the country. On his first visit to the company's U.S. headquarters in Marysville, Ohio, it looked to him as if there was not one woman or person of color working in the manufacturing plant. It was not long before the president of the company made it clear that everyone would be participating in Smith's workshops. The reverend says: "You get them to talk first. You acknowledge them, honor them. You say, 'I know you don't want to be here, but we're here, so let's talk. Why don't you want someone like me to come talk with you?' And they heard themselves. They realized, to stay in this job, I will have to embrace some of it. They had to sit in an all-day session with me."[48]

Starting in 1999, Rev. Smith also began to work closely with Marc Burt, an African American executive hired to help develop Honda's diversity policies. Within seven years, Burt says, "we became thought leaders in the industry."[49] In 2007, they formed the Office of Inclusion and Diversity, and Burt became senior manager of the department. A few years later he was promoted to system vice president, and in 2013 his office moved to Marysville.

Most often, Burt says, Smith was a listener and adviser: "He's a confidant that I can bounce things off of, that's pretty obvious and pretty frequent. But he also sits in on all of our strategic meetings relative to diversity. His purpose there is to act as an outside voice, an outside counsel . . . we would rather have those who give counsel be part of what we do."[50]

Smith recalls an occasion when twelve Honda executives had dinner with him and Andrew Young in an effort to educate them about the African American experience in this country. Young invited the guests to his midtown New York office where the memorabilia from his years with Martin Luther King Jr. is on view. Smith says it is always a powerful experience for people to see those materials and hear about them from Young himself.

Burt has learned a great deal about the unconscious level at which bigotry operates. "We have to allow each other to be curious. One of the reasons why we have this really, really bad epidemic of unconscious bias in this country is because if we don't know each other . . . we unconsciously fill in the gaps because we've not really engaged."[51] He suggests instead, "If we don't know, we ask. That's all. People can tell if you are faking. You really have to be genuine."[52] Nonetheless, the work can be difficult: "I tell people all the time that what we are involved in is culture change. And culture change is never fast and it's never easy."[53]

Over the years, Burt and Smith have helped Honda develop distinctive programs that contribute more broadly to the public good. One of these, the Honda Campus All-Star Challenge, celebrates the HBCUs.[54] The contest pits the HBCUs against each other in friendly quiz-show competition for the prize of top school in a given year. Jeffrey Smith says the event has been held "for more than twenty years. Graduates include nuclear physicists, astronauts, brain surgeons. . . . They are young people who are academically plugged in, ambitious, [and] want to strut their stuff for their school."[55]

Another annual event sponsored by Honda for the HBCUs is now being called "HBOB" or the "Honda Battle of the Bands." The event has been held every year since 2003 at the Georgia Dome in Atlanta.[56] It combines pride in the HBCUs with the enormous popularity of marching band and drum line performances. Bands compete during football season and then some are invited to meet in Atlanta in January to perform in the Invitational Showcase. Grants are awarded, and an HBCU recruitment fair is held.

Throughout his years with Honda, Rev. Smith has attended many of these performances. In 2012, something more than his general counsel was suddenly needed. That year, he was asked to visit with the family of a young drum major named Robert Champion who had been fatally beaten by his Florida A&M band mates in a hazing ritual that occurred the previous November.[57] The young man's parents had attended the HBOB event many times to watch their talented son perform. His mother recalls sitting on a couch with her husband in a suite at the Georgia Dome.

> We were introduced to many people, even John Lewis. They all expressed their deepest sympathy and offered to help us if needed. Then we were introduced to Rev. Dr. Paul Smith. We had no knowledge of who he was, but little did we know that was not important to him.
>
> He pulled up a chair and placed it closely in front of us and sat down facing us both. He took my hand and looked deep into my eyes and the tears began to fall. It was as if he could sense my pain and agony through my tears. He did not say a word at first; he just sat there to absorb what we were feeling; what I was feeling. And he began to speak. He told me it was okay to cry and hurt, don't try to hold it back. I wondered how he knew this was what I had been doing since my son's death. He talked in a low soft voice and seemed to have said all the right words we needed to hear.
>
> He provided so much comfort to us and encouragement. No one has ever taken the time to do what he did for us. He took the time to [acknowledge] our pain and agony, while conveying God's inviting words of comfort . . . [what] I will never forget was his unspoken words of compassion while he held my hand and looked deep into my eyes.[58]

Smith's compassion and empathy were also deeply reassuring to one of New York's most famous residents: the African American tennis champion and activist Arthur Ashe. Ashe, of course, had a celebrated athletic career, which included three Grand Slam championships and holding the No. 1 ranking in men's professional tennis.[59] After giving up tennis in 1980 due to heart disease and later contracting AIDS from a blood transfusion after surgery in 1983, Ashe used his fame to help fight apartheid and to raise awareness about HIV/AIDS.

Ashe knew David Dinkins well, and Andrew Young was a close friend who had performed Arthur and wife Jeanne's wedding ceremony. After Smith moved to New York, it was inevitable that he and Ashe would cross paths. They discovered later they also shared a passion for the work of Howard Thurman. Ashe felt Thurman was "the supreme example of the black American's capacity for achieving spiritual growth and maturity despite the incessant blows of racism."[60] Ashe and others helped get Thurman's birthplace in Florida recognized as a National Historic Register site.[61]

Smith and Ashe began to study Howard Thurman's work together around 1990, after Andrew Young asked Smith if he would consider being Ashe's pastor. When Smith asked why Ashe needed a pastor, Young revealed the AIDS diagnosis to him. At that point, almost no one, not even David Dinkins, had heard the devastating news.[62]

Through Young, Ashe expressed a desire to obtain a copy of Thurman's *Jesus and the Disinherited*, which had gone out of print. Smith sent his own autographed copy via Young. Though Smith has many famous friends, the chance to meet the tennis great had special resonance for Smith. The prayer in his journal reveals his thoughts before the meeting. "Tomorrow I will visit with Arthur Ashe. Lord help me to be used by you and to keep my channels open to your spirit. I must remember it is his need that is important; mine can surely wait. . . . More than anything Lord, please work your miracle in his life and in the life of members of his family. Help us find a cure for the disease of AIDS. Hold Arthur in your hands and bless him and heal him Lord, by the power of your holy spirit."[63]

After his encounter with Ashe in a restaurant the next day, Smith wrote again in his journal.

> Met with Arthur Ashe today. It was a sacramental moment. He is a follower of and a believer in Andy Young. They met across a tennis fence in Washington, D.C., when Andy was a Congressman. . . .
>
> We began with our introductions of each other. . . . I also gave him my copy of *The Negro Spirituals Speak of Life and Death* by Howard Thurman. We had a wonderful time sharing stories and exchanging ideas. He mentioned that he had considered going to Calvin Butts' church[64] but felt now that God had

brought us together through Andy—and that as a result we would be seeing more of each other. He is clearly an outstanding and caring person. I especially liked his simplicity and his care for his 2½ yr. old daughter.... Before the time was up he had mentioned something about his adjustment to the "fact" of his illness.... He said it was "just one of those unfortunate circumstances and therefore, I don't think about it."

He spoke of moving back to Manhattan so he could be nearer his doctors at New York Hospital and that he would be taking things one day at a time.... We each began to see something deeper and more significant in our conversation. Roger Staubach came over and we were introduced—but clearly Arthur wanted to get back to our conversation. From that point on we looked one another in the eyes.[65]

Thereafter, the two men talked on the phone or met in person about once a month. At fireside meetings in Smith's wood-paneled study at First Church, Ashe and Smith read and discussed Thurman's writing and listened to audiotapes of the revered minister speaking. Ashe occasionally attended Sunday services at First Church. In his memoir, Ashe wrote warmly: "In the past months, I have spent some happy hours talking with Paul about Thurman and his works."[66] Ashe wrote with gratitude of a hospital visit by Smith and Andrew Young: "Before they left, in a moving moment, Paul, Andy, Jeanne and I held hands in a circle and prayed."[67]

Ashe was forced to go public with his health crisis in 1992 after journalists caught wind of the story. Unfortunately, when Ashe decided to give a press conference and tried to contact Smith to ask him to attend, the message went astray. Smith still feels badly that, as a pastor, he was not there to help as Ashe shared his terrible news under the glare of intense media scrutiny.

Just a few months before his death, Ashe established his Institute of Urban Health with the goal of helping the underserved to get access to community-based health care. It was Smith who helped Ashe connect with the State University of New York (SUNY) Health Science Center in Brooklyn where the institute was housed.[68] Smith was a founding member of the institute's board of directors, which came to include Ed Goldberg among other associates of Smith's. For many years, Smith helped raise funds for the institute, which addressed public health issues he has long held dear.[69]

The last time Smith saw Ashe, the athlete was giving him and Andrew Young a thumbs-up as he was wheeled into a hospital after collapsing near the end of his life. After Ashe's death in 1993, Smith participated in his

Paul Smith and Arthur Ashe, First Presbyterian Church, Brooklyn, New York, ca. 1991. Courtesy of the Smith Family.

Richmond, Virginia, funeral and the memorial service held at the Cathedral of St. John the Divine in New York City.

Smith's interest in community health is just one of the social justice issues that have been central in his life since the 1960s. His commitment to getting decent health care for people of color in urban areas made it natural for him to become involved in his local Brooklyn hospital. Until 2015, Long Island College Hospital (LICH) in Brooklyn Heights was a five-hundred-bed teaching hospital. With his experience teaching medical ethics in Atlanta, Smith was tapped to become a board member at the hospital soon after he settled in the neighborhood. Though he was impressed with the diversity of the medical personnel at LICH, he found himself, once again, the first and only Black trustee on the hospital's board. Dr. Smith has had occasion to step down from all-white boards that never made him feel welcome; however, at LICH, he was instead chosen to chair the Ethics Committee.

Serving that role put him in contact with John Wren, the CEO of Omnicom Group, one of the largest media and communications firms in the world. Smith says Wren initiated conversation with him at board meetings. It seemed Wren wanted to know how it felt being the only Black person in the room. Smith told him, "The races didn't start together. One had a head start."[70]

The two became friends and saw each other frequently at the hospital where the meetings were held. Eventually, Smith took Wren on one of his regular visits to the hospital wards. "One time at the LICH board meeting, I asked him, 'Would you go up to say hello to a young man who has AIDS and is dying?' About 8:00 pm, we went up on a ward to see the kid. Wren was deeply touched that I asked him. I wanted him to see how the hospital was caring for this AIDS patient. I don't think he ever forgot that."[71]

Smith recalls that as they sat by the man's bed, the dying man reached out and hugged Wren. Wren was surprised, but Smith had already demonstrated that there was nothing to fear in touching the very sick man. Wren later asked Smith to visit his own mother when she was at LICH during her final days. Smith did so and says he served as her pastor until she died. Smith's relationship with Wren flourished in the context of their mutual work at LICH. Over many years, dozens of physicians, benefactors, and community leaders like Smith worked to ensure that the 150-year-old institution remained open to serve community needs.

However, the hospital was not profitable and had begun to accrue debt. Its demise began in 2008, when the health-care company that owned and ran the facility proposed selling some of its buildings to pay its debts.[72] Smith and others fought to keep the much-needed emergency room and other medical services open. He rallied local Black churches to help save the facility.

It was the hospital's location near the Brooklyn waterfront that ultimately sealed its fate. Though formerly a stretch of nondescript commercial warehouses, a long-planned public park began to be built below the Promenade in the later 2000s. As development of the park proceeded, the real estate occupied by the hospital became extremely attractive to buyers who wanted to build high-end housing. A years-long battle was waged for control of the hospital and the rights to build on the site.

Eventually, a solution appeared to have been found; the hospital was purchased by the State University of New York (SUNY) Downstate Medical Center in Brooklyn. Smith was one of those behind the scenes who helped garner a $50 million commitment from Governor David Patterson's office to facilitate the merger. Then two years later, just when it seemed that the battle had been won, the SUNY board voted to close the hospital altogether. Labor and neighborhood groups challenged the decision with strident protests and action in court but to no avail.[73]

Lawyer Clayman describes Smith contributions to the effort: "I think he was very much the spiritual leader with a small 's' to get people to do, to move, to talk. He has a will of steel when he wants to."[74] Clayman sees Smith's success as flowing from "the nature of his personality, his intelligence, his ability to compromise, to understand how things go. . . . I think when people were approached by him and got to know him, they saw him as a man of God and that was important. But that was the beginning, not the end."[75]

As a veteran New Yorker, though, Clayman was not surprised when the huge community effort failed: "If you view the history of the city, there's the real estate interests and then there's everything else. That's the business of New York."[76] For Smith and many others who had given years of their time and raised enormous sums of money to buttress the institution, the closing of the hospital was a huge disappointment. However, they could not forestall the inevitable; in 2014, the SUNY Board approved the property's sale to Fortis Property Group for $240 million.[77] In a scenario that has repeatedly played out in New York City in recent years, a small hospital that served middle- and low-income residents in its immediate neighborhood could not stand against the tidal wave of real estate money unleashed by its closure.

CHAPTER 12

Legacy

On January 21, 2006, in a long, gently worded letter to the First Church congregation, Smith wrote the words no one wanted to hear: "The time has come to officially announce my retirement."[1]

Smith had already informed the Session of his plans in September 2005, the month he turned seventy. In the letter, Smith expresses both sadness and joy, saying he was excited to see what God had in store "not only for me but for you."[2] He writes that he and Fran wanted to spend more time with their daughters and grandchildren. He promises to continue his work on behalf of those "who live daily with their backs against the wall." He recalls that "we have brooded over each other; we have prayed together; and yes, we have made some very tough decisions together. We have enjoyed fun filled moments, which I will always carry close to my heart and spirit." In concluding, he delivers, one last time, his characteristic message:

> Let me thank every one of you for allowing me to be me without making it difficult for you to be you. Continue to pray for us as I shall be praying for all of you. And remember, there is in God, sufficient strength, whatever our needs may be.
>
> Your servant in Christ,
> Dr. Paul[3]

As the congregation came to terms with the news, a grand send-off was organized. Speakers at that occasion included local public officials, such as David Dinkins, Marc Morial, and Ed Goldberg. Angela Breland, an officer from the 84th Precinct, read the scripture. The program was laced with music, including Professor Murumba playing guitar and singing "I'll Never

Last Easter Sunrise Service, Brooklyn Promenade, Brooklyn, New York, 2006.
Courtesy of the Smith Family.

Let Go of Your Hand." Smith's sermon, titled "Following Your Yes," sounded a final optimistic note. His parishioners wrote in the program:

> During his time here Dr. Smith, using the guidance of his mentor Dr. Howard Thurman and his experience in the American civil rights movement, has created one [of] this country's most diverse churches. We who are members are enormously proud of this accomplishment and most determined to continue on the road Dr. Smith has shown us. . . . To say that Rev. Dr. Paul Smith will be missed would be to grossly understate. His love and leadership have caused the institution to flower. We hope to live up to the ideals he has shown us.[4]

As the news traveled, Smith's friend and fellow activist Rev. David Dyson of the nearby Lafayette Avenue Presbyterian Church sent a letter of congratulations. Rev. Dyson wrote, "It seems to me the end of an era here in Brooklyn. On behalf of this church, I want to thank you for standing by her in times of true trouble and craziness. This church could easily have gone down but your 'tough love' helped her to stay afloat."[5] Rev. Dyson added a personal note: "I am profoundly grateful to you. You have been a role model for me in so many ways. Your picture, on the day of my installation, sits right over my right shoulder as I sit at my cluttered desk. . . . That picture will stay there as long as I have anything to say about it. . . . So God speed on this next chapter in your amazing life."[6]

One measure of Smith's impact is the extent of the void created by his departure. It took more than ten years for First Church to find a replacement for Smith that they could wholeheartedly agree on. After twenty years of Smith's improvisations, some wanted to reassert the principles and procedures set down in the Presbyterian Book of Order. Others were resistant to reapplying the traditional guidelines too zealously. Three committees conducted searches during that decade. The community experienced significant conflict over the first two individuals who were formally called, and each case took time to resolve. The fact that one interim minister insisted that Rev. Smith not set foot in First Church for a year suggests she felt that some congregants had not really moved on.

Finally, in June 2016, First Presbyterian announced it had called a new pastor—Rev. Adriene Thorne. Having been a dancer in an earlier career, Rev. Thorne delighted the congregation by tap-dancing part of her installation sermon. Tall and elegant, warm and articulate, Rev. Thorne brings effortless style and an unforced reverence to her work. There is no doubt that First Church has found a new and inspiring leader.

After retiring, Rev. Smith was freed of the round-the-clock responsibilities that had structured his life for so many years. He and Fran moved out of the Henry Street manse and settled permanently in Maryland. They have traveled, visited their daughters, and spent time with their four grandchildren: Kathy's daughter Paula; Heather's son Lloyd; and Krista's two children, Stephen and Krista Ann.

Rev. Smith is frequently asked to preach, and he continues to advocate for better health and end-of-life care. In July 2007, he was the opening speaker at Marian Wright Edelman's thirteenth annual Samuel DeWitt Proctor Institute for Child Advocacy Ministry held at the former farm of Alex Haley in Tennessee. His contributions in Brooklyn were recognized the following year when Medgar Evers College made him a Legacy Award Honoree. In 2011, he returned to Talladega College as the invited speaker at the fourteenth annual Founder's Celebration.

Most significantly, as he was preparing to end his twenty years at First Presbyterian Church, Smith's relationship with John Wren of Omnicom turned in a dramatically new direction. Wren wanted to give back to his home borough and had been making contributions to First Church for some years. "John would ask how the church was doing. . . . If we were not okay, he gave me three blank checks with his signature. He said, 'You write in any amount to take care of any deficit and whatever else you want to do.

I want to make a contribution.' He never, ever questioned what the checks came out like. Wren did this at least three times. So there's a history of him trusting me with his money."[7]

Wren's unusual responsiveness became clear on another occasion when Smith was in South Africa visiting a former student and Presbyterian minister, Maake Masango.

> Maake asked me to come see his mother in Pretoria who was very sick. I've been around a lot. I've seen blight, poverty. . . . But I have never been anywhere like this hospital. I think it was the smell. I went to the bedside, prayed with Maake and his mom. I later told Maake I wouldn't send my cat to this hospital.
>
> So I called John in the U.S. . . . I said, "I don't know what you can do, but if you can send something. . . ." Wren said, "We have an office in Jo'burg." Two days later we go by their office, and there was a $25,000 check.[8]

The money helped Masango pay for better health care during the final days of his mother's life.[9]

As Smith approached his retirement, Wren made a remarkable offer: "[Wren] said, 'I want to make a proposition since you are retiring—I want to give you some money to do something in Brooklyn.' I said, 'I will need to talk to my wife—this is not what she has in mind.' John said, 'We'll do it formally.' So the three of us met in Wren's office. He said, 'You will have $5,000,000 at your disposal. I don't want you to have to ask me for money every month.' I was to use the money as I saw fit to help people."[10]

Smith said he was awed by the trust placed in him.

> Here is a corporate CEO, a white male, from Brooklyn, independently wealthy, and this African American minister who have come to know each other so well. He also wrote [a] check to LICH [Long Island College Hospital]. So he wasn't just doing this for me. I was one of his many charities.
>
> [Wren] never in five years asked me for a financial report. I sent it to him anyway, of course. It is extraordinary when you think about it. . . . He didn't have to do any of this.[11]

Founded in 2007, Healthy Families Brooklyn put the Brooklyn benefactor's money to powerful use for training community health-care aides.[12] Rev. Smith hired Dr. Necole Brown, a community health specialist then working at the Arthur Ashe Institute, to be the program director. Brown says, "Our main focus is to get people connected to a primary care physician to prevent disease."[13] The success of the program was detailed in a scholarly paper published in 2010.[14] Brown has shared the success of the model with health-care workers in Philadelphia among other places.

Brown has become one of the highly accomplished women Paul Smith calls his "surrogate daughters." When asked about Smith's influence on her, Brown says he taught her to "find what makes you come alive and go do that. The world needs people who are alive ... around Paul, you feel uplifted. You genuinely feel his love for you because it is real."[15]

Brown met Smith when she began working for the Arthur Ashe Institute in the mid-1990s. Her first project involved meeting with Brooklyn churches to share information about HIV/AIDS.[16] With Smith as her guide, her hope was that she could help Black churches develop ministries around a public health crisis in the Black community.[17]

Despite her strong communication skills and ardent concern for the communities involved, Brown made little progress. She did convince clergy to allow her to meet congregations, but when she arrived on the day of a scheduled workshop, no one came. She eventually discovered that she had to directly address the fact that HIV/AIDS was not just a disease of young homosexuals. Brown also found people within the Black community who were willing to share their experience with HIV/AIDS. One in particular became a powerful witness: a married mother and nurse, daughter of a preacher and a minister herself, who had discovered that her husband was HIV-positive. Here was the case of a woman "doing all the right things and still now HIV is *in* her home—not just knocking at the back door."[18] Brown finally made inroads after finding collaborators like the nurse.

The powerful mentor/mentee relationship that has flowered for nearly twenty years between Necole Brown and Rev. Smith exists with a number of other accomplished women as well. Smith remains in touch with former Attorney General Loretta Lynch. He regularly sees Lisa Mensah, who was undersecretary of agriculture in the Obama administration. Mensah grew up in Oregon with an African immigrant father and a mother from Iowa. Mensah earned her degrees at Harvard and Johns Hopkins universities,[19] and she frequently joins forces with Smith as he continues to preach and publicly support his causes. One might guess that Smith's closeness with these highly accomplished "daughters of Paul" could cause friction with Smith's real daughters. However, Krista says that her father makes these people part of the family, so they all learn to care for them too.

Dr. Smith continues to receive messages of thanks and spiritual uplift from former parishioners, colleagues, and friends. His enormous network is a model of deep diversity. Nonetheless, he is closest to his African American surrogate sons and daughters. One of the "sons" is attorney Jim Johnson, who is still a member at First Church. Johnson says his relationship with Smith became especially important when he was serving in Bill Clinton's administration. As assistant secretary and then undersecretary of the treasury, Johnson oversaw the Bureau of Alcohol, Tobacco and Firearms (ATF), the Secret Service, and the Customs Service. All told, twenty-nine thousand people reported directly or indirectly to him. He managed an operating budget of about $4.5 billion.[20]

At times, Johnson says, the responsibilities were overwhelming—"having the Secret Service report to you means you are responsible for the security of the President." Johnson's purview was extremely wide ranging, and he could never predict what task would fall to him. In 1996, he was asked to investigate the hundreds of Black churches that were being burned by arsonists all over the South. Johnson says, "The ATF was responsible for investigating those fires, and I was responsible for the ATF." President Clinton paired him with Deval Patrick,[21] director of the Civil Rights Division of the Department of Justice, as cochairs of the National Church Arson Task Force (NCATF).[22]

The NCATF's goals were threefold: to locate and prosecute the arsonists, to help rebuild the damaged churches, and to help local authorities prevent future incidents.[23] The task force that Johnson later led with Bill Lann Lee became exemplary for creating collaboration between the ATF and the Department of Justice, among other government agencies.[24] A database of church burnings was created, and a series of annual reports detailed the magnitude of the problem. In its first two-and-a-half years, "429 houses of worship had been destroyed by arson or bombing. African American churches were more than twice as likely to be destroyed as others."[25] While they did not find systematic coordination between the perpetrators of these acts, the NCATF unearthed abundant evidence that racial hostility was a common motivator.[26]

It was during this period that Smith became an essential adviser. Johnson says, "When you are in a senior position, there are few people you can really talk to on a confidential basis." When things got really bad, Smith dispensed tough love. "He would pull me back into perspective, sometimes in ways that were just sort of blunt. He'd say, 'You have an extraordinary privilege. This is hard, but we are not enslaved. There are people who have gone through things, a generation before, that were much harder. And part of this hardness is your own internal conflict; it is not what is happening to you on the outside.' ... He was very, very straight with me."[27]

More recently, Johnson has been working to build deeper relations between law enforcement and the communities. He helped found the New Jersey Institute for Social Justice, a group he says coalesced after Staten Islander Eric Garner was killed by a police officer and a grand jury refused to indict him. People came to Johnson saying they wanted to do something more meaningful than another vigil or protest. He helped to broker an agreement between the NAACP and the New Jersey State Associations of Chiefs of Police to work together to build bridges.

Johnson has learned to create community forums that encourage people "to come into relationship with each other—not just talking *at* each other, but relationship. And then developing a practice of engagement.... Basically the work of diversity is close-in work ... trying to understand racial profiling is about understanding not just bigotry and the conscious decisions that are wrong but also the unconscious biases that we have and why we make split-second decisions that can be horrific. And then how do we train against that?"[28]

In 2015, to honor the fiftieth anniversary of the marches in Selma, Johnson invited Smith to speak at his law firm, Debevoise and Plimpton. With him was Dick Leonard, the white Unitarian minister who had replaced James Reeb in the marches after Reeb died. Leonard and Smith had never met, but together, the two civil rights veterans brought the struggle of the 1960s to life for people too young to have experienced it. Johnson says of his mentor's honesty about his experiences at Selma, "It just points up that nonviolence is very, very hard.... It creates a space. It says we're not perfect. And [Paul's] power is in his imperfection and willingness to own it and challenge himself and everybody else."[29] In the spring of 2017, Johnson ran in the Democratic primary for governor of New Jersey. While he lost the primary to a better-known candidate,[30] Johnson made a strong showing as a newcomer to state politics with a message of economic equality and social justice.

Another one of the "sons of Paul" is investment banker John Utendahl. Now executive vice chairman at Bank of America, Utendahl is best known for having founded the Utendahl Group, one of the largest African American investment banking companies in the United States.

Utendahl first met Smith when he and his wife attended First Church in the early 1990s on the spur of the moment one Easter Sunday. His story of their first encounter is vintage Smith.

We walk in and see a Black preacher, a predominantly white congregation, a diverse population of Black and white. Paul was preaching. He didn't sound like Calvin Butts, but he had a delivery that was very effective and sincere.

[After the service] he walked by and we shake hands. He says, "How ya doing? You play tennis?" I'm six foot seven so I usually get asked about basketball. I was playing tennis a lot, so I said, "Yeah I do." And he said, "You want to play?" I was really into it. I said, "Yeah, sure. But I don't play outside in cold weather." He said, "Let's play in the Heights Casino."

I'd been trying to get in there! I couldn't figure out how. . . . Here I am supposed to be this big Wall Street banker, and I couldn't get in the door. He said, "I'm a member. Do you want to play?" I said, "Yeah," and he said, "Meet me over there at 3:00." That's how it all started.

To my surprise that man beat me that first day! I was expecting an old man game. Every serve was a first serve. He actually hit me with the ball. That set me back. My wife at the time said, "Did you take it easy on him?" And I said, "He beat me! And he hit me with the ball!" Then I went in my room and got quiet for about an hour.[31]

Smith and Utendahl have been speaking on the phone regularly ever since. When asked what the reverend has done for him, Utendahl says unequivocally, "Paul represents somebody who saved my life. I owe him a large part of my success. My perception and the way I look at things have a lot to do with Paul. There isn't a thing I wouldn't do for Paul. He's a hybrid. He can see me as a dear friend, and he can also see me as a surrogate son that he never had. . . . It is a very close relationship, very special. . . . Paul is a rare individual who perhaps has no equal. He's a force of nature."[32]

Smith and Utendahl have served on boards together, and the banker says he too was invited to visit some of the terminally ill patients at Long Island College Hospital.

There was one morning he asked if I would go with him on a normal morning run to LICH. It was six in the morning. He was spending time talking with AIDS patients, early on before we knew very much about AIDS.

I've got to admit I was nervous. I was like, "Let's do this." But I was thinking, am I supposed to fear death? And that answer is no, given my religion. I was thinking, am I going to catch this? I remember going into the room, greeting everybody. Most of them were in bed. Paul went over and hugged a particular guy. I looked at him and that individual. I thought this is truly a special, special man, if he is a man at all. I don't know anyone, even in the movies, a man like this. He gave me so much strength to accept, recognize the flaws in my thinking.[33]

Like Smith, Utendahl has daughters, so child-rearing is another subject of their conversations. Utendahl says that his mentor has helped him develop a daily practice that sustains him. "He has insisted, the way out of good and bad times is to keep my routines, keep my faith strong. I get up at five, five-fifteen, having a sip of espresso, take a nutrient drink, reading the Bible for about an hour, exercising for about an hour. If I do that routine every day, it allows me to deal with any problem, any situation."[34]

More than anything, Smith supports Utendahl's understanding of his Christian faith.

> I don't know how I could get through any day, any moment without God and Christ. Paul has literally been the rudder of that ship for me. He has helped me keep a consistent thought, routine, strength through moments when it's been very challenging. I had to endure divorce, which was very traumatizing for me. I've had moments where I wouldn't say it challenged my religious beliefs, but it did challenge my views on individuals. . . . Paul has said, "You're human. You will have moments when your judgments have been challenged." . . .
>
> Everybody has some talent, skills, and then you have gifts . . . . The gifts are the things that separate you from anybody else. Paul is always telling me to focus on the clues . . . those gifts are God. It is there. You have to access it. You have to start to believe. It is interesting when you find that thing and you can believe, how many doors open up and how hope becomes even visible, very visible.[35]

Since moving to the Washington, D.C., area in retirement, Smith has grown close to Mossi Tull, who is chief operating officer of Jackson and Tull, his family's engineering firm. The clan is impressive; Tull is a descendant of college graduates in the South four generations back on both sides of his family.[36] He and Smith met at a gathering of their Boulé chapter in the fall of 2015. Tull says he likes to talk to his elders, so he struck up a conversation with Smith and soon found Smith had gone to Talladega. Tull was a Morehouse graduate.

Upon learning that Smith was a minister, Tull, who is an avid reader, said, "Can I ask you a personal question?" Smith said yes. Tull then asked, "Do you understand Howard Thurman?" Smith burst out laughing and said he couldn't claim to understand everything Thurman had written but that he and Thurman were friends. Tull has been in close touch with Smith ever since.

When asked about Smith's impact on him, Tull quotes Warren Buffett's business partner Charlie Munger, who said of Buffett that he had "an exponential impact on my life." Smith's "transcendent faith" has touched every one of Tull's endeavors from his professional work to being a husband and a father. He says, "Rev. Paul allows you to dig deeper into things." Asked how Smith compares to other Black ministers, Tull says men like Rev. Mordecai Johnson of Howard University, nineteenth-century AME leader Bishop Turner, or Dr. Benjamin Mays each contributed to their community in their own way. He believes Smith does the same. Tull recalls what Dr. Mays said at the Morehouse funeral oration for Dr. King: "No man is ahead of his time. Every man is within his star. Each man must respond to the call of God in his lifetime and not somebody else's time."[37]

Tull is not a regular churchgoer, and he finds it remarkable that Smith does not proselytize, saying, "I went to Morehouse, so I *know* ministers." He also finds the fact that Smith has worked deep within the power structure of white majority institutions since the mid-1960s surprising and impressive. He admires Smith's complete lack of interest in parading his own accomplishments. Asked whether Smith should be seen as a mystic like Dr. Thurman, Tull says simply, "Of course. Completely."[38]

Smith's legacy is also carried forward by Howie Hodges II, whose parents Smith knew in Buffalo. Hodges is still chauffeuring Smith to conferences and family events. Asked to describe Smith's impact on him, Hodges says:

> I guess the word to use is grace. Just being able to talk to and appreciate that everybody's got value. Everybody's got something to offer.
>
> I'd say before [college], I was slightly less than listening. I thought that I was like BMOC, Big Man on Campus. But then when I got to Morehouse, not only just the school, but the academic regimen, molded you into something bigger. To think of more than just yourself. To be more compassionate.[39]

Hodges, who lives in the District, drove regularly to Charlottesville, Virginia, to care for his mother before she died and still visits his elderly aunt who is Smith's former classmate from Talladega. Smith often rides along. "I get a lot of quiet time with him in the cars driving. . . . I drive and he's in the passenger seat and we talk about life, relationships, how he and Fran met, the things that he hoped to instill in his kids and his grandkids. He talks about things that he fears or I'd say, is concerned about, at this age."[40]

Asked what kinds of things Smith is concerned about, Hodges mentions:

> Just being prepared. Not being a burden on his children. Not being a burden on his wife. Wanting to have the best health as long as possible.

So I'm there listening. I think the thing that probably struck me the most was, on one of these trips when we're going to visit my mom and my aunt, he says, "Howie, I've really admired how you watch and take care of your mom and your aunt. I'm taking notes!" He always says that, "I'm taking notes." I said, "I'm here for you," and he said, "I know."[41]

Hodges recalls with frustration that he was out of town and unable to come when Smith called for help after having a heart attack in the fall of 2014. Smith soon learned he had life-threatening heart disease in addition to the diabetes he has dealt with for years.[42] After several more minor heart attacks, he underwent triple bypass surgery in November 2015, just after his eightieth birthday.

Smith had no warning when he was abruptly told about the surgery. Nonetheless, he says, "I had not one iota of fear. I felt, it is going to be taken care of or not. And if not, I won't know about it! Fran was able to walk with me until the last thirty feet or so into the operating room. I had faith in the medical system, having been around it so much in my life."[43] Smith is a bit rueful when he reveals that immediately afterward, he was more focused on the next dose of morphine than he was on God! But he says he never had any doubts about God's role in helping him meet these health challenges. His view of life, death, medicine, and God at this point is pragmatic: "I have seen that when I go into a hospital room with a very sick person and I pray for them and they don't make it, I have done the same thing, prayed the same way, as when they do make it. It can't be that God chooses [to respond] or not. When my brother was dying, he was at the emaciated stage of AIDS, and I knew God was not going to change that state he was in. So I prayed for God to comfort him, to ease his pain."[44]

Dr. Smith has been diligent in his recovery, consistently keeping up with his physical rehabilitation and exercise. While he admits to moments of frustration over his physical limitations, he asks for help without embarrassment or apology. He has not resisted changing his life to meet his current circumstances. He has given up tennis, for example, saying he'd be really sorry if he fell and broke a hip. Happy to be regaining his strength, Smith is not complaining. Slowing down has allowed him to see that those he has helped are ready to support him in return. This is fortunate, as in the last few years he has faced some of the darkest days of his long life.

CHAPTER 13

Black Lives Matter

Martin Luther King Jr. was born on January 15, 1929. If he had not been assassinated at age thirty-nine, he would now be over ninety years old. Paul Smith, who was born six years later, belongs to King's generation. In a penetrating article about the history of Black leadership, Harvard scholar Nathan Irvin Huggins has noted that Black leaders up until the 1930s were reluctant to wield direct action as a political tool.[1] The NAACP, which was founded as an interracial social justice organization in 1909, has generally worked through the courts, banking on "the fundamental rightness of the American society and the system's ability to reform itself."[2] Perhaps the pinnacle of success for those wielding these methods was the 1954 *Brown v. Board of Education* Supreme Court decision, which "shattered the legal and constitutional rationale which had protected racial caste patterns."[3]

Through hard experience, however, mid-twentieth-century Black leaders like King were forced to discover new methods through which to advance their cause. Guided by the counsel of Howard Thurman, who had been to India and met with Mahatma Gandhi, King and his contemporaries came to believe that "civil disobedience was the proper course for the righteous."[4] King was very clear about why and when he was willing to use direct action to force political change. He asserted that "a just law is a man-made code that squares with the moral law or the law of God." An unjust law is "out of harmony" with that.[5] He followed Gandhi in asserting that "one who breaks an unjust law must do it *openly, lovingly* . . . and with a willingness to accept the penalty." For King, this was "expressing the very highest respect for law."[6]

While iconoclastic and willing to defy injustice, Smith, like King, has never been driven to bring down the system. He is a builder and a healer, not a destroyer. For Smith, equanimity, compassion, and aversion to violence are integral to his being—part of a moral compass guided by the justice of a Higher Power. He admits to moments of anger and cynicism, yet he works hard to pacify such emotions in himself.

Given all this, Smith has been deeply shaken by recent evidence that American racial violence is as pervasive as ever. In 2012, Black teenager Trayvon Martin was killed by a white vigilante who walked free, hiding behind Florida's new "stand-your-ground" statutes. After that, Smith like so many others struggled to make sense of a relentless string of ordinary citizens being publicly killed with impunity by police officers. The list included Eric Garner in Staten Island, Michael Brown in Ferguson, Ezell Ford in Los Angeles, and twelve-year-old Tamir Rice in Cleveland in 2014; and Freddie Gray in Baltimore, Walter Scott in South Carolina, and Sandra Bland in Texas in 2015. In 2016, there was a terrifying crescendo when Alton Sterling died in an encounter with law enforcement on Tuesday, July 5; Philando Castille was shot and killed during a traffic stop in St. Paul on Wednesday, July 6; and then on July 7, five Dallas police officers were killed by a Black shooter raging over the deaths of these young men at the hands of police. Talking about these events on Sunday, July 10, 2016, Smith's eyes filled with tears. He paused and collected himself, then explained:

> I'm surprised at my anger and disappointment. I was never afraid when I was in the civil rights movement. Even when that guy spat in my face. I'm afraid now. That's the difference. It is so toxic. Other friends say the same —"I don't know if someone will go off if they simply see me or hear me." I decided not to drive to Atlanta for the memorial [of Atlanta colleague Joann Nurss]. I don't want to be a Black man in a Mercedes driving down to the South. Someone said he'd come with me, but then we'd be two Black guys in a Mercedes driving to Atlanta! I was never afraid. Open-heart surgery—never afraid. I'm afraid now. And when you're afraid, you're dangerous.[7]

As a Black person, Smith felt he was at risk of being shot and killed for no reason at all. The cellphone videos of these deaths, while riveting public attention on the problem as never before, also made it nightmarishly clear how quickly and easily this could happen. Smith has suffered acutely over these news stories. As a dear friend says, he's "too empathic . . . all that feeling manifests in his body. . . . He internalizes everything he can't fix."[8]

Like so many people in this country, Smith was full of joy and optimism when Barack Obama was elected president in 2008 and 2012. Something that had heretofore seemed impossible to people of color—a Black man sitting at the Resolute Desk—had actually happened. Yet Smith has struggled mightily with the election of Donald Trump in 2016 and the Republican Congress's overt declaration that they would prioritize undoing everything Obama accomplished. As far back as 1989 in New York City, Smith wrote in his journal: "These are difficult days for white men. The world is changing their power base. Once that happens they may be willing to fight to hold onto what they have."[9]

During Obama's eight years in office, Smith says he felt an uptick in openly racist behavior as well as "micro-aggressions," the hurtful everyday interactions between people from different racial groups based on negative stereotypes. In 2013, he wrote of a visit to his daughter's home in suburban New Jersey:

> President Obama's two-time election as POTUS has opened up a huge backlash of resentment and anger by mostly white men. I am a target for this anger and resentment. As I was walking to my car which I had parked at a [commuter train] lot in Summit, N.J., a white man walking a few steps in front of me was also looking for his car. . . . I was dressed with a suit and tie and was carrying my briefcase. It did not matter. The white man turned and asked me if I would move the cars blocking his! I was stunned momentarily until he said, "Aren't you the parking attendant?" 2013, a black man dressed professionally could only be an attendant. . . . [But] I would not describe him as a white racist. He is used to black people in menial jobs. . . . What else could a black man be in Summit, N.J.?[10]

Without a consistent pulpit to speak from, Smith has begun posting on a blog created for him by Sue Carlson, a former First Church elder.[11] The death of seventeen-year-old Trayvon Martin, the young man in a hoodie with Skittles in his pocket, hit especially close to home. On August 1, 2014, Smith posted on his blog: "I am mortified by the events taking place around the world and within our own country. . . . Trayvon Martin who was murdered was the age of my grandsons. His death could easily have been my own grandsons. . . . Most disturbing for me was the comments from Mayor de Blasio and Police Commissioner Bratton who said 'race was not a factor' in the death of Mr. Garner. Who do they think they are kidding?"[12]

After Martin's death, Smith wrote to his grandsons with instructions about how to behave when they interact with police. Lloyd and Stephen, the sons of Smith's daughters Heather and Krista, respectively, were both born in 1998. In the fall of 2016, both left home for college. As devastating as the loss of a child would be to any family, people of color also know that their son, daughter, or grandchild could die at the hands of the very people paid to protect them. Granddad Smith says, "Regardless that they are middle-class kids, they need to be aware of what to do, how to act, when and if they are stopped by cops. First thing, be respectful. 'Yes, sir. No, sir.' You need to be sure to say to them, 'I'm going in my pocket now to get what you asked me for.' . . . Follow their instructions. . . . Do not be argumentative even though you know you are right. Get the day, time, officer's name . . . write it down afterwards. . . . Let [the police] know that your parents are concerned."

Smith himself continues to be subject to unwarranted police surveillance. Several times in recent years, he has been stopped by police in his understated black Mercedes four-door that he loves to drive.

> I got stopped twice on the way to Columbus [Ohio]. . . . A policeman was following me. The first question he asked me was, "Is this your car?" They are not supposed to ask that, but he has the gun! . . . It was 1:30 in the morning and I didn't put my directional on. The cop says, "You can't do that in this town."
>
> The [second] police officer said, "The reason I stopped you is because you were driving too close to the person in front of you." On Interstate 70. In my Mercedes. . . . He's already pissed because I'm driving a Mercedes. This car almost drives itself. . . . It won't *let you* get too close to the car in front of you![13]

On one of these occasions, Smith was asked to open his trunk. One can only hope that it gave the officer pause when all he discovered there were the clerical robes Smith had worn at a funeral earlier that day.

On another recent work-related road trip, Smith handed his reservation printout to the counter clerk at a Hampton Inn, a chain the Smiths regularly patronize. She asked him to verify his address without looking at it. Smith paused and said, "Why are you asking me this?" According to Smith, "[the clerk] said, 'I just want to know who is staying in my hotel.' I could feel the anger coming up. She asked, 'What kind of car are you driving?' I said, How do you know I'm driving? She said, 'If you left your lights on, then I could contact you.'" Smith was furious, but says he knows "you can't do what your anger tells you. I felt like slapping the lady and going up to my room and waiting for the cops to come and get me!" It made matters worse that a white man standing there was treated quite politely. "It was obvious to him what was going on," Smith said. "They never asked him those questions. I gave them the license plate of my car."[14]

Public protest—the expression of long-repressed anger over the utterly mundane yet potentially fatal nature of these racially driven encounters—shifted into a new gear after Trayvon Martin's death. August 9, 2014, was the next milestone in the awakening of the rest of America to these realities. That day, the news broke that unarmed eighteen-year-old Michael Brown had been killed by police officer Darren Wilson in Ferguson, Missouri. The encounter was triggered after Brown and a friend were seen on a video camera stealing a package of cigarillos in a nearby convenience store. The young men left the store and were walking back to an apartment complex in an eastern corner of town when Officer Wilson, who had heard a dispatch describing the robbery suspects, spotted them.[15]

Wilson radioed that he thought he'd seen the men, followed them, and blocked their path with his car. There was an exchange of words, and a physical struggle ensued with Brown outside the car and Wilson still in it. Wilson discharged his gun twice, one bullet grazing Brown's thumb. Brown began to run away, and Wilson got out of the car and followed. After going some distance, Brown turned to face him and, Wilson says, charged toward him. Wilson shot ten more times, hitting Brown in at least six places. Brown died face down in the street, more than 150 feet from Wilson's car.[16] It took hours for his body to be removed. His only crime had been petty theft, and for that he had not even been charged.

As news of Brown's death spread, crowds gathered and vigils of remembrance were organized. Over the next few days, there was looting and vandalism. Businesses were damaged, and a QuikTrip and a gas station were set on fire and destroyed. Daily protest marches led to angry confrontations between local people and the police. Activists began organizing regular demonstrations that went on for months, attracting supporters from all over the country.[17]

The militaristic police response—including helicopters, SWAT teams, and heavily armed police in riot gear—shocked many observers. Smith wrote about it in a blog post two weeks later. "Like many of you I have been watching the events taking place in Ferguson, Missouri and wondering whether common ground can ever be found. I confess that early on the images of armored vehicles, rubber bullets along with tear gas being thrown at the police could easily have been anywhere in the Middle East. It was not the Middle East rather it was an American city where 52 years ago I spent time as a very young pastor."[18]

Of central concern to Rev. Smith was the fact that the multiracial nature of protests in the 1960s seemed to be absent. "What is troubling me is the seeming lack of white ministers and whites in general at the protest marches. I raise the question, where are they? Did the civil rights organizations try to reach out to them? If not why not? Whatever is or is not negotiated going forward will necessarily have to include white people. They must be at the table to make sure they hear the plaints of blacks and vice versa. Dr. King was always open to sitting at the table with the oppressor. Why can't we?"[19]

Smith gave voice to his frustration and wrote yet again of tempering his anger.

> As I prepared to preach at a predominantly white congregation last week in Bethesda, Maryland, I realized I had not gotten over some of my own personal anger and outrage over the shooting deaths of Michael and Eric by the guns of white policemen.[20] I was a real mess until I received two e-mails from close friends and colleagues who ended their message to me with these words: "There is still reason to celebrate." . . . I turned immediately [to] 1 Corinthians 13 Paul's letter to the church in that city. The words of Scripture spoke volumes about how I was approaching my situation in the wrong way. It has been said this particular epistle is the best definition of love ever printed. I allowed Paul's words to touch my head and my heart and it made a difference in my feelings. I knew there was no way for me not to be open and prayerful in my tone. I had to provide an opening for myself before I could find an opening for others.[21]

A few weeks later, Smith was lifted up by a surprise—he received an email from one of those white ministers. Rev. Mike Trautman, his former student at Columbia Seminary in Atlanta, is now senior pastor of First Presbyterian Church of Ferguson. He had found Smith's post online and wrote back asking for advice. He had not been in close touch since Rev. Smith preached his ordination sermon in 1982. After twelve years pastoring at other St. Louis churches, Trautman had been called to Ferguson in 2001.

Trautman wrote to say he was going to demonstrations but was looking for insight and support, having found himself in a town that had gone from ordinary to infamous overnight. Trautman said later, "Especially, when Ferguson began to be torn apart—at that point I felt I had to reach out to Paul. I reread Thurman's *Jesus and the Disinherited*. It was a really important book to reread, to see what kind of opportunities for ministries were happening. I reached out [to Smith] in a deeper way, saying here's what I'm thinking and feeling. And he started connecting me with people from all over. They were people who have been through things like Ferguson. . . . He offered to get me connected with [then Attorney General] Loretta Lynch, another 'daughter' of his."[22] Smith put Trautman in touch with Jim Johnson, who had experience dealing with racial issues in policing. Johnson in turn circulated Mike's name as a possible contact for other locals trying to find solutions to the conflict.

Rev. Smith wrote again about Ferguson late in September 2014. In a blog post titled "The Need for Constancy, Not Consistency," he airs his frustration over the state of America's race relations.

> In listening to the residents and others expressing their thoughts on [Michael Brown's] tragic death which has torn apart its citizens one thing is quite clear: the great racial divide with blacks and whites in America continues. One need only listen to comments from both sides to realize America has a long ways to go. . . . Without constancy in addressing our issues I am afraid it will be difficult to reach any sort of agreement. . . .
>
> Constancy is preferred because the God of my life is constant in loving me, in correcting me, in nudging me, in encouraging me to launch out into the deep. . . . And if you do not believe in God that is your right and privilege and you would be welcomed at my table. I will not cut you off from dialogue and conversation as so often is the case. I believe now is the time for us to recapture the dreams of those on whose shoulders we stand.[23]

Rev. Trautman was grateful for Smith's help and responded using the language of Smith and Thurman: "I hear you about that need to be constantly moving on the path to forgiveness, risking listening to the sound of the genuine that alone can break down the barriers that divide us. I realize that I haven't created the space within me to allow that God sound that comes through the voice of the 'other' to find a resting place with me."[24]

Smith wrote back a few days later with questions intended to guide his former student through the crisis.

> Who is working with the Ferguson Police Department on strategies of working with the protesters? Who has done sensitivity training for the 53 police officers? . . . Is there an identifiable leader or organizer of the protesters? Is there a central place where protesters can gather to rest, discuss, refresh and otherwise get information as to next moves? Would your church be such a place? . . .
>
> As one on the outside looking in the police are making some huge mistakes and that only irritates the protesters. Protesters are also on edge and must have someone they may work with that can intervene on their behalf. Are there off-camera meetings, conversations taking place with officials, protesters and clergy? These are just a few thoughts coming up for me that I pass

on to you. . . . Hope you are holding up and doing well in this entire situation. You and your colleagues remain in my prayers. Paul.[25]

Some of what Smith was asking about was in fact occurring. Leah Gunning Francis, a professor at Smith's own Eden Theological Seminary, has chronicled the ways that local clergy acted to support the protesters.[26] They spoke to officials, prayed for police, visited activists who had been arrested, helped get activists released from jail, and opened their churches to protesters organizing as the weeks went on.

Ferguson is not the urban tinderbox it appeared to be in the incessant television coverage that followed. Presently, Ferguson is now home to a mix of Black and white families living in small, tidy houses. The center of the community is the stretch of South Florissant Road where the city hall and police station are located. There are strip malls, churches, and a historic railroad station. To all appearances, it is an entirely ordinary American town.

Trautman says he has seen "some successful living together of African Americans and Anglos" there: "The sad tragedy of Ferguson is that you never hear about that. In the seventies and eighties lots of people were active to get laws against redlining and to get the integration of the schools. Many whites left, going to places like Chesterfield and St. Charles. But there were people who stayed even as the African American community grew in numbers. They wanted to live in communities that were diverse."[27]

Rev. Trautman's church, First Presbyterian, is just two blocks away from the epicenter of the 2014 protests. His parishioners are mostly white homeowners who had planned to ride out the demographic shift. As the protests over Brown's death settled into a pattern of nightly demonstrations, his congregants were upset and surprised by the way things were unfolding. "Most of them are lifetime residents who have been here through thick and thin, and there is great dismay at how quickly things unraveled. . . . People who once talked easily across the fence are now more guarded. They're fearful of saying the wrong thing, of not being sensitive. But they're trying to come together."[28]

Despite some efforts to address police brutality against people of color, Ferguson was already "known as a place where the police don't mess around."[29] Interviewed shortly after Brown's death, Trautman identified perhaps the most painful part of the episode for people of color: "It was bad enough that Michael Brown was shot and killed, but to have his body lay on the ground four and a half hour[s] was inexcusable. That reminded so many folks of the power of lynch[ing], when the bodies of victims were intentionally left on display."[30]

Asked what could be done to improve race relations in the community, Trautman emphasized that conversations are needed in which hard truths can be acknowledged. "People need to hear of the pain and the hurt and the history of black oppression. And we don't want to hear white folks say, 'Well, it is not my fault.' . . . That's where churches can be helpful. It's a place where, at our best, we are able to bear this kind of hard conversation."[31] Trautman advises having these conversations *before* a crisis unfolds. He suggests that people should "leave your anger at home, and just open your hearts and hear what is going on.[32]

Weeks later, on October 13, 2014, Trautman participated with other clergy in a protest known as "Moral Monday."[33] On that day, several hundred people assembled in the rain to march from Wellspring Church to the police station a few blocks away.[34] The clergy had explicitly decided to support the younger activists, not to lead them. They took up positions opposite the line of police officers in full riot gear stationed outside the police station. Many said afterward that it was in that moment of confrontation that they felt the presence of God and the rightness of their participation.[35]

Despite such well-meaning interventions, when word came in November that Officer Wilson would not be indicted—as has been true of most police who kill in the line of duty—violence erupted for the first time upon businesses on South Florissant Road. Trautman says that white residents who had been sympathetic to the protesters became angry that the central part of town was being damaged. An "I Love Ferguson" countercampaign flared up. Whites and Blacks were becoming more and more polarized.

In March 2015, a brutally frank Department of Justice (DOJ) report was released, excoriating both the police department and the court system in Ferguson.[36] It took a full year for the DOJ and the Town Council to agree on how to implement the recommendations in the report. One step toward the "entire reorientation of law enforcement in Ferguson"[37] was the hiring of a new police chief. In May 2016, Major Delrish Moss, an experienced Black officer from a small city in Florida, took up his new post. He was succeeded after two-and-a-half years by an African American police captain from Atlanta.[38]

Shortly after Brown's death, the deeper causes of this urban unrest began to be explored.[39] There is a decades-long history of federal, state, and local policies that converged to create the volatile encounter between Michael Brown and Darren Wilson. These same processes have contributed to urban poverty and unrest all over America.[40]

Ferguson started out early in the century as one of many unincorporated residential neighborhoods in St. Louis County. In the 1930s, white residents incorporated the village of Berkeley so that they could keep their schools separate from those of Kinloch, the adjacent Black community. After the separation of the tax bases, Kinloch and its schools deteriorated. In 1975, federal courts mandated that the towns integrate their school systems.[41]

Trautman relates that around that time, a coalition of local clergy had formed who were disturbed by the effective segregation of Kinloch from the white neighborhoods. Until the 1970s, he reveals, there was a fence marking the border between Kinloch and Ferguson, and the only road linking the two was gated and locked at night. The ministers believed that allowing that arrangement to continue wasn't who they were "called to be as people of faith."[42] The group went to court and got permission to have the fence removed, but the work never got done. Finally, the mayor of Kinloch and the clergymen got together one night and tore the fence down themselves.[43]

Historian Richard Rothstein's exhaustive study demonstrates that "St. Louis was segregated by interlocking and racially explicit public policies of zoning, public housing and suburban finance, and by publicly endorsed segregation policies of realty, banking and insurance industries."[44] Many of these intertwined regulations and practices have been abolished, but their effects continue to play out.

After huge downtown St. Louis developments like Pruitt-Igoe were demolished in the 1970s, inner-city residents looked to places like Ferguson for a better quality of life. Privately developed low-income apartment complexes, such as Canfield Green where Brown lived, were an attractive place to start. Yet all the low-income housing was clustered on the eastern edge of town, and over the years, those developments became overcrowded. The result was the formation of "one of the highest concentrated areas of low-income housing in the state of Missouri."[45]

Crime in the poor, densely populated neighborhood brought heightened police surveillance and that contributed to residents' feelings of being targeted and denigrated.[46] The fact that around the time of Brown's death, "police [had] blocked off nearly all access roads to the apartments with concrete barriers, fences and gates,"[47] is chillingly similar to the approach used to control Kinloch decades ago.

There is a complex patchwork of police jurisdictions around Ferguson that contributes to residents' sense of being continually stopped, harassed, and subjected to police surveillance. As Rev. Trautman points out, "[There are] one hundred and sixteen different taxing districts in the County of St. Louis . . . most of the little communities at one time had their own police force and then they would share . . . fire departments, things like that. [So] you've got all these little municipalities with their own self-interests and their own little fiefdoms and many of them were reliant on the revenues [generated by law enforcement]."[48] While progress is being made in Ferguson, there is still a long way to go toward a more humane kind of community policing.[49]

Recent scholarship addresses the effects such conditions have on young men of color in particular.[50] Marc Lamont Hill argues incisively that to fully understand the plight of Michael Brown and others like him, one has to recognize that they are being treated as a "disposable class." He writes: "[Brown's] physical presence on Canfield Drive was due not only to his personal experiences and choices but also a deeply rooted set of policy decisions, institutional arrangements, and power dynamics that made Ferguson, and Canfield, spaces of civic vulnerability."[51] Isabel Wilkerson pushes the analysis much further in her new book *Caste*. In a detailed argument, she makes the case that America has a caste structure like that of India, which strands ordinary Black people at the bottom of the hierarchy—permanently. While we are taught to believe that everyone has a chance to succeed in our society, her analysis powerfully illuminates the multifaceted, entrenched, and bigoted worldview that undergirds American social structures and institutions.[52]

It was during the months-long protests in Ferguson that the hashtag #BlackLivesMatter began to circulate in earnest on social media platforms like Twitter and Instagram. The moniker stuck and became the rallying point around which a broader and more organized civil resistance movement took shape. Instrumental in this process were three leading lights—Alicia Garza, Patrisse Cullors, and Opal Tometi.[53] All had been active in protest movements before they joined forces in earnest after Ferguson. Yet these young women of color have broken the mold used by previous civil rights leaders. Garza has been quoted as saying, "The model of the black preacher leading people to the promised land isn't working right now."[54] They do not subordinate themselves to male leadership; they have strong ties to the LGBTQ community; and their movement is self-consciously democratic, not hierarchal. They do not claim the right to speak for the movement as a whole, and they have only loosely guided the local chapters of Black Lives Matter that have arisen all over the country.

This radical decentralization has been facilitated by cellphone technology and the use of social media. Yet today's activism is still susceptible to some of the same difficulties that have beset protest movements throughout history. Organizers cannot control the behavior of everyone at events they endorse, and Black Lives Matter has been vilified in the conservative press for appearing to endorse or encourage violence against police and destruction of property. Reading Cullors's personal story makes clear how deeply her commitment to nonviolent resistance goes.[55] But she has been clear about the scope and purpose of Black Lives Matter: "We're talking about more than police brutality. We're talking about incarceration, health care, housing, education and economics—all the different components of a broader system that has created the reality we see today. . . . Black lives should matter in all stages of life—and to honor that truth, we must radically transform the system from its roots."[56]

In the spring of 2015, another young man's death caused another anguished uproar, this time in Baltimore, Maryland, closer to Dr. Smith's home. Freddie Gray was pulled out of a police van with a spine so badly mangled he later died. There were injuries, arrests, and buildings set aflame before a state of emergency was declared and the city quieted a few weeks later.

Shortly thereafter, Smith's mediation skills were called into play. Rev. Christa Burns of the city's Faith Presbyterian Church went on sabbatical, and Dr. Smith was asked to fill in during her three-month leave. He said later, "Baltimore was a powder keg at that time. I met with probably fifteen ministers at Christa Burns's request. And we just talked. Kind of like what we did with the 84th Precinct in Brooklyn. Why couldn't they do something like that? . . . It's a model."[57]

Smith made himself available to anyone who needed his advice. "Jim Johnson . . . told the chaplain, community relations officer, and a third person that they needed to talk to me when they came to Baltimore. They came and they were really learning and listening. They were people, police officers [from] communities outside of Baltimore. So they came to see what they needed to learn." Still, no one was surprised that all the charges against law enforcement personnel involved in the death of Freddie Gray were eventually dropped.[58]

In June 2015, Smith had an occasion to celebrate. He wrote proudly in a blog post about the success of one of his surrogate daughters. "A couple of weeks ago I was invited to the swearing in ceremony of Loretta Lynch, our new Attorney General and a dear friend. There was hardly a seat in the Warner Theatre in Washington, D.C., where the ceremony took place. President Obama was at his very best in praising Loretta whom he has known for a long time. I had not seen the president so happy and it showed on his face and in his interaction with the crowd who had come to witness the ceremony."[59]

The post then had to jarringly reverse course to address a particularly horrifying episode of racist violence against upstanding Black citizens. On June 17, 2015 nine Christian worshippers were murdered by a white supremacist during Bible study in their Charleston church.

> Little did any of us know how soon the President's smiling face would quickly turn to one of grief and frustration upon hearing of the massacre in Mother Emanuel AME Church in Charleston, South Carolina. The President's cup like my own had "runneth over." What does one do when one's cup overflows with unbearable agony and grief upon hearing the news of the tragedy? That the tragedy occurred inside of a house of worship during bible study is unimaginable and too hard to understand. So, what do you and I do?[60]

Rev. Smith wrote that first, he had to recognize that the event had actually taken place to begin to deal with his pain. Second, he had to "acknowledge my anger was real, so real that I was ashamed of myself longer than I am willing to admit. My anger is the same kind of anger all of us have and when it gets out of control we become as dangerous as Dylann Roof."[61] Third, he found he had "learned about the real essence of forgiveness and faith coming from [those in Charleston] who had lost the most.... My flow began to stop when I heard the testimonies and I saw how the God of my life and theirs is the only answer to the experience of the tragic fact. Scripture tells us: weeping may endure for the night but in the morning cometh joy. And morning did come."[62]

In mid-2016, Smith spoke of finding his public voice in these difficult times.

> I think my role is emerging. Calvin Butts spoke at our convention of the Boulé. ... They asked me if I would do the scripture and the prayer at the end. For a lot

of these guys, if they are not the main speaker, they don't want to do scripture and do the prayer. . . . So they came to me. The good news was that they could come to me. Calvin spoke and [people] were literally up cheering at points. He was fantastic and erudite. . . . It was like when you make a basket in the last two seconds of the game? "The crowd goes wild!" I had to follow that.[63]

But rather than try and compete with the nationally renowned speaker, Smith says he followed his instincts.

Here's 2000 people been brought to the mountaintop. So I get up. You could feel that energy. [It was] all on the jumbotrons. I just closed my eyes and said nothing for 10 seconds. Then I began with Aretha's "When your soul is in the lost and found, who comes along to claim it?" I said, "My soul is in the lost and found. The question is: who will we allow to come along and claim it? Do we even know who we will let save it?" I'm just moving by the spirit. I hear Calvin say, "Yeah, yeah!" I ended by saying, "I want the God of your life and mine to come along and claim you."[64]

Smith is developing new ways to address the fear and anger simmering in the wake of these events. Early in 2016, he was contacted by John Wygal, a congregant from First Congregational Church (FCC) in Darien, Connecticut. Wygal and his minister, Dale Rosenberger, had been talking about how to create a context for discussing race issues at their all-white church. At first, Smith says, he felt tired. He did not want to take up the challenge. "I said, 'I don't want to help white people to do what they know they need to do!' Wygal tried again. He said, 'At least talk to my pastor.' So I went up to Darien and met [Rev. Dale Rosenberger]. I had a beautiful time. In July I finally met John Wygal in the flesh. He said, 'You're everything that my pastor said you were.' We sat and planned the whole service."[65]

The event was shaped by the fact that FCC's sanctuary needed repairs and could not be used. Instead, Smith told him about the "Under the Tent" events at Ghost Ranch. Rosenberger was enthusiastic, predicting Smith would have more people in the tent than were normally in the sanctuary. Smith invited his friend, composer/musicologist Nolan Williams Jr., to participate in the service. For years, Rev. Williams has created joyous musical performances on Martin Luther King Jr. Day at Washington's Kennedy Center. Williams suggested teaching some new music to FCC's choir would be a powerful way to get the existing congregation involved. He volunteered to drive up to Darien the Friday before the event to work with the choir. That Sunday, he brought musicians to support the performance. As had become his custom, Dr. Smith invited the author to attend.

On Sunday, September 18, 2016, Smith and friends convened for "Under the Sacred Canopy: A Racial Reconciliation Sunday," a special service at First Congregational Church. About 160 people joined Rev. Rosenberger and his associate ministers for an outdoor service built around music, a sermon by Rev. Smith, a conversation facilitated by diversity expert Dr. Steven Jones, and a panel discussion that included a "daughter of Paul," Lisa Mensah.[66]

Many of the attendees had shared a meal at John Wygal's home the night before the event. Smith related to the author that

> it reminded me of 30 years ago. We talked, celebrated, disagreed. A couple of Trump supporters felt they could speak their mind because I was there.
>
> What happened in that potluck dinner was so enriching. I want to be healthy enough to do more of that. Somebody said, "If you go with me, I'll try anything." It was like he was saying, "If you were working with us, I could change." It was almost confessional. He had been waiting for the opportune time to say that.[67]

The Sunday service opened with Williams leading the First Congregational choir singing "See Something, Say Something," an arrangement of the music he had used on a much larger scale in Washington. The upbeat refrain conveys the heart of his message: "Bad things happen when good people do nothing, say nothing, just turn and walk away. Do something, say something, I say, hey."[68]

In the sermon, Rev. Smith used Dr. Thurman's metaphor of the deep-sea diver to ask people to make contact with their own emotional and spiritual depths. He guided the congregation through a meditation, leading them inward toward what Thurman called "the luminous darkness." That is the realm, Smith said, "where there is neither male, nor female, where you don't have to pretend. God asks us to be still—this is the level where God is. This is the level where it is all right to be me without making it hard for you to be you."[69]

It was the lyrics "Hands up, don't shoot" in Rev. Williams's song that brought deeper matters into the discussion afterward. Michael Brown was rumored to have uttered these words just before he was killed, and they subsequently became a chant used by protesters. One person at FCC said he didn't like hearing those words; another said he had no problem with them; a third said she thought it brought the media into the discussion in an unwelcome way. Several others expressed their concern for both innocent people getting shot and cops getting hurt in the line of duty. One of the performers noted that the term "reconciliation" has to be defined. She said that if someone's idea of reconciliation does not include taking account of harm done, it is not a useful concept for creating real change.[70]

As Rev. Smith commented on the discussion: "I pastor people. That's really what I do. Under the tent, we pastor. I embraced so many people; it was an opening for them. Someone said, 'If you keep looking so deeply into me, I will want to cry.'"[71] Rev. Rosenberger told Smith afterward that he had never seen his congregation speaking the way they had that day. Thus, Smith and his colleagues are developing a new and powerful kind of activism that has promise for the future. Smith says, "We want to . . . create a paradigm that can be used, replicated . . . [to address] the fears that keep you from talking—maybe, just maybe, a song that we sing together will loosen up your tongue, open up your heart, touch your spirit."[72]

Despite all the apparent progress that had been made, however, the last word in Darien was a question asked in the parking lot by a middle-aged white man of me, the author, a middle-aged white woman. He said in a confidential tone, "But don't you *really* think that big Black men are scary?" I asked *him* a question: "Do you really think that people like Paul's grandsons could be scary?" I then told him how in my university teaching I had had occasion to teach all kinds of people and learned over and over how deceiving appearances can be. Then I answered: "No, if Black men ever seemed scary to me, I learned better. It is white people who need to learn to *see* Black people differently." He turned away, unable to respond.[73]

As this book goes to press, it is November 2020 and President Donald Trump is contesting the legitimacy of Joe Biden's lawful election to the presidency. Dr. Smith has had to work hard over these past four years to manage his anger over Trump's unwillingness to denounce white supremacist violence and overt bigotry among some of his devoted followers. 2020 has brought not only the frightening coronavirus pandemic but also more people of color dying after encounters with law enforcement. The catalyst for a nationwide surge of protests was the horrible public death of George Floyd in Minneapolis on May 25. Cellphone videos viewed by millions show a dying Floyd repeating over and over, "I can't breathe," while being pinned to the ground with a police officer's knee on his neck.[74] His death followed closely upon that of Georgian Ahmaud Arbery, who was shot and killed in February after jogging past the homes of armed neighborhood vigilantes,[75] and Breonna Taylor in March, who was killed in her bed as a result of a misdirected police raid on her Louisville apartment.[76] All this has left Smith "in a place I've never been before. It must be age-related too, but I am disappointed in America. I'm angered and befuddled."[77] Despite all the evidence that change is desperately needed, the deep personal and communal work that will create social and cultural change has only just begun.

In a heartfelt book, *Tears We Cannot Stop*, Rev. Dr. Michael Eric Dyson, a minister and sociologist, directly and carefully addresses the heart of the problem—the mutually reinforcing system of beliefs, behaviors, and institutions that have come to be called "white privilege." This worldview poses an enormous obstacle to addressing our society's egregious wrongs, past and present. Dyson describes the devastating fear and sadness he faces discussing with his children the fact that there are fellow Americans who may subject them to indignities, violence, and even death for simply being who they are.[78] In a book that is part-prayer, part-entreaty, Dyson asks white Americans, whom he addresses as "beloved," to think deeply about how whiteness and Blackness are ideas with consequences, not concrete realities: "Beloved, let me start by telling you an ugly secret; there is no such thing as white people. . . . Please hear me out . . . I'm talking about the politics of whiteness. . . . You don't get whiteness from your genes. It is a social inheritance that is passed on to you as a member of a particular group. And it's killing us, and, quiet as it's kept, it's killing you too."[79]

Dyson goes on to describe the devastating power held by white Americans as a group: "Beloved, to be white is to know that you have at your own hand, or by extension, through institutionalized means, the power to take black life with impunity. It's the power of life and death that gives whiteness its force, its imperative. White life is worth more than black life."[80] Dyson pleads for an opening of consciousness on the part of white Americans about this reality. "The most radical action a white person can take is to acknowledge this denied privilege, to say, 'Yes, you are right.'"[81] He points the way forward in his Benediction: "Empathy must be cultivated. . . . Imagine how you would act if you were us. Imagine living in a society where your white skin marks you for disgust, hate and fear. Imagine that for many moments. Only when you see black folks as we are and imagine yourselves as we have to live our lives, only then will the suffering stop, the hurt cease, the pain go away."[82]

Toward the end of his life, James Cone's relentless truth-telling about race relations in our country found its most eloquent and devastating expression in *The Cross and the Lynching Tree*. Only Cone would have had the courage to write this book that places "the cross . . . alongside the lynching

tree [to] help us to see Jesus in America in a new light, and thereby empower people who claim to follow him to take a stand against white supremacy and every kind of injustice."[83] Despite the enormity and gravity
of his mission in this book, he concludes with a surprisingly hopeful, if
challenging, message:

> Blacks and whites are bound together in Christ by their brutal and beautiful
> encounter in this land. Neither blacks nor whites can be understood fully
> without reference to the other because of their common religious heritage
> as well as their joint relationship to the lynching experience. What happened
> to blacks also happened to whites. When whites lynched blacks, they were
> literally and symbolically lynching themselves—their sons, daughters, cous-
> ins, mothers and fathers, and a host of other relatives. Whites may be bad
> brothers and sisters, murderers of their own black kin, but they are still our
> sisters and brothers. We are bound together in America by faith and trag-
> edy. All the hatred we have expressed toward one another cannot destroy the
> profound mutual love and solidarity that flow deeply between us.... No gulf
> between blacks and whites is too great to overcome, for our beauty is more
> enduring than our brutality. What God joined together, no one can tear apart.
> ... If America has the courage to confront the great sin and ongoing legacy
> of white supremacy with repentance and reparation there is hope "beyond
> tragedy."[84]

In his final book, an autobiography, Cone called America "a 'Beloved
Community' in the making, a human family, with all kinds of people in it—
different races and sexual orientations, different sizes and shapes, both able
and differently able, and a whole lot of other things."[85] Through his writing
and that of others who have honestly addressed the poisonous history of
race in America, we can see that a beloved community is not a heaven-like
dream. It must be a union that is based on the truth of human equality,
alive to the common human condition of suffering, ever alert to the ways
we cause, and have caused, suffering in others, and committed to putting
concern for the common good ahead of our own desires for ever more
power, safety, and comfort. That is the kind of beloved community that Rev.
Dr. Paul Smith has helped to construct—a sometimes unruly but evolving
coalition that is constructed mindfully, humbly, and joyfully by willing participants, day by day, here on earth.

CHAPTER 14

Sacramental Moments

While Dr. Smith freely shares the wisdom of his African American culture, his spiritual generosity is even deeper and more personal. Ever since the elderly German parishioner in Buffalo reached out to him for succor in his final days of life, Dr. Smith has known that he has a gift for supporting people coming to terms with death. It is one of the most delicate responsibilities of any religious leader. Americans' religious heterogeneity and cultural aversion to discussing or having contact with the dead pose special challenges to clergy. Smith's pragmatism and emotional honesty help him overcome such obstacles.

As a leader of intentionally diverse congregations, Smith knows well that the absurdities of our belief in the reality of "race" are especially clear in our postmortem practices. He exclaims:

> You know racism goes even for burial! Blacks are buried in Black cemeteries and whites in white cemeteries.[1]
>
> Strange that white undertakers and Black undertakers bury their own. . . . I have never witnessed a Black person being prepared at a white funeral home. It is rare indeed for a white person to be funeralized by a Black undertaker. Unconsciously we go about our business as two separate societies. . . . There is something very wrong about this, yet it happens more than we care to acknowledge.[2]

The same has been true of graveyards: "Until the 1950s, about 90 percent of all public cemeteries in the U.S. employed a variety of racial restrictions."[3] As recently as ten years ago, white and Black caretakers tended separate sections of one public cemetery in Waco, Texas. Though some town leaders considered a change long overdue, it was only in 2016 that a chain-link fence dividing the two areas was finally removed.

Over the years, Smith has taken opportunities to confound expectations on this score. In Atlanta in 1983, he broke with tradition when he stepped up to lead the funeral of a white parishioner. He wrote about it in his journal at the time.

> At Turner's Mortuary on N. Decatur Rd. a few weeks ago the test was given. I was the only black person there and of course it was never assumed that I could actually be the minister—just a friend of the family. Mr. Turner's face said it all when I watched him enter the chapel where the family had gathered. George [McMaster], the other pastor[,] was equally observant and was sensitive to the situation. I asked the service to begin by making an announcement and then asking George to pray. The ice was broken, however the stares were there; amazement resided with most of the family friends. The family has long since dealt with the issue and have been supportive and open from the first day of my pastorate at Hillside.[4]

Even in the final years of the twentieth century, a Black pastor serving white congregants in their final days was not acceptable to everyone. At First Church in Brooklyn, a strong-willed white southern parishioner accompanied Rev. Smith to a local funeral home to ensure that he could fulfill his pastoral duties for a white parishioner who had died. Smith remembers, "Even in Brooklyn Heights, I had to win people over."[5]

There is some evidence that attitudes are slowly changing. Local heritage groups are beginning to attend to forgotten burial grounds.[6] The mortuary business is beginning to see some overlap between how whites and Blacks use funeral homes.[7] Yet without a conscious effort to change things, it appears likely that the segregation of the dead in America will continue.

Rev. Smith understands the absurdity of this better than most. In his book *The Deep Calling to the Deep: Facing Death*, published in 1998, Smith shares from his decades of pastoral experience with both Black and white people. In the introduction, he reveals that helping people face death is an aspect of ministry that "for me has been exceptionally rewarding and has shed a light on all the other parts of my work."[8] He believes there is much to learn from the terminally ill that "can make our living richer and their dying more peaceful."[9]

Over the years, Smith has come to see that there is something extraordinary about the final days and hours of people's lives. He writes, "There is a clarity of thought and a stark honesty that tends to take over when a person is dying—as if, as the person loses strength and energy he saves all his resources for that which is essential. This is the deep speaking to the deep. Put another way, it can be defined as 'soul-talking.' When we speak from the deep in our souls, there is no need for pretense or denial. The soul is laid bare before our Creator and before ourselves."[10]

In his book, Smith discusses six cases from his long years of pastoring. Of Dr. John Edson, a physician and colleague of Smith's from Long Island College Hospital, he writes:

> Once at lunchtime, I asked the nurse if I could feed John. I still don't quite know why I made this request, except that at the time it seemed the natural thing to do. There was something very special and deeply moving about the experience. I still remember the quietness in the room as I got into the rhythm of lifting the spoon to his mouth just as he opened it. This became a sacramental moment for me, symbolizing the Lord's Supper or the Holy Communion of the Christian tradition.[11]

Smith finds Howard Thurman's concept of becoming "centered" profoundly useful for both the dying person and those attending to them. Smith writes, "By 'centering,' I mean opening myself up to hear what God is saying to me and thereby enabling me to hear what John was saying to me too. Each time I took John's [Edson's] hand, he and I immediately entered spiritual ground.... His experience of the agony seem[ed] to become more bearable as he and I centered. In centering, we opened ourselves to each other. There were no pretenses. We [laid] ourselves bare before each other and before God."[12]

In pastoring Jean Young, the first wife of Andrew Young, Smith suggested her family keep a notebook handy in the hospital so they could write down her thoughts and instructions. They learned to "adjust to the timeframe" of a person near the end—to slow down and listen when she spoke from the depths of her being. He finds that "people who are dying speak slowly and purposefully in a particular and characteristic cadence and rhythm. Listening to them requires great focus and attention—the things they have to say tend to be profound, yet they are often somewhat concealed by the symbolism and poetic brevity with which they are expressed."[13] One of Smith's Boulé brothers wrote of *Facing Death*, "I am less fearful of death today thanks to Paul's writing. I now know what I had hoped for all my life was possible, that I might be able to face death without fear, with dignity, knowing that closure is just a continuum of life itself."[14]

Over the years, Dr. Smith's pastoring has become even more quiet, precise, and practical. He advises everyone to think ahead and make a record, an advance directive, of what kinds of care they want or don't want at the end of their life. These decisions can include whether to be resuscitated, intubated to help with breathing, fed through a tube, given antibiotics, and so on. The alternative is to allow the body's processes to take their own course. If one's wishes are known, family members are relieved of the fear, uncertainty, and guilt that can come with having to make all these decisions themselves.

Smith knows that his physical presence is sometimes all he can offer and all that is needed. He is unafraid to physically reach out to the dying person or to the grieving, knowing how powerful simple touch can be. He can often tell a family when it appears the end is near, so familiar is he with the way impending death affects the body. Sometimes he anoints the body of the dying person with oil while praying with the family. Most of all, he advises the dying and their families to speak while there is time, to ask their questions, to affirm their love, and to make their peace.

Rev. Smith can be quite direct in his counseling: "People always say, 'What happens if she dies and I'm not here?' And I say, 'What happens if you are here? Death is death. It doesn't make any difference whether someone is there or not.'"[15] He has learned that, at some point, he must explain to people in plain language what will happen after their loved one's death. He makes sure people understand that the undertaker's employees will arrive and, without any ceremony, load the body of the deceased into a zippered bag. He warns the family that this process is entirely impersonal; the workers are simply doing a job they perform multiple times a day. Smith has found that knowing such mundane details makes it easier for people get through the first hours and days of bereavement.

After the death in 2010 of Prince Rivers, Smith's dear friend and colleague from Hillside Church in Atlanta, Prince Rivers's son, Prince Raney Rivers, posted on a Duke Divinity School blog about Smith's pastoring. Rev. Prince Raney Rivers is himself a minister who writes that he has "preached more funerals than I care to remember."[16] Having been informed that his father had acute kidney failure, Rev. Rivers knew he had to call his father's old friend. "By his patient listening and thoughtful reflection, Paul reminded me that we make a mistake when we equate caring with fixing. He never told me how I *should* feel. He gave me the room to rattle off a litany of contradictory emotions.... Paul had more questions than answers. After a few particularly insightful questions, he said he was 'taking my temperature...'

Years of walking beside people in their pain equipped him to listen from many different angles."[17]

Rev. Smith's approach surprised Rev. Rivers in other ways. Smith asked him,

> "What hard questions do you want to ask your dad?" That was such a blessing to hear. It sobered me to the urgency of the moment long enough to think clearly about anything unsaid or unasked....
>
> Paul ... arrived a few days before Dad died. He invited everyone to sit around my dad's bed and tell stories about him....
>
> [Paul] helped us know that death was not the worst thing that could happen to Dad. Paul interceded for us, blessed my father, and stepped aside. He prayed a prayer that afternoon that can only be described as "deep calling unto deep" (Psalm 42:7). From that moment forward I stopped waiting for death and began to anticipate life. Thank God for good pastors.[18]

Particularly with those whose loved ones have met an untimely death, Smith has developed his own forms of solace. As he wrote recently in an email to a man who had lost his daughter to multiple sclerosis, "God's gift to the human spirit in times of loss is the gift of memory. With memory you will recall the date of [your daughter's] birth and the joy you felt as you held her for the very first time. With memory you can recall her own joy with the birth of her children (your grandchildren). With memory you can recall those very special moments that only a father can feel being with their daughters.... Thank God for the gift of memory."[19]

A natural extension of Smith's pastoral work is his concern for end-of-life management of pain and suffering. Rev. Smith has written and spoken about the underuse of palliative care and hospice services by African Americans.[20] In his view, people should not deny themselves the comforts of hospice services because they believe it is somehow inimical to their faith. As chair of the ethics committee of the board at Long Island College Hospital, Smith helped create policies for families deciding whether to remove someone from life support.

Responding especially to his brother Willie's difficult death in 1990, Smith has become an advocate for end-of-life rights. In a recent article, he explains his approach.

> For some, death comes suddenly and unexpected. For others, like the terminally ill, death comes slowly—as if approaching over the horizon. It can be seen coming and even be predictable.

Such was the case for my youngest brother, William Rollie Smith, who died of AIDS many years ago. I've been bedside for many deaths, and my brother's was among the worst I've seen. So agonizing was his pain that he begged his doctors to amputate his aching limbs. Time and again he asked our mother and me to help him die, but we told him it just wasn't an option. But it should have been.[21]

For about twenty years, Smith has served on the board of Compassion & Choices, a national nonprofit organization that advocates for end-of-life options.[22] Through their efforts, "Death with Dignity" legislation has become law in California, Colorado, the District of Columbia, Hawaii, Maine, New Jersey, Oregon, Vermont, and Washington.[23] The idea appears to be gaining general acceptance. While the Catholic Church and some other religious institutions strongly object to this trend, Smith's openness to such options emerges out of his lifetime's work supporting the dying in their final days.

Barbara Coombs Lee, president of Compassion & Choices, says of her work with Smith: "Over the years Paul has graciously offered me and my staff emotional support, strategic advice, important connections and a voice in prominent forums, including the pulpit of his own church. But his most important gifts have been his abiding belief in the rightness of our cause and the prayers and benedictions that have sustained us through years of toil and countless challenges."[24]

If there is any single font of wisdom that has fed Smith's pastoral practice, it is surely Howard Thurman's *Deep River: The Negro Spiritual Speaks of Life and Death*.[25] This slim volume contains two essays celebrating the genius of the music of the enslaved.

The second essay explores the meaning of the spirituals and the elemental wisdom of the enslaved. For them, Thurman says, death was "a fact, inescapable, persistent. For the slave, it was extremely compelling because of the cheapness with which his [or her] life was regarded. The slave was a tool, a thing, a utility, a commodity, but he [or she] was not a person. . . . The notion of personality . . . had no authentic application in the relationship between slave and master."[26]

Thurman lays bare the trauma inherent in this extreme imbalance of power: "Death at the hands of another human being makes for panic in the mind and outrages the spirit. To live constantly in such a climate makes the struggle for essential human dignity unbearably desperate. The human spirit is stripped to the literal substance of itself."[27]

Historically, Thurman notes, everyone was much more familiar with death than we are today. He finds that "therapeutic effects are missed" when we avoid encountering the dying or the dead.[28] "The creators of the Spirituals [had contact] with the dead [that] was immediate, inescapable, dramatic. The family or friends washed the body of the dead, the grave clothes were carefully and personally selected or especially made. The coffin itself was built by a familiar hand. . . . In the case of death from illness all the final aspects of the experience were shared by those who had taken their turn 'keeping watch.'"[29]

Using words that have been central to aspects of Rev. Smith's most profound life's work, Thurman asks, "How significant is death? Is it the worst of all possible things that can happen to an individual? . . . Obvious indeed is it here that death is not regarded as life's worst offering. There are some things in life that are worse than death. . . . A radical conception of the immortality of man is apparent because the human spirit has a final word over the effect of circumstances."[30]

Thurman believes that the lyrics of the spirituals express a deeply affirming, transcendent view of God's plan. "[The songs] express the profound conviction that God was not done with them, that God was not done with life. The consciousness that God had not exhausted His resources or better still that the vicissitudes of life could not exhaust God's resources, did not ever leave them. This is the secret of their ascendancy over circumstances and the basis of their assurances concerning life and death. The awareness of the presence of a God who was personal, intimate and active was the central fact of life."[31]

With great delicacy, Thurman illuminates the reality that death is not a catastrophic endpoint but rather one moment in an ongoing flow of existence: "The significant revelation is in the fact that death, as an event, is spatial, time encompassed, if not actually time bound, and therefore partakes of the character of the episodic. . . . There is, therefore, an element of detachment for the human spirit, even in so crucial an experience."[32]

Thurman concludes (his emphasis): "Death is an experience *in* life and a man, under some circumstances, may be regarded as a spectator *of*, as well as a participant *in*, the moment of his own death."[33] Like Thurman, Smith believes "God is the 'ground of being.'"[34] As Rev. Marvin Chandler[35] puts it, "Dr. Thurman saw God in everything, and Paul sees that as well . . . in the sense [that] there is a presence in life that nothing in life can snuff out. Paul sees that energy, that life is dynamic."[36]

Thurman scholar Dr. Luther Smith Jr. said recently of Smith, "One would be hard pressed to find many whose lives and sense of vocation have been [affected more] than Paul by Thurman's witness."[37] The two men shared many aspects of their theology and their worldview.

Following Thurman, Smith challenges the church to move beyond sectarianism and dogma. Like his mentor, Smith believes in the power of sustained, face-to-face relationships where love and antiracism are overtly cultivated and appreciated. He has dedicated his life to uprooting racism because it distorts the personality and poisons society as a whole.

Like Thurman, Smith's ability to speak from his heart without pretension attracts people to him. Smith powerfully positions himself *alongside* others in dealing with the vicissitudes of life. He listens intently. He speaks fearlessly. He urges people to grow in the service of creating community. He empowers people to push beyond their limits, to be more than they may have imagined they could be.

As Luther Smith Jr. has written of Howard Thurman, Smith's hope emerges from "the feeling of security, power and meaning received through religious experience. [His] mysticism, his reliance upon the God-encounter, assure[s] him that love can be experienced in the midst of hate, meaning in chaos, peace in the midst of turmoil, fulfillment in non-supportive circumstances, and unity and wholeness within separateness and fragmentation."[38]

Rev. Smith further knows that there is healing for *all* people—not simply people of color—in recognizing and embracing the profound wisdom of African American culture in this country. He agrees with Luther Smith Jr. that "in ignoring and oppressing blacks, American religionists have ignored and oppressed the group of people who reveal in distinctive ways the truth of Jesus. . . . Whites can learn from and be evangelized by the spirituality which is found in the black religious experience."[39]

Paul Smith believes it is significant that Howard Thurman himself had a mystical end-of-life experience. On April 9, 1981, Smith received a middle-of-the-night phone call from a frightened Anna Lee Scott in St. Louis, saying that Thurman's daughter, Anne, had called her in great distress. Rev. Smith called Anne and learned that she had been called to the hospital and was present when her father had had a kind of dream during which he seemed completely out of touch with reality. He seemed so unlike himself and unreachable that his daughter was deeply afraid. The doctors later said he had survived two close encounters with death that night. Smith's journal reveals some of what Thurman's daughter told him her father had said out loud. "[Thurman said,] I know my redeemer lives; he lives in my soul. He kept repeating that phrase during intervals. Over and over again he spoke to his creator. He kept pointing to something. His eyes became yellow and fixed. He did not know me; he cried like a baby and I kept saying 'I know, I know' and I hugged him. What he had believed all of his life seemed to be of no avail."[40] Smith went on in his journal to note that "I have heard experiences similar to this one, yet there was something quite different and special about it. Perhaps some of it is due to the particular relationships I share with the Thurmans. Whatever, it has reaffirmed my belief and interest in 'walks through death.'"[41]

In early April 1981, about a week before his death, Thurman talked to his assistant Joyce Sloan about his experience in the hospital. Fortunately, she recorded the conversation. Smith says he played that tape over and over for Arthur Ashe. They strained to understand what was said, because Dr. Thurman was speaking softly and the cassette tape was of such poor quality. It was not until after Ashe died that Smith learned from Thurman's wife Sue that a transcript of the tape existed. Smith felt badly that he had not known that but says, "I am convinced that even in that poor quality audiotape [Ashe] heard something important. . . . His reading of Thurman's work . . . and his discussions with me all helped Arthur find the courage to face his death."[42]

The transcript of the tape appears to have been hastily typed, but it shows how Thurman came to interpret his night at the hospital. He did not mention sadness or fear. He stated firmly that he had not had an out-of-body experience. Rather, his explanation of what had occurred in his hallucinatory state was more forthright.

> This is an account of something that may not ever have happened or could not happen but did happen. It has to do with an experience, one experience of illness that took me where, I am not sure. . . .
>
> The problem there was the fight that I was having with death. I did not understand what death was about and I wanted to know who or what was ultimately responsible. . . . Who called the shots? Who said this person lives and that person dies? I went all through the evening asking that question and trying to get an answer because I wanted to face the person who had ultimate responsibility for life or death over all living things. . . .
>
> I wanted to know from him, "Was there ultimately any difference between the colors of people?" Because this is my concern of how you deal with the question of a black person as over against a white person. Are there elements

known only to you by which you judge? And if that's the case the whole scheme of creation is evil. . . .

And when I found I could not have much discussion then I said, "Who are you? Are you God? Are you a Creator of things or are you the Creator of existence itself? And if so, ultimately what is the difference between black and white? Now if there's no answer then why perpetuate the sense of ultimate separation—separateness? If there is an answer give us the secret so that when we observe your behavior pattern we can do it without judgment and know that it is not an evil thing. . . ."

I feel there is something evil about a distinction . . . between human beings if it's just a capricious thing. Is there some valid hidden secret that makes differences between black and white, because that's what I'm concerned about. . . . Now, I said, I'm going to follow you to the ends of existence until you give me an answer to these questions. . . .

I was wrestling with that thing all night long because I couldn't find any ultimate authority that would take responsibility of making the difference between black and white. And I felt there was some hidden reason why I couldn't do it. And I was determined to bird dog it throughout all the universe.[43]

It is unclear who the great theologian believed he was talking to—God or Death or some other entity. Nonetheless, it is entirely in keeping with Thurman's character that he seized the opportunity to ask whether racial inequality was built into the order of creation. For him, at the end of a long and actively religious life, an affirmative answer would have been devastating. Nonetheless, Thurman had the courage to demand an explanation when he saw the chance.

Rev. Smith calls this "Thurman's unfinished business." He finds it inspiring that his spiritual guru was "bird-dogging" an existential explanation of race even from the beyond. Smith has said, "At the very end, he was asking the questions nobody else has had the guts to ask!"[44]

From his earliest journal writing to the present day, Rev. Smith has been probing the meaning and nature of racism and of death. And like his mentor before him, Smith's instinct is that evil is *not* at the heart of the cosmos. His experience shows that in life and in death, the only real differences between people are those we ourselves create. He knows that harmony, patience, and forgiveness can and must be cultivated. He has seen through the myths and knows that it is human fear, anger, avarice, and ideology that have so destructively separated us. But it is not God who must rid us of this scourge.

From left: Hon. David Dinkins, the author, and Paul Smith, Union Theological Seminary, New York, New York, 2018. Courtesy of the author.

As it has been since the founding of this country, it is people who have defined themselves as "white" who have had the power "to infuse their racial prejudice into the laws, policies, practices, and norms of society."[45] So it is "white" people who must do the reflective work, gain the experiences, and have the discussions that are necessary to acknowledge the past and rebuild our society on a new foundation. Some are already doing so. But all of those who benefit from belonging to the dominant group need to undertake this work for the good of all.[46]

As African American scholars Karen Fields and Barbara Fields have succinctly written: "Race is ideology and ideologies do not have lives of their own.... If race lives on today, it does not live on because we have inherited it from our forebears of the seventeenth century or the eighteenth or nineteenth, but because we continue to create it today.... Nothing handed down from the past could keep race alive if we did not constantly reinvent and re-ritualize it to fit our own terrain."[47]

Postlude

It took ten years for First Presbyterian Church of Brooklyn to find new leadership; it also took ten years for Paul Smith to fully let go of First Church. Driving from Maryland on a frequent basis or talking on the phone, his pastoring has still tied him closely to his Brooklyn parishioners. He regularly visited two of his closest First Church associates, Dorothy Turmail and Dorothy Gill, until their deaths in 2012 and 2014. He presided over both their funerals.

In early 2016, his dear friend and colleague from Atlanta, Joanne Nurss, was diagnosed with a fast-progressing cancer. Her illness was particularly difficult for Smith. Dr. Nurss had seen his daughters grow up, had been a stalwart member of the Session in Atlanta, and had visited the sick in hospital rooms with him. The irony was not lost on either of them that she now needed the end-of-life care she had helped him dispense to others. Smith recorded his thoughts throughout the months he ministered to her. At the end, they had two final days of conversation and contemplation. He says now, "We covered everything that two human beings could talk about before someone dies."[1]

At Dr. Nurss's request, Rev. Smith took an unusually active role in managing her care. When the physical therapy she was getting in preparation for chemotherapy became too painful, it was Smith who asked the hospital administration to change the treatment plan. Following his friend's wishes, he helped her review and finalize her affairs. While Joanne was in hospice, she insisted he stay at her home. He says, "That was like a second home for me. . . . We had discussions there; it shaped my ministry. There were intellectual battles, teas, gatherings, all kinds of things."[2]

In pastoring Dr. Nurss, Smith invited Rev. Beth Waltemath to join him. Waltemath and Rev. David Lewicki are copastors at Nurss's Atlanta church. This collaboration served them all. As Dr. Smith explains, "When I left, Joanne could see me through Beth. Beth learned how to ask the hard questions—questions like—'When you see your body deteriorating, what does that say to you?' She could see herself wasting away. Beth said, 'You can ask that?' . . . What I was able to do was to get [Joanne] to understand that everything I had taught her about God would be coming into play right now. I read to her from my journal about her. I was keeping notes and prayers, every day."[3]

Rev. Waltemath was due to have a child six weeks later, and Smith knew he could acknowledge to both of them that the child was the future. He recalls, "I put my hand on Beth's belly and said, 'The birth of a child is life's dramatic answer to death. Here's the new light. Your light is about to go out.' Joanne knew but knew it even better after I came."[4]

Dr. Nurss died in May 2016, and her memorial was held the following July. Overwhelmed with news about deaths in the Black community and for a time afraid to even drive his car for fear of being harassed by police, Rev. Smith made the decision not to officiate. He had seen all their friends and colleagues on his visits to Dr. Nurss's hospital room and felt he had done all he was needed to do.

A few short months later, a remarkable confluence of events convinced Rev. Smith that it was time to step back. He had been invited to return to Brooklyn on November 17 to receive a lifetime achievement award from his colleagues in the Brooklyn hospital and health-care community. A few days before the event, he received word that Dorothy Turmail's husband Dick, one of the First Church stalwarts, had died of a heart attack while playing tennis. Smith was asked to participate in the memorial service and declined, but he was unsure about his decision.

Significantly, Rev. Adriene Thorne, Smith's successor at First Church, had just been installed at First Presbyterian on November 13. Looking for clues as to his proper path forward, Smith took the opportunity to walk alone through First Church on a visit to Brooklyn. There, he was surprised to find cloth bags hanging on each pew. Upon further investigation, they proved to be "gratitude bags." Suddenly he found the insight he had sought when he came there. "I realized this was her imprimatur. That's who she is. That's why I walked through. It confirmed for me that it's about Adriene now. It *was* about Paul—now it is about Adriene. I was not at the installation because I had had my time. Now it was her time."[5] Smith realized clearly that since Rev. Thorne had been Dick Turmail's pastor in his final days, it was right that she should lead his memorial service. Smith finally felt comfortable moving on.

The gala event at which Smith was honored for his years-long contributions to Brooklyn health care was held in a beautifully restored warehouse on the waterfront in Brooklyn. The soirée and fundraiser brought together people from the tightly knit health-care community in Brooklyn.[6] Hosting the event was the former CEO of Cobble Hill LifeCare, Olga Lipschitz. Guests included Smith supporters who had not seen each other in years—Honda executives, First Church board members, and doctors who had worked at Long Island College Hospital. Dear friends like Lenny Wilkens and his wife Marilyn were among those who bought a page in the event's souvenir book. The books contained letters conveying the best wishes of New York governor Andrew Cuomo, Mayor Bill de Blasio, Congressman Hakeem Jeffries, and others. About forty of Smith's family and friends were seated at a very long and boisterous table.

Compounding the emotion that evening was the fact that Donald Trump had been elected president ten days earlier. Having Trump succeed Obama has seemed the ultimate insult to Smith. The level of his dismay rivals what he felt about the appointment of Clarence Thomas to Thurgood Marshall's seat on the Supreme Court in 1991. In both cases, the contrast between a departing giant of the Black community and the man chosen to replace him could not have been more stark. Smith expressed fury over the Clarence Thomas decision in his journal. The ascension of an overtly bigoted candidate to the presidency has been even more devastating.

After presenting the other awards and quieting the hundred or so guests, Mrs. Lipschitz shared her regard for Rev. Smith while speaking from her personal experience of the Holocaust.

> Believe me, in my life, I have seen evil. I have looked at the face of [Adolf] Eichmann and he looked at me ... this was in Auschwitz. And because of that, I have seen his face, even though I was a child, for that was the face of evil.
>
> And here, my friend Dr. Smith is a face of goodness and when he opens his mouth, all the good things come out. . . . So ladies and gentlemen, here is a man who is a pastor, who is a friend, who has done more kindness for human beings than anyone that I know.[7]

As Smith rose to speak amid applause, a woman at his table called out, "You go, Paul!" and there was laughter. An inscription on the plaque presented to Smith was read aloud: "In tribute to you for many years for bringing joy, peace and love to communities in service; for compassion and respect for every person who crosses your path . . . we salute you for decades of significant achievements and wish you good health, strength and happiness for many years to come."[8] Then Rev. Smith took his place at the microphone, full of gratitude but also aware of the heaviness of the mood.

> Well, thank you so very much. To my co-honorees, I thank you for all of the contributions you have made to the community that we all love so much. I also want to thank Olga, who in the midst of so many battles that we took on, she was always there supporting, putting together contacts that made it possible for us to do the things we were able to do.
>
> Three months ago one of my former students asked me—how did I make my ministry so successful? That is easy—you get a whole lot of people who are a lot smarter than you, [and then] you can do anything that you want to do! And I mean that. So I am surrounded by a host of witnesses who have come to join me in this award this evening.
>
> One of the beautiful things about being pastor is that you have a lot of surrogate sons and daughters, and many of them are here this evening. But I do want to give thanks for [two] of my four grandchildren are here, my son-in-law is here, my daughter is here. But most of all my wife of fifty-six years this year [applause] . . . she keeps saying that if you want to make fifty-seven, there are some conditions! So I honor that and make sure that I make number fifty-seven.[9]

Speaking more slowly and with greater emotion, Rev. Smith began to pray over the remarkably heterogeneous crowd.

> So let me just say this, we need to understand that what's in this room tonight is what our purpose is—our God. In Thee, we are more loving, we're stronger, we're more likable. We're more reflective when we can be together like we are in this room right now. And there are times when the water in the well is low, there are times when we wonder what role, what voice we are going to take, and yes, there are times when you just want to wring your hands and say, "I've had it." I'm here to tell you that all that is part of life; we all experience that.[10]

Looking out at the now-hushed crowd, Smith was aware of the profound sadness, anger, and fear the election results had engendered in people so dear to him. He searched his heart for the words with which to entreat them to not lose hope (his emphasis).

> If there has been any kind of success that we've all had, and we've seen it in this community, it is that we all come together to make our community great. To make the institutions we work for great. For the people in our lives who give us meaning, that's why we are here and that's what's in common with us. . . .
>
> We believe that it is always possible to accomplish anything we wish to accomplish so long as we recognize our oneness—*our oneness.*
>
> I haven't preached for a long time [laughter], so let me just—one of the things that really holds me together other than daughters, wife and grand-children and the love of friends, is the awareness that the God of my life and yours makes all things *new.* . . . Walk tall all of you who are in the room, because *I have not come this far for God to leave me!*[11]

When his turn comes, Paul Smith will have his eyes and his heart open as he journeys into the unknowable. There will be joy in going "wherever Jesus is" but also sadness about those he leaves behind. As he wrote a few years ago:

> What makes me cry and tear up is the fact that death takes me down from the mountain called life. It is here that I have enjoyed all of God's many blessings to me. I don't want to leave my daughters or my wife or my beautiful grand-kids. I thoroughly enjoy life even with its challenges. . . . I know I cannot stay here forever. I know my days on the planet will soon be over. That is what makes me cry—knowing it all must come to an end someday. The second chance I have been given to help raise our grandkids fills my soul. Growing older with Fran and enjoying each other as we age brings untold happiness to me. I want to be the first to go before Fran or any of our grandkids and our daughters. I don't think I could stand living without Fran. I feel she would handle my death better than I would handle hers.
>
> As I write, I continue to be more and more curious about what is on the other side of life as I know it. If anything, I am being drawn to the edge and I want to be pushed over that edge so I can begin to fly. . . . O God, I pray that I may die easy when I die. May I soar about the clouds and discover Your Presence as I learn how to fly in that other place—the place on the other side of life. And so it is![12]

Acknowledgments

Writing this book would not have been possible without the warmth, cooperation, and support of Rev. Dr. Smith and his family. I am grateful to Dr. Paul for being my colleague and friend; for making his records, contacts, and journals available to me in my research; and for inspiring me to undertake this project in the first place. Dr. Paul made himself available on dozens of occasions to answer my questions and graciously included me in all his activities whenever we spent time together. Frances Smith has freely offered her incisive wisdom, patience, and hospitality over the years it has taken to finish this project.

Starting in late 2014, I visited key sites in Smith's life and interviewed many of his family members, friends, and colleagues. Family members who were especially generous with their time include Marlene Smith Wright, who spent a day with me in South Bend, and Kathleen Smith Randolph, who was my guide in St. Louis. Krista Smith Clapp and her husband John provided quiet space for many conversations with Dr. Paul. Smith's cousin Bernard Streets shared background material on "Granny" in telephone calls and email correspondence.

I am profoundly grateful to have had the opportunity to meet and get to know the amazing people in Dr. Paul's spiritual circle. Rev. Marvin Chandler was one of the first people I called when I started doing background research, and the enormous motivational boost I received just speaking with him on the phone carried me through the entire project. I said to him, "Writing this book is going to change me," and it has. Rev. Chandler and his wife Portia were gracious hosts at their home in Indianapolis.

Marsha Larner has given freely of her warmth and spirit, quickly becoming my supporter as well as Dr. Paul's. Dr. and Mrs. Kenneth and Marge Smith welcomed me into their house full of history in St. Louis and had much to say about their work and worship with Dr. Smith at Second Presbyterian Church. Leonard Wilkens generously spoke about the enduring friendship with Smith that began in St. Louis and has continued over decades.

I am grateful that the late Dr. Joanne Nurss was able to spend hours talking with me about all that was accomplished at Hillside Church in Decatur, Georgia. Dr. Luther Smith Jr., whose family attended Hillside, offered his incisive thoughts on Smith's work there and in St. Louis. Jo Moore Stewart, who heard the Spelman College Convocation speech by Thurman in 1980, has graciously given permission to reprint her photograph of Smith, Thurman, and others that day.

I appreciate Rev. Mike Trautman for taking the time to talk at length on several occasions and for showing me around Ferguson. Thanks to Howie Hodges II, Mossi Tull, and John Utendahl for eloquently sharing their thoughts on being among the "sons of Paul."

Many present and former First Presbyterian Church parishioners contributed enormously to this project, enthusiastically sharing details about their years with Dr. Paul in Brooklyn. They include Janet Dewart Bell, Sue Carlson, Fred Davie, Nathan Dudley, Jim Johnson, David Lewicki, Sam Murumba, Amy Neuner, Ellen Oler, Marcia Smith, John Utendahl, and Mercia Weyand. The congregation as a whole extended its characteristically warm welcome to me and my husband on the occasions when we attended First Church. Charles Clayman shared freely about his relationship with Smith, his Brooklyn Heights neighbor and fellow tennis player.

I am grateful that The Honorable David Dinkins and Ambassador Andrew Young, who are in demand for interviews despite their advancing years, were able to speak with me about their dear friend and colleague. Barbara Coombs Lee responded quickly to my request for comment on her years with Dr. Smith.

The late Ed Goldberg, Marc Burt, and Jeffrey Smith discussed at length their working relationships with Dr. Smith in corporate settings. They described their experiences with him in remarkably similar and effusive terms. Ed was especially devoted to this project. He also masterminded a celebration of Smith's story at Macy's that brought together many of Smith's New York media and political supporters. The opportunity at that event to have live jazz performed with narration by Dr. Paul was extraordinary. I thank Pam Champion for being willing to share her experiences with Dr. Paul under tragic circumstances.

I acknowledge the Brooklyn campus of Long Island University for providing travel funds in the spring of 2015 and sabbatical leave in the spring of 2016. Fellow LIU faculty who have been good friends and generous colleagues throughout the years include: Nic Agrait, Syed Ali, Larry Banks, Hal Barton, Leah Dilworth, John Ehrenberg, Dalia Fahmy, Stacey Horstmann-Gatti, Kimberly Jones, Yusuf Juwayeyi, Haesook Kim, Arthur Kimmel, Kevin Lauth, Maria McGarritty, Mark Pires, Gustavo Rodriguez, Jose Sanchez, Joram Warmund, Lester Wilson, and Yafeng Xia.

The collegiality of historian Terry Anne Scott, who suggested I contact Walter Biggins about publication at the University of Georgia Press, was wonderful gift. Walter's expertise and enthusiasm were essential to bringing this work to fruition; I thank him for his belief in Paul's story. More recently, Nathaniel Holly has brought his knowledgeable and energetic assistance to the process of readying the manuscript for production. The patience and expert advice of Jon Davies and Kay Kodner in the final stages of manuscript editing were much appreciated. Everyone at the UGA Press has been a pleasure to work with, even during the difficult months of the coronavirus national shutdown.

I offer special thanks to UGA's anonymous reviewers who invested many hours reading and commenting on this text. Their interest and expertise have been invaluable. Likewise, the constancy and optimism of my dharma friends and fellow writers Michele Martin and Karen Lucic have sustained me through the long process of bringing this narrative to publication.

Special thanks go to Howie Hodges II and Necole Brown for being there at key moments in this process. Their comradeship and generosity have been most welcome. Howie's warmth and friendship have been especially important to keeping this project on track. His intuitiveness and empathy during what appeared to be a setback will not be forgotten.

I thank my closest readers and supporters for their patience and hard work. They include Helen Heinrich, Holly Hendrickson, Andrew Hendrickson, Virginia Herron Lanoil, Jesse Lanoil Edelman, Judy McKee, Max McKee, and Louis Raveson.

I owe the most to my husband, Andrew McKee, who has been an integral part of the research and writing that created this book. He has patiently read and reread many drafts over many months and kept me going with his fantastic cooking. Thank you, Andy, for forgiving the many times my head was too deeply buried in writing to come up for air. Your belief, perseverance, and good judgment as we have traveled along this path together have been invaluable. Any errors or omissions that may remain in this text, of course, are solely my own.

Note on the Sources

Paul Smith's Journals

Dr. Smith has kept diaries on and off since the late 1950s. What he calls his "journaling" is an important part of his meditative practice. He has made his collection of more than eighty notebooks available as a resource for this biography. Included are two journals dating from the late 1950s into the 1960s, one started in the 1970s, and then more than twenty journals per decade thereafter. The notebooks are frequently inscribed with a note about who gave them to Dr. Smith. No two are alike, and all are unpublished. Most are now stored at the home of Smith's daughter Kathleen in St. Louis.

Listed here in rough chronological order are descriptions of the journals from which quotes have been taken for this biography. All of these are on loan to the author. Quotes were chosen because they refer to key events like weddings, the births of Dr. Smith's children, and changes of jobs, or because they refer to recurring concerns such as his relationship with Rev. Dr. Howard Thurman, political events, or media reports of violence against people of color. The journal titles were given either by Smith or by the author. Light editing and correction of typos and punctuation has been applied to the quotes.

Paul Smith. Hartford Journal

3/21/57–3/10/65. This is one of two notebooks containing Dr. Smith's earliest entries. These cover the period during which Dr. Smith was studying at Hartford Seminary in Connecticut as well as his early pastorates in Buffalo and St. Louis. This small black and burgundy "Record" book includes notes written while Smith was driving to his wedding in California in 1960 and a note made after his experiences in Selma in 1965.

Paul Smith. Federal Supply Service Journal.

1959–1968. This is the second notebook containing very early entries. Eight entries were written by Smith in 1959 while he was at seminary. Entries then stop until 1967 when Dr. Smith was living and working in St. Louis. This notebook contains Smith's reactions to Dr. Martin Luther King Jr.'s death in 1968. This oversized, government-issue, light green "Record" book is partially water damaged but mostly legible.

Paul Smith. Atlanta Journal No. 1.

1/29/82–11/21/87. Entries were made during Smith's years working at Morehouse College in Atlanta and Hillside Presbyterian Church in Decatur, Georgia. This small notebook has a unicorn tapestry reproduced on the cover. This and some other notebooks in the collection have "No." labels attached by Dr. Smith at some point in the past.

Paul Smith. Atlanta Journal No. 3.

11/14/78–6/17/89. Dr. Smith wrote in this journal during his final months at Hillside Church in Atlanta and his first several years at First Church in Brooklyn, New York. This large dark-brown notebook has a large gold star on the cover.

Paul Smith. Brooklyn Journal No. 15.

3/6/89–11/30/89. Entries were made in this medium-sized notebook with a wool tweed cover during one of Smith's early years at First Church in Brooklyn, New York. This diary contains entries pertaining to Smith's pastoring of tennis champion Arthur Ashe before his death from AIDS in early 1993.

Paul Smith. First Church Journal.

8/2/91–10/22/06. Entries cover fifteen of Dr. Smith's twenty years at First Church in Brooklyn, New York. This very large, thick journal with a brown speckled cover contains many inscriptions to and about babies Smith baptized, couples he married, and people whose funerals he performed. It seems to have functioned as a kind of unofficial record of his work with First Church parishioners.

Paul Smith. Ghost Ranch Journal.

6/15/91–9/24/91. Dr. Smith started this journal on his way to one of a number of retreats he and his parishioners enjoyed at a Presbyterian Church property, the "Ghost Ranch" in Abiquiú, New Mexico. This small spiral notebook has clear plastic covers imprinted with hieroglyphs.

Paul Smith. Urban League Journal.

5/29/13–9/26/13. This notebook is typical of the many made after Smith's 2006 retirement from First Presbyterian Church in Brooklyn. It is full from cover to cover, and it was written over a period of about four months. This notebook is small, red, and embossed with the words "New York Urban League."

Collected Papers of Paul Smith

Most of Dr. Smith's collected professional papers were loaned by him to the author to be preserved and used as source material for this narrative. They include letters, church programs, photographs, and scrapbooks. These are here cited as "collected Smith papers on loan to the author."

Included among these documents are original news articles that were saved as mementos. Many are trimmed as if to be placed in a scrapbook, causing the publication date, newspaper name, and byline to be lost. These will be identified in the end notes as "news-clippings." Any citation details that are extant, or that can be reconstructed from their context, will be noted in the end note.

Also quoted in this biography are entries from "the diary of Odie Wingo," Dr. Smith's maternal grandmother. This diary, which appears to be the only surviving one written by Odie, was found among Smith's papers. The unpublished document covers a period of about six months between December 5, 1901 and May 31, 1902. Odie was age eighteen at the time and living in southwestern Kentucky where she was born. Dr. Smith received it as a gift from his cousin. It has been transcribed and lightly edited by the author.

Preservation of and Access to These Materials

It is hoped that all these materials along with the author's interview recordings and transcriptions will be made available to other scholars when they are housed in an appropriate library or historical archive. At the time of publication, these plans have not been finalized.

Notes

Author's Note

1. Vaughn, "History of Diversity."
2. Thurman, "The Sound of the Genuine."

Chapter 1. Answering Dr. King's Call

1. Paul Smith, "In Search of Common Ground," blog post, August 23, 2014. See Paul Smith website, http://www.revdrpaulsmith.org.
2. Branch, *At Canaan's Edge*, 60.
3. Ibid., 73.
4. King, *I Have a Dream*, "Letter," 85.
5. George Wallace, "Inaugural Address," January 14, 1963, https://digital.archives .alabama.gov/digital/collection/voices/id/2952.
6. Pratt, *Selma's Bloody Sunday*, 50.
7. Lewis, *Walking with the Wind*, 343.
8. Branch, *At Canaan's Edge*, 78.
9. Paul Smith, email message to the author, September 8, 2015.
10. Quoted in Pratt, *Selma's Bloody Sunday*, 74.
11. Paul Smith, email message to the author, February 23, 2015.
12. Ibid.
13. Ibid.
14. Dudley, "Second American Revolution." Used with permission.
15. Ibid.
16. Branch, *At Canaan's Edge*, 80–81.
17. Smith email, September 8, 2015.
18. None of them lost their jobs over responding to Dr. King's call. But some politically active Presbyterian ministers elsewhere did. See Heuser, "Presbyterians and the Struggle," 9.

19. Johnson, "Voting Rights Act Address."

20. Lewis, *Walking with the Wind*, 361–62.

21. Ibid., 363.

22. *Shelby County v. Holder*, 570 U.S. 2 (2013).

23. May, *Bending toward Justice*.

24. Weiser and Feldman, *State of Voting*.

25. Hay and Borter, "North Carolina Orders New U.S. House Election."

26. Pratt, *Selma's Bloody Sunday*, 4.

Chapter 2. On Granny's Porch

1. Paul Smith, interview with the author, July 29, 2014.

2. Paul Smith, *Facing Death*, 2–3.

3. Almost completely bounded by rivers including the Mississippi, this region had been purchased for the United States by Andrew Jackson and Isaac Shelby via treaty with the Chickasaw Indians in 1818. See Harrison and Klotter, *New History of Kentucky*, 20–21.

4. Downey, *Images of Rail*, 7.

5. "Wingo," Graves County Communities, Official Website of Graves County, Kentucky, https://www.gravescountyky.com/relocation/communities/wingo/.

6. Bernard Streets, email message to the author, June 15, 2016.

7. "Wingo."

8. Streets email, June 15, 2016.

9. Ibid.

10. Ibid.

11. For more details about this diary and other original documents quoted in this narrative, see Note on the Sources, 223–25.

12. No other diaries by Odie Wingo have been found.

13. Diary of Odie Wingo (see Note on the Sources). Entry dated December 1901, day not specified. In collected Smith papers on loan to the author.

14. Clearly, this did not have the same meaning in 1901 that it has today.

15. Diary of Odie Wingo (see Note on the Sources), December 6, 1901. In collected Smith papers on loan to the author.

16. Diary of Odie Wingo (see Note on the Sources), December 7, 1901. In collected Smith papers on loan to the author.

17. This appears to have been shorthand for Sunday School.

18. Diary of Odie Wingo (see Note on the Sources), December 8, 1901. In collected Smith papers on loan to the author.

19. One of two portraits labeled "Photo by Taylor, 1889, Dawson Springs, KY" is seen on p. 19.

20. Wright, *Racial Violence in Kentucky*.

21. Harrison and Klotter, *New History of Kentucky*, 235.

22. Ibid., 247.

23. Craig, *Kentucky Confederates*.

24. Wright, *Racial Violence in Kentucky*, 72–73.

25. Harrison and Klotter, *New History of Kentucky*, 180.

26. Wright, *Racial Violence in Kentucky*, 10–11.

27. Ibid., 70ff.

28. Ibid., 72–73.

29. Ibid., 251.

30. "All Mayfield Under Arms: Excitement over the Kentucky Race War," *New York Times*, December 23, 1896.

31. Wright, *Racial Violence in Kentucky*, 75.

32. "All Mayfield Under Arms."

33. "Peace Reigns at Mayfield: Colored People Petition for Harmony and the Race War Is Over," *New York Times*, December 24, 1896.

34. Robinson, *Better Homes of South Bend*, 34.

35. Ibid.

36. Ibid., 35.

37. "Negro Killed by Freight Train," November 5, 1927. This undated newsclipping in Bernard Streets's possession was most likely published in the *South Bend News-Times*.

38. Bernard Streets, email message to the author, July 23, 2016.

39. Paul Smith, email message to the author, July 29, 2015.

40. Smith interview, July 29, 2014.

41. Paul Smith, interview with the author, August 3, 2016.

42. Ibid.

43. Despite activists staging protests starting in the 1920s, most northern cities barred people of color from pools and beaches into the 1950s. See Sugrue, *Sweet Land of Liberty*, 154ff.

44. Robinson, *Better Homes of South Bend*, 24.

45. Healy, "We Stand on His Shoulders," 6.

46. Thornbrough, *Indiana Blacks in the Twentieth Century*, 35.

47. Smith interview, July 29, 2014.

48. Gordon, *Negro in South Bend*, 77.

49. Robinson, *Better Homes of South Bend*, 27ff.

50. Thornbrough, *Indiana Blacks in the Twentieth Century*, 103.

51. Ibid., 35.

52. Ibid., 42–43.

53. Tucker, *Notre Dame vs. the Klan*.

54. Dr. Eugene Carson Blake, who led the United Presbyterian Church in the U.S.A. as Stated Clerk of the General Assembly in the mid-1950s, was also well known for his public civil rights activism. See Heuser, "Presbyterians and the Struggle" ("in the U.S.A." is part of the official title of this branch of the Presbyterian Church).

55. Thornbrough, *Indiana Blacks in the Twentieth Century*, 92–93.

56. Robinson, *Better Homes of South Bend*, 45.

57. Thornbrough, *Indiana Blacks in the Twentieth Century*, 42.

58. Robinson, *Better Homes of South Bend*.

59. Smith interview, July 29, 2014.

60. Ibid.

61. Ibid.

62. Thornbrough, *Indiana Blacks in the Twentieth Century*, 49.

63. Smith interview, July 29, 2014.

64. Lewis, *Walking with the Wind*, 27.

65. Smith interview, July 29, 2014.

66. Paul Smith, interview with the author, October 6, 2014.

67. Mitchell, *Black Preaching*.

68. Ibid., 95.

69. Ibid., 103.

70. Ibid.

71. Mitchell, *Black Preaching*, 112.

72. Shelton and Emerson, *Blacks and Whites*, 8–9.

73. Paul Smith, interview with the author, October 11, 2014.

74. Ibid.

75. Paul Smith, interview with the author, July 10, 2016.

76. Ibid.

77. Ibid.

Chapter 3. Riding the Hummingbird into the Fire

1. William Smith, Paul Smith's father's father, worked as one of A. Philip Randolph's train porters.

2. Paul Smith, interview with the author, July 29, 2014.

3. Auchmutey, "Guess Who's Coming to Worship?," 24.

4. Smith interview, July 29, 2014.

5. "Our History," About Talladega, Talladega College, https://www.talladega.edu/history.asp.

6. Ibid.

7. Paul Smith, interview with the author, June 5, 2015.

8. Ibid.

9. "Gray," Obituary, *Chicago Tribune*, June 25, 1979.

10. Paul Smith, interview with the author, October 11, 2014.

11. Ibid.

12. Ibid.

13. Undated letter from Paul Smith to Leonard Smith Sr. In collected Smith papers on loan to the author.

14. Paul Smith, interview with the author, February 10, 2016.

15. Ibid.

16. Paul Smith, interview with the author, January 16, 2015.

17. Ibid.

18. Paul Smith, "Athens Alabama Musings." Undated talking points for a speaking engagement. In collected Smith papers on loan to the author.

19. Ibid.

20. Smith interview, July 29, 2014.

21. Ibid.

22. Smith interview, January 16, 2015.

23. Andrew Young, *Easy Burden*, 96.

24. Graham, *Our Kind of People*, 85.

25. Ibid., 86.

26. The oldest Black women's sorority, Alpha Kappa Alpha, was founded in 1908 at Howard University. Vice President Kamala Harris is a member.

27. Paul Smith. Federal Supply Service Journal (see Note on the Sources), April 28, 1968.

28. Andrew Young, *Easy Burden*, 97.

29. Branch, *Parting the Waters*, 217.

30. Frances Smith, interview with the author, January 17, 2015.

31. Ibid.

32. Ibid.

33. Smith interview, June 5, 2015.

34. Ibid.

35. Paul Smith, "A Comparison of the Baptist and Congregationalist Denominations," 33.

36. Ibid., 1.

37. Ibid., 58.

38. Ibid., 62–63.

39. Ibid., 71–72.

40. Ibid., 47, 56.

41. Ibid.

42. Paul Smith, email message to the author, October 4, 2016.

Chapter 4. First Rites

1. Paul Smith, interview with the author, October 10, 2016.

2. Branch, *Parting the Waters*, 417–18.

3. Smith interview, October 10, 2016.

4. Ibid.

5. Ibid.

6. Ibid.

7. Paul Smith, "Athens Alabama Musings." In collected Smith papers on loan to the author.

8. Ibid.

9. Letter from Dr. Raymond Pitts to Paul Smith, February 2, 1958. In collected Smith papers on loan to the author.

10. Paul Smith, interview with the author, October 11, 2014.

11. Ibid.

12. Pitts letter, February 2, 1958.

13. Ibid.

14. Ibid.

15. Ibid.

16. Ibid.

17. Ibid.

18. See the Hartford Theological Seminary website, http://www.hartsem.edu.

19. The Kennedy School of Missions, the Hartford Theological Seminary, and two other schools in the Hartford Seminary Foundation have since merged.

20. Paul Smith, interview with the author, July 29, 2014.

21. Ibid.

22. "Seminary Students Perform Important Church Service," news-clipping; most likely from the *Hartford Courant*, 1957 (see Note on the Sources).

23. Ibid.

24. For more details about Dr. Smith's journals, see Note on the Sources.

25. Paul Smith, Hartford Journal (see Note on the Sources), dated March 21, 1957.

26. These earliest entries are grouped together in the center of the notebook. Smith seems to have gone back to this notebook much more formally and consistently in 1959 while he was studying at Hartford Seminary.

27. Ibid., November 16, 1959.

28. Smith is quoting from *J.B.: A Play in Verse* by Archibald MacLeish that was based on the Book of Job and received a Pulitzer Prize in 1959.

29. Paul Smith, Hartford Journal (see Note on the Sources), December 1959, day not specified.

30. Ibid., June 12, 1960.

31. Ibid., February 3, 1961.

32. Ibid., July 1961, day not specified.

33. Ibid., March 10, 1965.

34. Paul Smith, Federal Supply Service Journal (see Note on the Sources). Entry dated March 21, 1957.

35. Ibid., 1959, month and day not specified.

36. Ibid., October 1959, day not specified.

37. Ibid.

38. This was an annual event sponsored by the Federal Council of Churches from the 1920s until the 1960s to encourage ministers to publicly address race issues. See Sugrue, *Sweet Land of* Liberty, 7–8.

39. Paul Smith, Hartford Journal (see Note on the Sources), February 14, 1960.

40. Ibid., undated entry; must have been early June 1960.

41. Paul Smith, Hartford Journal (see Note on the Sources), June 12, 1960.

42. Ibid.

43. Frances Smith, interview with the author, February 10, 2016.

44. Paul Smith, Urban League Journal (see Note on the Sources), June 12, 2010.

45. Ibid.

46. Paul Smith, Hartford Journal (see Note on the Sources), August 5, 1960.

47. Ibid.

Chapter 5. Urban Alliances

1. The Evangelical and Reformed churches of which Salem United was a part were then joining with the Congregational churches to form the United Church of Christ (UCC).

2. Paul Smith, interview with the author, October 11, 2014.

3. Ibid.

4. Ibid.

5. Ibid.

6. Ibid.

7. Kraus, *Race, Neighborhoods, and Community Power.*

8. Ibid., 24ff.

9. "New Pastor Is Assigned: Rev. Paul Smith Named Assistant Minister," news-clipping; most likely from the *South Bend Tribune*, 1960 (see Note on the Sources).

10. Smith interview, October 11, 2014.

11. Auchmutey, "Guess Who's Coming to Worship?"

12. Ibid., 25.

13. Ibid.

14. Ibid.

15. Smith interview, October 11, 2014.

16. Ibid.

17. Martin Luther King Jr., *I Have a Dream*, "Facing the Challenge," 22. See https://www .thekingcenter.org/The King Philosophy.

18. Ibid.

19. Ibid., 21.

20. Paul Smith, telephone interview with the author, March 10, 2015.

21. Ibid.

22. Herbeck, "Buffalo's Crimes of the Century."

23. Donald Hartnett quoted in Herbeck, "Buffalo's Crimes of the Century."

24. Smith interview, March 10, 2015.

25. Branch, *Parting the Waters*, 418.

26. Andrew Young, *Easy Burden*, 141.

27. The site that came to be called the Dorchester Center was used as a staging ground for the critical Birmingham campaign protests of 1963. Andrew Young, *Easy Burden*, 188–90.

28. Andrew Young, *Easy Burden*, 143.

29. Andrew Young, telephone interview with the author, August 31, 2016.

30. Andrew Young, *Easy Burden*, 147–48.

31. Ibid., 149.

32. Young interview, August 31, 2016.

33. Smith interview, October 11, 2014.

34. Still, "Preacher."

35. The *JET* article mentions a thesis Smith wrote at Hartford titled "Jazz, Religion and the Beat Generation," but no copies are extant.

36. MacLean, *Freedom Is Not Enough*.

37. Ibid., 42.

38. "Ex-Resident Gets Urban League Post," news-clipping; most likely from the *South Bend Tribune*, October 1963 (see Note on the Sources).

39. See the National Urban League website, https://www.nul.org/mission-and -history.

40. Paul Smith, interview with the author, July 29, 2014.

41. MacLean, *Freedom Is Not Enough*, 77.

42. Paul Smith, Federal Supply Service Journal (see Note on the Sources), undated entry ca. 1968. The job sites are given as IBM, Krey Packing, and Project Equality.

43. MacLean, *Freedom Is Not Enough*, 339.

44. See U.S. Equal Employment Opportunity website, https://www.eeoc.gov.

45. MacLean, *Freedom Is Not Enough*, 8.

46. Ibid., 2.

47. Paul Smith, email message to the author, September 3, 2019.

48. Paul Smith, email message to the author, September 8, 2015.

49. Ibid.

50. See Rochester Black Freedom Struggle Online Project—Marvin Chandler, https://rbscp.lib.rochester.edu/rbfs-Chandler.

51. Marvin and Portia Chandler, interview with the author, March 31, 2016.

52. One of the techniques Chandler still uses starts with several listeners choosing one musical note each on the piano. From those notes, Chandler improvises a complete piece of music on the spot. The effect is literally to create

harmony out of dissonance, thereby delivering at an almost subconscious level the ministers' fundamental message about the human potential for unity. It is an unforgettable demonstration.

53. Marvin and Portia Chandler interview, March 31, 2016.

54. Ibid.

55. Ibid.

56. Ibid.

57. Ibid.

58. MacLean, *Freedom Is Not Enough*, 105.

59. See Rochester Black Freedom Struggle Online Project—Marvin Chandler.

60. Marvin and Portia Chandler interview, March 31, 2016.

61. Thompson, *Blood in the Water*.

62. Marvin and Portia Chandler interview, March 31, 2016.

63. Ibid. Chandler also spoke of seeing Malcolm X in Rochester shortly before X's assassination. Chandler remembers: "He was so disappointed with the lethargy of Black people in those days. . . . He didn't understand that not all Black ministers were social[ly] conservative. He didn't understand what we were doing. He didn't have the patience." On the assassination, see Branch, *Pillars of Fire*, 597ff.

64. See the Hartford Institute for Religion Research website, http://hirr.hartsem .edu/about/dudley.htm.

65. Frances Smith, interview with the author, January 17, 2015.

66. Paul Smith, email message to the author, March 17, 2016.

Chapter 6. Prophets of Multiracial Christianity

1. Sweets, "Laclede: An Experiment."

2. Looker, *BAG: "Point from Which Creation Begins."*

3. Ibid., 23.

4. Ibid., 25.

5. Carl S. Dudley, "My Experience." Used with permission.

6. Sweets, "Laclede: An Experiment."

7. Allen and Kolk, "Painful Persistence."

8. Kathleen Smith Randolph, interview with the author, April 2, 2016.

9. Ibid.

10. Sweets, "Laclede: An Experiment."

11. Looker, *BAG: "Point from Which Creation Begins,"* 23.

12. Nathan Dudley, "Laclede Town," 17.

13. Paul Smith, telephone interview with the author, March 10, 2016.

14. Ibid.

15. Ibid.

16. Randolph interview, April 2, 2016.

17. Nathan Dudley, "Laclede Town," 15.

18. Emerson with Woo, *People of the Dream*, 35–36.

19. Emerson, "Cracks in the Christian Color Wall," reports that twenty-first-century Protestant churches with more than 1,000 members are becoming more multiracial.

20. DeYoung et al., *United by Faith*, 168.

21. Ibid., 169.

22. Ibid., 175ff.

23. Emerson with Woo, *People of the Dream*, 97.

24. Emerson and Smith, *Divided by Faith*.

25. Ibid., 133. As recently as 2018, a group of evangelical Christians led by pastor John MacArthur produced a formal document asserting emphatically that making social justice a central Christian concern amounts to heresy. See Gerson, "Christians Are Suffering."

26. Emerson and Smith, *Divided by Faith*, 184.

27. Jones, *White Too Long*, 187.

28. Ibid., 232.

29. Ibid., 170.

30. Smith also wrote resolutions and statements circulated by the national denomination.

31. Smith, "In Search."

32. Paul Smith, interview with the author, August 3, 2016.

33. Joanne Nurss, interview with the author, January 15, 2015.

34. Paul Smith, interview with the author, June 10, 2019.

35. Wilmore, *Black and Presbyterian*, 25.

36. Wilmore, "Identity and Integration," 210.

37. See Wilmore, "Identity and Integration."

38. Smith interview, August 3, 2016.

39. Carl S. Dudley, "Second American Revolution"; "My Experience."

40. Nathan Dudley, interview with the author, January 26, 2016.

41. Carl S. Dudley, "Second American Revolution."

42. Lang, *Grassroots at the Gateway*, 209.

43. Smith interview, August 3, 2016.

44. Ibid., 184. After many such actions, a job discrimination suit filed by Green against McDonnell Douglas was decided in his favor by the Supreme Court in 1973. Lang, *Grassroots at the Gateway*, 241–42.

45. "The Christian Response to Death," booklet prepared for Berea Presbyterian Church by the Board of Deacons with Pastors Carl Dudley and Paul Smith, Easter 1965. In collected Smith papers on loan to the author.

46. Paul Smith, interview with the author, February 10, 2016.

47. "Christian Response" booklet.

48. Paul Smith. Federal Supply Service Journal (see Note on the Sources), April 1967, day not specified.

49. Luther E. Smith Jr., telephone interview with the author, June 22, 2015.

50. Carl S. Dudley, "Second American Revolution."

51. Paul Smith. Federal Supply Service Journal (see Note on the Sources), April 20, 1967.

52. Paul Smith. Federal Supply Service Journal (see Note on the Sources), April 1967, day not specified.

53. Ibid.

54. Ibid.

55. Ibid.

56. Carl S. Dudley, "Second American Revolution."

57. Sweets, "Laclede: An Experiment."

Chapter 7. Black Employment, Black Theology, and Black Power

1. James Forman,"Black Manifesto," issued by the Black Economic Development Council, April 26, 1969. See the Student Nonviolent Coordinating Committee website, https://snccdigital.org/events/jim-forman-delivers-black-manifesto-at-riverside-church/.

2. Forman, "Black Manifesto," 7.

3. Ibid.

4. Ibid., 11.

5. The Manifesto was supported by the Black Presbyterians United but rejected by the Presbyterian Church's General Assembly of 1969. Wilmore, "Identity and Integration," 227. However, the General Board of the National Council of Churches supported its "call to repentance." Detailed plans were made for a social and economic development fund that could address the Manifesto's demands. Just as that fund was about to be launched in January 1971, however, it was deemed a bad risk by the new management of the company where the fund was being developed. After that, the entire scheme fell flat. Similar efforts in other denominations also failed to materialize. Findlay, *Church People in the Struggle*, 216ff.

6. Coates, "Case for Reparations."

7. Stolberg, "At Historic Hearing."

8. Paul Smith, interview with the author, June 7, 2019.

9. Ibid.

10. Paul Smith, "Relation," 20–21.

11. MacLean, *Freedom Is Not Enough*, 66.

12. Ibid.

13. Auchmutey, "Guess Who's Coming to Worship?," 25.

14. See "Timeline and Milestones," 2014 Roadmap to Empowerment, Urban League St. Louis Annual Report,https://www.ulstl.com.

15. Paul Smith, interview with the author, March 27, 2015.

16. Ibid.

17. Ibid.

18. MacLean, *Freedom Is Not Enough*, 77.

19. Ibid., 335.

20. Ibid., 77.

21. Ibid., 76.

22. The EEOC still hears claims brought by field officers from all over the country.

23. MacLean, *Freedom Is Not Enough*, 337.

24. Ibid.

25. Ibid., 338.

26. Ibid., 339.

27. Leonard Wilkens, telephone interview with the author, September 11, 2017.

28. Ibid.

29. Ibid.

30. Frances Smith, interview with the author, February 10, 2016.

31. Kathleen Smith Randolph, interview with the author, April 2, 2016.

32. Cone, *Black Theology and Black Power*.

33. Cone, *Black Theology and Black Power*, 53–54.

34. Ibid., 65.

35. Ibid., 68.

36. Ibid., 69.

37. Ibid., 74.

38. Ibid., 147–49; his emphasis.

39. Paul Smith, interview with the author, July 29, 2014.

40. Ibid.

41. Ibid.

42. Ibid.

43. Ibid.

44. Ibid.

45. See the Second Church Presbyterian Church USA website, https://secondchurch.net/about/history/.

46. Marge and Kenneth Smith, interview with the author, November 10, 2018.

47. Ibid.

48. Ibid.

49. Ibid.

50. "Washington U. Post for the Rev. Paul Smith," news-clipping; most likely from the *St. Louis American*, 1970 (see Note on the Sources).

51. "Paul Smith, Wash. U. Vice Chancellor," news-clipping; most likely from the *St. Louis American*, 1974 (see Note on the Sources).

52. Smith, "Black Church."

53. Lang, *Grassroots at the Gateway*, 202.

54. Smith, "Black Church."

55. Graham, *Our Kind of People*, 130.

56. Letter from Paul Smith to Leonard Smith Sr., October 14, 1977. In collected Smith papers on loan to the author.

57. Paul Smith. Atlanta Journal No. 3 (see Note on the Sources), April 9, 1983.

Chapter 8. Undermining Everything That Separates

1. Luther E. Smith Jr., *Howard Thurman*, 13.

2. See Thurman, *With Head and Heart*.

3. Paul Smith, interview with the author, July 30, 2014.

4. Ibid.

5. Cone, *Said I*, 98–100.

6. See Thurman, *Footprints of a Dream*.

7. DeYoung et al., *United by Faith*, 63–65.

8. Cited in ibid., 63.

9. Ibid., 65. While being led by Thurman, the racial composition of Fellowship Church is said to have been 60% white, 35% African American, and 5% Asian and Hispanic.

10. Smith interview, July 30, 2014.

11. Thurman, *Jesus and the Disinherited*.

12. Ibid., 13.

13. Thurman, *With Head and Heart*, 113–14.

14. Thurman, *Jesus and the Disinherited*, 34.

15. Ibid., 41.

16. Ibid.

17. Thurman, *Jesus and the Disinherited*, 65; his emphasis.

18. Ibid., 72.

19. Ibid., 75.

20. Ibid., 76.

21. Ibid.

22. Thurman, *Jesus and the Disinherited*, 80.

23. Ibid., 82–83.

24. Ibid., 101.

25. Ibid., 98.

26. Ibid.

27. Ibid., 106.

28. Luther E. Smith Jr., *Howard Thurman*.

29. Ibid., 85.

30. Ibid., 105.

31. Ibid., 194.

32. Letter from Howard Thurman to Paul Smith, January 29, 1975. In collected Smith papers on loan to the author.

33. Letter from Paul Smith to Howard Thurman, February 12, 1975. In collected Smith papers on loan to the author..

34. Ibid.

35. Ibid.

36. Letter from Howard Thurman to Paul Smith, February 18, 1975. In collected Smith papers on loan to the author.

37. Paul Smith, "Relation of Black and Jewish Students," 29.

38. "Report of the National Advisory Commission on Civil Disorders," 1, https://www.ncjrs.gov/pdffiles1/Digitization/8073NCJRS.pdf.

39. See Gooden and Myers, "Kerner Commission Report."

40. Paul Smith, "Relation of Black and Jewish Students."

41. Smith notes in his dissertation that he served as president of Freedom of Residence in St. Louis from 1965 to 1967, hearing complaints about housing from Black West End residents. Ibid., 20–21. This local advocacy group should be distinguished from the Fellowship of Reconciliation (FOR), an international network of peace activists that was founded in the United States during World War I and remains active today. See https://forusa.org/who-we-are/history/.

42. Paul Smith, "Relation of Black and Jewish Students," 49.

43. Ibid., 51.

44. Ibid., 52.

45. In addition to overgeneralizing about Jews as landlords, Smith also states flatly that Jews control the media.

46. Paul Smith, "Relation of Black and Jewish Students," 31.

47. These were exactly the kind of "contacts devoid of fellowship" that Thurman had found at the heart of the modern problem of intergroup hatred.

48. Paul Smith, "Relation of Black and Jewish Students," 70–71.

49. Ibid., Addendum 1.

50. Paul Smith, "Relation of Black and Jewish Students."

51. Ibid., 1.

52. Ibid., 4.

53. Ibid.

54. Paul Smith, "Relation of Black and Jewish Students," 5.

55. Ibid., 10–11.

56. Hillel is a nationally known, campus-based Jewish student organization.

57. Paul Smith, "Relation of Black and Jewish Students," 7–8.

58. Ibid., 15.

Chapter 9. Listening for the Sound of the Genuine

1. Luther E. Smith Jr., *Howard Thurman*, 6.

2. See Morehouse University website, https://www.morehouse.edu/about /prominent_alumni.html.

3. Mel and Thel, "We're Telling," *St. Louis American*, May 1978.

4. Ibid.

5. See Morehouse University website.

6. Howie Hodges II, interview with the author, April 14, 2016.

7. Ibid.

8. Ibid.

9. Ibid.

10. Ibid.

11. Ibid.

12. Paul Smith, interview with the author, January 16, 2015.

13. Howie Hodges II, interview with the author, April 14, 2016.

14. Paul Smith, interview with the author, January 16, 2015.

15. Hodges interview, April 14, 2016.

16. Smith interview, January 16, 2015.

17. Ibid.

18. Hodges interview, April 14, 2016.

19. Paul Smith, Atlanta Journal No. 3 (see Note on the Sources), January 29, 1979.

20. Thurman, *With Head and Heart*, 77.

21. Paul Smith, Atlanta Journal No. 3 (see Note on the Sources), January 29, 1979.

22. Paul Smith, Atlanta Journal No. 3 (see Note on the Sources), August 20, 1979.

23. Chaves, American Religion, 88ff.

24. Lisa Demer, "More Than Surviving: Hillside Stands Out with Whites, Blacks Together."

25. Barbara Brown, "Pastor in Transitional Church Must Be Creative, Courageous, Compassionate."

26. Letter from Search Committee to Fellow Hillsiders, October 1, 1979. In collected Smith papers on loan to the author.

27. Paul Smith, Atlanta Journal No. 3 (see Note on the Sources), August 13, 1980.

28. Sharon Bailey, "White Church Takes Itself a Black Pastor."

29. Paul Smith, Atlanta Journal No. 3 (see Note on the Sources), August 13, 1980.

30. Bailey, "White Church."

31. "Black Pastor Tackles Job: A Declining White Church," *Miami Herald*, December 27, 1979; Jeff Prugh, "White Church in South Picks Black Pastor," *Los Angeles Times*.

32. Prugh, "White Church in South Picks Black Pastor."

33. Jim Auchmutey, "Guess Who's Coming to Worship?."

34. Prugh, "White Church."

35. Brown, "Pastor in Transitional Church."

36. Paul Smith, interview with the author, June 6, 2019.

37. Ibid.

38. Ibid.

39. Brown, "Pastor in Transitional Church."

40. Ibid.

41. Demer, "More Than Surviving."

42. Shelton and Emerson, Blacks and Whites, 8–9

43. Demer, "More Than Surviving."

44. Ibid.

45. Ibid.

46. Joanne Nurss, interview with the author, January 25, 2015.

47. Ibid.

48. Ibid.

49. Ibid.

50. Paul Smith, Atlanta Journal No. 3 (see Note on the Sources), March 31, 1983. Agnes Scott is an elite women's college in Decatur, Georgia.

51. Ibid.

52. Ibid.

53. Charles Austin, "North-South Rift of Presbyterians Healed by Merger," *New York Times*, June 11, 1983, https://www.nytimes.com/1983/06/11/us/north-south-rift-of-presbyterians-healed-by-merger.html.

54. Ibid. In the end, some forty congregations in the South did not join the reunited denomination.

55. Ibid.

56. Paul Smith, Atlanta Journal No. 1 (see Note on the Sources), June 10, 1983.

57. Paul Smith, Atlanta Journal No. 3 (see Note on the Sources), October 23, 1983.

58. Paul Smith, Atlanta Journal No. 3 (see Note on the Sources), March 31, 1983.

59. Ibid.

60. Ibid.

61. Paul Smith, Atlanta Journal No. 1 (see Note on the Sources), February 1, 1982.

62. Mike Trautman, telephone interview with the author, February 17, 2016.

63. Ibid., April 4, 2016.

64. Burch, "Who Killed Atlanta's Children?"

65. McInnish, "Ministers Relate Williams Case."

66. Mike Trautman, interview with the author, April 3, 2016.

67. Ibid.

68. Trautman interview, February 17, 2016.

69. Ibid.

70. Ibid.

71. Thurman, "Sound of the Genuine."

72. Ibid.

73. Thurman, Luminous Darkness, 109–11.

74. Ibid., 111.

75. Ibid.

76. Flyer written by the Howard Thurman Enrichment Circle, Atlanta, Georgia, 1980. In collected Smith papers on loan to the author.

77. Scrapbook presented to Dr. Smith by the Howard Thurman Ethical and Enrichment Circle, Atlanta, Georgia, 1986. In collected Smith papers on loan to the author.

78. Paul Smith, Atlanta Journal No. 3 (see Note on the Sources), April 10, 1981.

Chapter 10. Building a Beloved Community, 1986–2006

1. Pearl, "Paul Smith."

2. Bird, "Amid Some Unease."

3. Ibid.

4. Ibid.

5. Paul Smith, Atlanta Journal No. 3 (see Note on the Sources), October 27, 1985.

6. Paul Smith, interview with the author, June 10, 2019.

7. Paul Smith, Atlanta Journal No. 3 (see Note on the Sources), January 12, 1986.

8. Ibid.

9. Ibid.

10. Bird, "Amid Some Unease."

11. Ibid.

12. Ibid.

13. Ibid.

14. Paul Smith, interview with the author, July 30, 2014.

15. Ibid.

16. Bird, "Amid Some Unease." Cox led First Presbyterian Church of Brooklyn from 1837 to 1854. Ibid.

17. Paul Smith, interview with the author, January 16, 2015.

18. Dr. Smith served as Moderator of the Presbytery of New York City in the year 2000.

19. Alvis, "Presbyterian Dilemma," 208.

20. Smith, interview, January 16, 2015.

21. Pearl, "Paul Smith."

22. Program: "The Installation of the Reverend Dr. Paul Smith as the Fourteenth Pastor of the First Presbyterian Church of Brooklyn by the Presbytery of New York City." September 21, 1986. In collected Smith papers on loan to the author.

23. The fact that the Korean congregation soon moved elsewhere was an early disappointment to Dr. Smith in Brooklyn. However, his journal entries show that he felt they evinced little interest in joining the kind of diverse community he was hoping to build.

24. Installation program, First Presbyterian Church, September 21, 1986.

25. Pearl, "Paul Smith."

26. Ibid.

27. Andrew Young, telephone interview with the author, August 31, 2016.

28. Marcia Smith, interview with the author, June 22, 2016.

29. See Emerson and Smith, *Divided by Faith*; DeYoung et al., *United by Faith*; Christerson, Korie, and Emerson, *Against All Odds*; Emerson with Woo, *People of the Dream*; Shelton and Emerson, *Blacks and Whites in Christian America*.

30. Smith's instincts in this regard have been in keeping with Americans' increasing acceptance of religious difference since the 1970s. See Chaves, *American Religion*, 20ff.

31. Ellen Oler, interview with the author, May 23, 2016.

32. Mercia Weyand, interview with the author, June 10, 2016.

33. Sam Murumba, interview with the author, June 22, 2016.

34. Weyand interview, June 10, 2016.

35. Marcia Smith interview, June 22, 2016.

36. Murumba interview, June 22, 2016.

37. Weyand interview, June 10, 2016.

38. Paul Smith, Ghost Ranch Journal (see Note on the Sources), August 7, 1991. SANE was the National Committee for a Sane Nuclear Policy.

39. Paul Smith, interview with the author, July 10, 2016.

40. David Dinkins, interview with the author, July 23, 2019.

41. Ibid.

42. Charles Clayman, interview with the author, January 29, 2016.

43. Ibid.

44. Ibid.

45. Ibid.

46. Ibid.

47. See Roberts, "Jon Lester."

48. Clayman interview, January 29, 2016.

49. Yarrow, "In Brooklyn Heights."

50. Smith interview, June 10, 2019.

51. This organization is now called NARAL Pro-Choice America.

52. Toner, "Abortion Marchers Gather in Capital."

53. Nathan Dudley, interview with the author, January 26, 2016.

54. Ibid.

55. Ibid.

56. Jim Johnson, interview with the author, November 11, 2015.

57. Ibid.

58. Fred Davie, interview with the author, May 20, 2015.

59. Ibid.

60. Ibid.

61. Ibid.

62. Ibid.

63. Smith interview, June 10, 2019.

64. See Patrick D. Heery, "What Same-Sex Marriage Means to Presbyterians," Presbyterian Church U.S.A., March 20, 2015, https://www.pcusa.org/news/2015 /3/20/what-same-sex-marriage-means-presbyterians/.

65. Murumba interview, June 22, 2016.

66. Paul Smith, First Church Journal (see Note on the Sources).

67. Marcia Smith interview, June 22, 2016.

68. Ibid.

69. Ibid. Meeting minutes, financial data, membership lists and other records had to be submitted to the Presbytery on a regular basis.

70. Smith interview, January 16, 2015.

71. Ibid.

72. Marcia Smith interview, June 22, 2016.

73. See Bell, *Lighting the Fires of Freedom.*

74. Transcript of address to First Church by Janet Dewart Bell, May 7, 2006. Used with permission.

75. Ibid.

76. Ibid.

77. Ibid.

78. Murumba interview, June 22, 2016.

79. Ibid.

80. Reeves Carter quoted in Aplin, "Rev. Dr. Paul Smith."

81. Young interview, August 31, 2016.

82. Paul Smith, Ghost Ranch Journal (see Note on the Sources), August 7, 1991.

83. Krista Smith Clapp, interview with the author, March 20, 2016.

84. Murumba interview, June 22, 2016.

85. Ibid.

86. Powers, "Two-Fold Mission."

87. Amy Neuner, telephone interview with the author, June 21, 2016.

88. Carpenter and Williams, *African American Heritage Hymnal.*

89. Amy Neuner, email message to the author, June 28, 2016.

90. Neuner interview, June 21, 2016.

91. Ibid.

92. Ibid.

93. Murumba interview, June 22, 2016.

94. Neuner interview, June 21, 2016.

95. Weyand interview, June 10, 2016.

96. See Derrick Bell's official site, https://www.professorderrickbell.com.

97. Sue Carlson, interview with the author, July 5, 2016.

98. Oler interview, May 23, 2016.

99. Video recording made by The Riverside Church of the memorial service for Dr. Derrick Bell, November 3, 2011. The CD is on loan to the author.

100. Ibid.

101. Oler interview, May 23, 2016.

102. "METRO DATELINES; Dalai Lama Receives Humanitarian Award," *New York Times*, September 30, 1987.

103. Murumba interview, June 22, 2016.

104. Norsen, "Seminar."

105. Ibid., 17.

106. E.g., "In Conversation: Tolerance Plus," Telecare—Channel 25 program #011.

107. Letter to Paul Smith from M. and M. Avram, January 19, 1999. In collected Smith papers.

108. Neuner interview, June 21, 2016.

109. Weyand interview, June 10, 2016.

110. Ibid.

111. Carlson interview, July 5, 2016.

112. Paul Smith, interview with the author, July 10, 2016.

113. Carlson interview, July 5, 2016.

114. Paul Smith, Ghost Ranch Journal (see Note on the Sources), June 25, 1991.

115. Ibid.

116. Ibid.

117. Marvin and Portia Chandler, interview with the author, March 31, 2016.

118. Ibid.

119. Ibid.

120. Marvin Chandler, telephone interview with the author, August 17, 2014.

Chapter 11. Speaking Truth to Power

1. See Chambers, "Grand Jury."

2. See Roberts, "Jon Lester."

3. See McFadden, "Brawley Made Up Story."

4. See Wilson, "Trump Draws Criticism."

5. See Rich Schapiro and Ginger Adams Otis, "Crown Heights Erupts in Three Days of Race Riots after Jewish Driver Hits and Kills Gavin Cato, 7, in 1991," *New York Daily News*, August 13, 2016, *https://www.nydailynews.com/new-york /brooklyn/crown-heights-erupts-days-race-riots-1991-article-1.2750050*.

6. When Smith was interviewed on national television in 1989 about the Central Park Jogger case, he did not claim to know whether the defendants were guilty or not. Rather, he assailed Trump's open malevolence toward the young

men. Trump's ad called the boys "muggers and murderers" who should "suffer" and "be executed." Despite the ugliness of these public statements, Trump never apologized to the boys.

7. Paul Smith, interview with the author, July 10, 2016. In collected Smith papers on loan to the author. One of Dorothy Turmail's banners honored the 84th Precinct.

8. Ibid.

9. Ibid.

10. Ibid.

11. Three news-clippings mentioning this event are extant. They were presumably published in 1994 in local papers like the Brooklyn Heights Press (see Note on the Sources). In collected Smith papers on loan to the author.

12. See The Violent Crime Control and Law enforcement Act of 1994, https://www.congress.gov/bill/103rd-congress/house-bill/3355/text.

13. Alexander, *New Jim Crow*, 99ff.

14. Ibid.

15. Ibid., 57.

16. Ibid., 58.

17. Paul Smith, interview with the author, May 28, 2015.

18. Smith and Hutchinson, "Gristedes Says 'Sorry' to Reverend."

19. Smith interview, July 10, 2016.

20. Ibid.

21. Ibid.

22. Paul Smith, interview with the author, February 11, 2016.

23. David Lewicki, email message to the author, February 3, 2015.

24. Paul Smith, interview with the author, June 6, 2019.

25. Paul Smith, interview with the author, June 7, 2019.

26. See Macy's corporation website, https://www.macysinc.com.

27. Edward Goldberg, interview with the author, June 15, 2016.

28. Edward Goldberg, email message to the author, August 1, 2016.

29. Goldberg interview, June 15, 2016.

30. Goldberg email, August 1, 2016.

31. Edward Goldberg, interview with the author, September 16, 2015.

32. Goldberg email, August 1, 2016.

33. Goldberg interview, September 16, 2015.

34. Halla, "Macy's Donates to First Presbyterian."

35. The *Amistad Murals* by revered artist Hale Aspacio Woodruff were commissioned by Talladega College in 1938. See Talladega College website, http://www.talladega.edu/academics/amistad.asp.

36. Elliott, "Macy's Settles Complaint"; Feuer, "Macy's to Pay $650,000."

37. Goldberg interview, June 15, 2016.

38. Christman and Mark, "Guidelines on Dealing."

39. Elliott, "Macy's Settles Complaint."

40. Ibid.

41. Goodman, "Macy's and Barney's."

42. Paul Smith, telephone interview with the author, August 2, 2016.

43. Jeffrey Smith, telephone interview with the author, June 14, 2016.

44. Ibid.

45. Ibid.

46. Ibid.

47. Ibid.

48. Smith interview, February 11, 2016.

49. Marc Burt, interview with the author, January 25, 2015.

50. Ibid.

51. Ibid.

52. Ibid.

53. Ibid.

54. See Honda Campus All-Star Challenge website, https://www.hcasc.com.

55. Jeffrey Smith interview, June 14, 2016.

56. See invitational showcase page on the Honda Battle of the Bands website, https://www.hondabattleofthebands.com/invitational-showcase.

57. See Tom Watkins, "FAMU Band Leader Drummed Out in Wake of Death Linked to Hazing," CNN News, November 24, 2011, https://www.cnn.com/2011/11/23/us/florida-hazing-death.

58. Pamela Champion, email message to the author, February 2015. Used with permission.

59. See Arthur Ashe Legacy Fund at UCLA website, https://arthurashe.ucla.edu/life-story/.

60. Ashe and Rampersad, *Days of Grace*, 321.

61. Ibid., 320.

62. David Dinkins, interview with the author, July 23, 2019.

63. Paul Smith, Brooklyn Journal #15 (see Note on the Sources), April 16, 1989.

64. Rev. Dr. Calvin Butts leads the Abyssinian Baptist Church in Harlem, New York.

65. Paul Smith, Brooklyn Journal #15 (see Note on the Sources), April 17, 1989.

66. Ashe and Rampersad, *Days of Grace*, 320.

67. Ibid., 311.

68. Ibid., 302.

69. See the Arthur Ashe Institute for Urban Health website, https://www.arthurasheinstitute.org.

70. Paul Smith, interview with the author, July 29, 2014.

71. Ibid.

72. Hartocollis, "Nurses."

73. Frost, "SUNY Board Official."

74. Charles Clayman, interview with the author, January 29, 2016.

75. Ibid.

76. Ibid.

77. Frost, "SUNY Board Official."

Chapter 12. Legacy

1. Letter from Paul Smith to The Members and Friends of First Presbyterian Church, Brooklyn, January 21, 2006. In collected Smith papers on loan to the author.

2. Ibid.

3. Ibid.

4. "Celebrating the Ministry of Rev. Dr. Paul Smith," First Presbyterian Church of Brooklyn program. In collected Smith papers on loan to the author.

5. Letter from Rev. David Dyson to Paul Smith, May 31, 2006. In collected Smith papers on loan to the author.

6. Ibid.

7. Paul Smith, interview with the author, July 29, 2014.

8. Ibid.

9. Masango's own story is remarkable. While growing up under apartheid, he made the most of the few educational opportunities available to him and was eventually ordained by the Presbyterian Church of Southern Africa. In the mid-1970s, a Presbyterian patron then helped him get to the United States to further his studies. Masango enrolled at Columbia Seminary in Decatur, Georgia, because he wanted more experience studying and working with white people. Unexpectedly, it was there that he met and studied under Dr. Smith, a fellow Black boundary-breaker. Following his mentor's path, Masango was later called to lead an all-white church in Johannesburg and taught for many years as a professor of practical theology at the formerly all-white University of Pretoria. Incisively, Masango has said: "You cannot be called into ministry in a racist way. I had to learn to love the people I hated." See Jerry Van Marter, "The Call to Ministry Is Above Rejection," Presbyterian Mission Agency, November 18, 2014, https://www.pcusa.org/news/2014/11/18/call-ministry-above-rejection/.

10. Ibid.

11. Ibid.

12. Eileen Elliott, "New Healthy Families' Program."

13. Necole Brown, telephone interview with the author, August 4, 2016.

14. Brown et al., "Healthy Families Brooklyn."

15. Brown interview, August 4, 2016.

16. Ibid.

17. See "Black Americans and HIV/AIDS: The Basics," Kaiser Family Foundation, February 7, 2020, https://www.kff.org/hivaids/fact-sheet/black-americans-and-hiv-aids.

18. Brown interview, August 4, 2016.

19. For more on Mensah, see https://ofn.org/sites/default/files/resources/PDFs/Leadership%20Bios/Lisa%20Mensah%20bio.pdf.

20. Jim Johnson, interview with the author, November 11, 2015.

21. Patrick later served as governor of Massachusetts from 2007 to 2015.

22. Johnson interview, November 11, 2015.

23. For more information, see https://clinton.presidentiallibraries.us.

24. Day, "Black Church Burnings," 263.

25. Ibid., 262.

26. Ibid., 264. Despite the fact that church burnings have continued, the work of the Task Force ended during the George W. Bush administration.

27. Johnson interview, November 11, 2015.

28. Ibid.

29. Ibid.

30. Phil Murphy became governor of New Jersey in 2018.

31. John Utendahl, telephone interview with the author, August 3, 2016.

32. Ibid.

33. Ibid.

34. Ibid.

35. Ibid.

36. Mossi Tull, telephone interview with the author, September 9, 2019.

37. B. E. Mays, "King Eulogy," April 9, 1968, http://americanradioworks.publicradio.org.

38. Tull interview, September 9, 2019.

39. Howie Hodges II, interview with the author, April 14, 2016.

40. Ibid.

41. Ibid.

42. Smith's father also had heart disease and diabetes. The complex reasons why Black men's health outcomes consistently rank lower than those of other groups of Americans are finally being analyzed in terms of the distinct and powerful stressors they are subject to in our society. See, for example, Keon L. Gilbert et al., "Visible and Invisible Trends in Black Men's Health 2016," https://www.ncbi.nlm.nih.gov/pmc/articles/PMC6531286/.

43. Paul Smith, telephone interview with the author, May 24, 2020.

44. Ibid.

Chapter 13. Black Lives Matter

1. Huggins, "Afro-Americans," 108.

2. Ibid.

3. Ibid., 111.

4. Ibid., 108.

5. King, "Facing the Challenge," 89.

6. Ibid., 90; his emphasis.

7. Paul Smith, interview with the author, July 10, 2016.

8. Marsha Larner, interview with the author, February 2, 2016.

9. Paul Smith. Brooklyn Journal No. 15 (see Note on the Sources), March 3, 1989.

10. Paul Smith, Urban League Journal (see Note on the Sources), June 28, 2013.

11. For more information, see www.revdrpaulsmith.org.

12. Paul Smith, "I'm Back." It took five years to bring to justice the police officer who caused Garner's death, Daniel Pantaleo. He was fired by the NYPD on August 19, 2019. The Citizen's Complaint Review Board that played a key role in the process was chaired by Smith's longtime colleague, Rev. Fred Davie. See Southall, "Daniel Pantaleo."

13. Paul Smith, interview with the author, August 2, 2016.

14. Paul Smith, interview with the author, August 3, 2016.

15. See "What Happened in Ferguson?," New York Times, updated August 10, 2015, https://www.nytimes.com/interactive/2014/08/13/us/ferguson-missouri -town-under-siege-after-police-shooting.html.

16. Ibid.

17. Gunning Francis, Ferguson & Faith.

18. Paul Smith, "In Search of Common Ground."

19. Ibid.

20. Garner died as the result of a chokehold, not due to a gunshot.

21. Paul Smith, "In Search of Common Ground."

22. Mike Trautman, telephone interview with the author, February 17, 2016.

23. Paul Smith, "Need for Constancy, Not Consistency."

24. Mike Trautman, email message to Paul Smith, September 28, 2014.

25. Paul Smith, email message to Mike Trautman, September 29, 2014.

26. Gunning Francis, Ferguson & Faith.

27. Trautman interview, February 17, 2016.

28. Quoted in Chu, "We Don't Need Peace."

29. Scanlon, "Unrest in Ferguson."

30. Ibid.

31. Ibid.

32. Ibid.

33. Moral Mondays are part of a civil disobedience movement were started by Rev. William Barber II, whose influential work has included the group Repairers of the Breach and the revival of Dr. King's Poor People's Campaign.

34. Gunning Francis, Ferguson & Faith, 94.

35. Ibid.

36. U.S. Department of Justice, *Investigation of the Ferguson Police Department*, 6.

37. Ibid.

38. Byers, "After 2½ Years "; Robles, "New Ferguson Chef."

39. See Bogan, Hollinshed, and Deere, "Why Did the Michael Brown Shooting Happen Here?"; Bogan and Moskop, "As Low-Income Housing"; Hannah-Jones, "School Segregation"; Rothstein, "Making of Ferguson."

40. Rothstein, *Color of Law.*

41. Rothstein, "Making of Ferguson," 3.

42. Trautman interview, April 3, 2016.

43. Trautman interview, February 17, 2016. Evidence of that segregation history remains in the street grid under Ferguson. There are still unnecessary dead-ends where roads from Kinloch could have crossed into Ferguson. And there here is only one road, now named Martin Luther King Blvd., that leads from the old Black neighborhood into Ferguson's town center. It is no longer gated and locked.

44. Rothstein, "Making of Ferguson," 30.

45. Bogan, Hollinshed, and Deere, "Why Did the Michael Brown Shooting Happen Here?"

46. Ibid.

47. Ibid.

48. Trautman interview, April 3, 2016.

49. In the years since Brown's death, the police force has become more diverse, and officers now wear body cameras. A community center has been built where one business was destroyed. But some have found it hard to sell their homes, and taxes have gone up while services and jobs have been cut to help balance the budget. See Bosman and Healy, "Returning to Ferguson."

50. Coates, *Between the World and Me*; Younge, *Another Day.*

51. Hill, *Nobody: Casualties of America's War.*

52. Wilkerson, *Caste.*

53. Jelani Cobb, "The Matter of Black Lives."

54. Ibid., 37.

55. Patrisse Khan-Cullors, *When They Call You a Terrorist.*

56. Patrisse Cullors, "'Black Lives Matter' Is About More Than the Police."

57. Paul Smith interview, August 2, 2016.

58. Rector, "Charges Dropped."

59. Paul Smith, "When Your Cup Runneth Over."

60. Ibid.

61. Ibid.

62. Ibid.

63. Paul Smith, interview with the author, July 10, 2016.

64. Ibid.

65. Smith interview, August 2, 2016.

66. Author's notes, Darien, Connecticut, September 18, 2016.

67. Ibid.

68. Ibid.

69. Author's notes, Darien, Connecticut, September 18, 2016.

70. Ibid.

71. Ibid.

72. Smith interview, August 2, 2016.

73. Author's notes, Darien, Connecticut, September 18, 2016.

74. "What to Know about the Death of George Floyd in Minneapolis," *New York Times*.

75. Fausset, "What We Know About the Shooting Death of Ahmaud Arbery."

76. Oppel Jr, Taylor and Bogel-Burroughs, "What We Know About Breonna Taylor's Case and Death."

77. Paul Smith, telephone conversation with the author, November 5, 2020.

78. Dyson, *Tears We Cannot Stop*.

79. Ibid., 44.

80. Ibid., 104.

81. Ibid.

82. Dyson, *Tears We Cannot Stop*, 212.

83. Cone, *Cross and the Lynching Tree*, xix.

84. Cone, *Cross and the Lynching Tree*, 165–66.

85. Cone, *Said I*, 173.

Chapter 14. Sacramental Moments

1. Paul Smith, interview with the author, July 30, 2014.

2. Paul Smith, interview with the author, January 16, 2015. See also Severson, "Helpful Hands."

3. Jennifer Young, "Persistent Racism of America's Cemeteries."

4. Paul Smith, Atlanta Journal No. 3 (see Note on the Sources), February 6, 1983.

5. Paul Smith interview, January 16, 2015.

6. Holley, "Segregated Cemetery."

7. Ellis Smith, "Funeral Home"; Sapong, "Cultural."

8. Paul Smith, *Deep Calling to the Deep*, 1.

9. Ibid., 33.

10. Ibid., 8.

11. Ibid., 29.

12. Ibid., 52.

13. Ibid., 33. Smith's book also covers his pastoral work with Arthur Ashe.

14. Waldon, "Deep Like a River," 64.

15. Paul Smith, interview with the author, July 30, 2017.

16. Rivers, "Good Pastor."

17. Ibid.

18. Ibid.

19. Email message to Paul Smith, August 1, 2014.

20. Symposium held at Riverside Church in 2005; Smith, Malik, and Wright, "Theological Perspectives."

21. Paul Smith, "OPINION."

22. See Compassion & Choices website, https://www.compassionandchoices.org.

23. See Death with Dignity website, https://www.deathwithdignity.org/learn/death-with-dignity-acts/.

24. Barbara Coombs Lee, email message to the author, September 22, 2019. Used with permission.

25. Thurman, *Deep River*.

26. Ibid. (second essay), 13–14.

27. Ibid., 14–15.

28. Ibid., 19.

29. Ibid., 19–20.

30. Ibid., 15–16.

31. Ibid., 37–38.

32. Ibid., 17.

33. Ibid.

34. Luther E. Smith Jr., *Howard Thurman*, 73.

35. Rev. Marvin Chandler succeeded Howard Thurman as pastor at the Church for the Fellowship of All Peoples in San Francisco and later led the Howard Thurman Trust. In "*I Sing Because I'm Happy*," Chandler said of Fellowship Church: "It did not fit or feel like a church. I came to use the term, 'religious association,' in order to maintain the sense of a spiritual gathering without the burden of the term 'church.'"

36. Marvin Chandler, telephone interview with the author, August 17, 2014.

37. Luther E. Smith Jr., telephone interview with the author, June 22, 2015.

38. Luther E. Smith Jr., *Howard Thurman*, 214–15.

39. Ibid., 113–14.

40. Paul Smith, Atlanta Journal No. 3 (see Note on the Sources), April 9, 1981.

41. Ibid.

42. Smith, *Deep Calling to the Deep*, 136–37.

43. Unpublished transcription by Joyce Sloan; typos lightly edited here. In collected Smith papers on loan to the author.

44. Paul Smith, interview with the author, August 2, 2016.s

45. DiAngelo, *White Fragility*, 22.

46. See Anderson, *White Rage*; DiAngelo, *White Fragility*; Oluo, *So You Want to Talk*.

47. Fields and Fields, *Racecraft*, 146–47.

Postlude

1. Paul Smith, interview with the author, July 10, 2016.

2. Ibid.

3. Ibid.

4. Ibid.

5. Paul Smith, telephone interview with the author, November 24, 2016.

6. Katz, "Cobble Hill Health Center."

7. Recording transcribed by the author, Cobble Hill Health Center gala, November 17, 2016.

8. Ibid.

9. Ibid.

10. Ibid.

11. Ibid.

12. Paul Smith, Urban League Journal (see Note on the Sources), June 4, 2013.

Bibliography

Alexander, Michelle. *The New Jim Crow: Mass Incarceration in the Age of Color-blindness*. New York: New Press, 2010.

Allen, Michael R., and Heidi Aronson Kolk. "The Painful Persistence of Pruitt-Igoe's Long Goodbye." *Common Reader*, September 7, 2018. https://wwwcommonreader.wustl.edu.

Alvis, Joel L., Jr. "A Presbyterian Dilemma: Ecclesiastical and Social Racial Policy in the Twentieth-Century Presbyterian Communion." In *The Diversity of Discipleship: Presbyterians and Twentieth-Century Christian Witness*, edited by Milton J. Coalter, John M. Mulder, and Louis B. Weeks, 187–208. Louisville: Westminster/John Knox Press, 1991.

Anderson, Carol. *White Rage: The Unspoken Truth of Our Racial Divide*. New York: Bloomsbury, 2017.

Aplin, Beth. "Rev. Dr. Paul Smith, Pioneering B'klyn Heights Pastor, to Retire." *Brooklyn Daily Eagle*, June 27, 2006.

Ashe, Arthur, and Arnold Rampersad. *Days of Grace: A Memoir*. New York: Ballantine Books, 1993.

Auchmutey, Jim. "Guess Who's Coming to Worship?" *Presbyterian Survey* 7 (1980): 24–25.

Austin, Charles. "North-South Rift of Presbyterians Healed by Merger." *New York Times*, June 10, 1983.

Bailey, Sharon. "White Church Takes Itself a Black Pastor." *Atlanta Constitution*, November 5, 1979.

Bell, Janet Dewart. *Lighting the Fires of Freedom: African American Women in the Civil Rights Movement*. New York: New Press, 2018.

Bird, David. "Amid Some Unease, Brooklyn Church Takes a Black Pastor." *New York Times*, January 29, 1986.

Bogan, Jesse, Denise Hollinshed, and Stephen Deere. "Why Did the Michael Brown Shooting Happen Here?" *St. Louis Post Dispatch*, August 17, 2014.

Bogan, Jesse, and Walker Moskop. "As Low-Income Housing Boomed, Ferguson Pushed Back." *St. Louis Post Dispatch*, October 19, 2014.

Bosman, Julie, and Jack Healy. "Returning to Ferguson Five Years Later." *New York Times*, August 9, 2019.

Branch, Taylor. *Parting the Waters: America in the King Years 1954–63*. New York: Simon & Schuster, 1988.

———. *Pillar of Fire: America in the King Years 1963–65*. New York: Simon & Schuster, 1998.

———. *At Canaan's Edge: America in the King Years 1965–68*. New York: Simon & Schuster, 2006.

Brown, Barbara. "Pastor in Transitional Church Must Be Creative, Courageous, Compassionate." *Ministry & Mission* (1980): 4–5.

Brown, Necole, Nicole A. Vaughn, Alison J. Lin, Ruth Browne, Marilyn White, and Paul Smith. "Healthy Families Brooklyn: Working with Health Advocates to Develop a Health Promotion Program for Residents Living in NYC Housing Authority Developments." *Journal of Community Health* 36, no. 5 (2011): 864–73.

Burch, Audra, D.S. "Who Killed Atlanta's Children?" *New York Times*, April 30, 2019.

Byers, Christine. "After 2½ Years as Police Chief in Ferguson, Delrish Moss Is Leaving the Spotlight." *St. Louis Post-Dispatch*, November 13, 2018.

Carpenter, Delores, and Nolan E. Williams, eds. *African American Heritage Hymnal*. Chicago: GIA Publications, 2001.

Chambers, Marcia. "Grand Jury Votes to Indict Goetz Only on Gun Possession Charges." *New York Times*, December 22, 1985.

Chandler, Marvin. *"I Sing Because I'm Happy": Improvisational Moments That Have Shaped My Song*. Unpublished memoir, n.d.

Chaves, Mark. *American Religion: Contemporary Trends*. 2nd ed. Princeton: Princeton University Press, 2017.

Christerson, Brad, L. Edwards Korie, and Michael O. Emerson. *Against All Odds: The Struggle for Racial Integration in Religious Organization*. New York: New York University Press, 2005.

Christman, Steven M., and Jillian M. Mark. "Guidelines on Dealing with Suspected Shoplifters." *New York Law Journal*, May 19, 2104.

Chu, Jeff. "We Don't Need Peace—We Need Unrest." *Beaconreader*, August 20, 2014. https://www.beaconreader.com/jeff-chu/we-don't-need-.peace-we -need-unrest.

Coates, Ta-Nehisi. "The Case for Reparations." *The Atlantic*, June 2014. https:// www.theatlantic.com/magazine/archive/2014/06/the-case-for-reparations /361631/.

———. *Between the World and Me*. New York: Penguin Random House, 2015.

Cobb, Jelani. "The Matter of Black Lives." *New Yorker*, March 14, 2016.

Cone, James H. *Black Theology and Black Power*. 1969; reprint ed., New York: Harper & Row, 1997.

————. *The Cross and the Lynching Tree*. Maryknoll: Orbis Books, 2010.

————. *Said I Wasn't Gonna Tell Nobody: The Making of a Black Theologian*. Maryknoll: Orbis Books, 2018.

Craig, Berry F. *Kentucky Confederates: Secession, Civil War and the Jackson Purchase*. Lexington: University Press of Kentucky, 2017.

Day, Katie. "Black Church Burnings in the 1990s and Faith-Based Responses." In *From Every Mountainside: Black Churches and the Broad Terrain of Civil Rights*, edited by R. Drew Smith, 249–68. Albany: SUNY Press, 2013.

Demer, Lisa. "More Than Surviving: Hillside Stands Out with Whites, Blacks, Together." *Dekalb News/Sun*, June 2, 1982.

DeYoung, Curtiss Paul, Michael O. Emerson, George Yancy, and Karen Chai Kim. *United by Faith: The Multiracial Congregation as an Answer to the Problem of Race*. New York: Oxford University Press, 2003.

DiAngelo, Robin. *White Fragility: Why It's So Hard for White People to Talk about Racism*. Boston: Beacon Press, 2018.

Downey, Clifford J. *Images of Rail: Kentucky and the Illinois Central Railroad*. Charleston: Arcadia Publishing, 2010.

Dudley, Carl S. "The Second American Revolution: As Seen Through the Window of Berea Church 1962–1973." Facebook, September 19, 2007.

————. "My Experience with Dr. Martin Luther King Jr." Facebook, February 16, 2009 [2006].

Dudley, Nathan. "Laclede Town: The Life of a Great American Urban Renewal Project." Unpublished paper, Yale University, 1979.

Dyson, Michael Eric. *Tears We Cannot Stop: A Sermon to White America*. New York: St. Martin's Press, 2017.

Elliott, Andrea. "Macy's Settles Complaint of Racial Profiling for $600,000." *New York Times*, January 14, 2005.

Elliott, Eileen. "New 'Healthy Families' Program in Brooklyn." *NYC Housing Authority Journal* 37, no. 2 (February 2007): 5–6.

Emerson, Michael O. "Cracks in the Christian Color Wall." Faith & Leadership blog, Duke Divinity School, February 1, 2010. https://faithandleadership.com/michael-o-emerson-cracks-christian-color-wall.

Emerson, Michael O., and Christian Smith. *Divided by Faith: Evangelical Religion and the Problem of Race in America*. New York: Oxford University Press, 2000.

Emerson, Michael O., with Rodney Woo. *People of the Dream: Multiracial Congregations in the United States*. Princeton: Princeton University Press, 2006.

Fausett, Richard. "What We Know about the Shooting Death of Ahmaud Arbery." *New York Times*, November 13, 2020.

Feuer, Alan. "Macy's to Pay $650,000 to Resolve Bias Inquiry." *New York Times*, August 8, 2014.

Fields, Karen E., and Barbara J. Fields. *Racecraft: The Soul of Inequality in American Life*. New York: Verso, 2012.

Findlay, James F., Jr. *Church People in the Struggle: The National Council of Churches and the Black Freedom Movement, 1950–1970*. New York: Oxford University Press, 1993.

Frost, Mary. "SUNY Board Official Approves Sale of Long Island College Hospital to Fortis." *Brooklyn Daily Eagle*, June 25, 2014.

Gerson, Michael. "Christians Are Suffering from Complete Spiritual Blindness." *Washington Post*, September 10, 2018.

Gooden, Susan T., and Samuel L. Myers Jr. "The Kerner Commission Report Fifty Years Later: Revisiting the American Dream." *Russell Sage Foundation Journal of the Social Sciences* 4, no. 6 (2018): 1–17.

Goodman, J. David. "Macy's and Barney's among Stores to Post Shoppers' 'Bill of Rights.'" *New York Times*, December 9, 2013.

Gordon, Buford F. *The Negro in South Bend: A Social Study*. 1922; reprint ed., South Bend, Ind.: Wolfson Press, 2009.

Graham, Lawrence Otis. *Our Kind of People: Inside American's Black Upper Class*. New York: Harper Perennial, 2000.

Gunning Francis, Leah. *Ferguson & Faith: Sparking Leadership & Awakening Community*. St. Louis: Chalice Press, 2015.

Halla, Frederick A. "Macy's Donates to First Presbyterian." *Brooklyn Daily Eagle*, November 24, 1998.

Hannah-Jones, Nikole. "School Segregation, the Continuing Tragedy of Ferguson." *ProPublica*, December 19, 2014. Accessed April 9, 2016. https://www.propublica.org/article/ferguson-school-segration.

Harrison, Lowell H., and James C. Klotter. *A New History of Kentucky*. Lexington: University Press of Kentucky, 1997.

Hartocollis, Anemona. "Nurses Roam Empty Halls as Long Island College Hospital Is Prepared to Close." *New York Times*, July 18, 2013.

Hay, Andrew, and Gabriella Borter. "North Carolina Orders New U.S. House Election after 'Tainted' Vote." *Reuters*, February 21, 2019.

Healy, David H. "We Stand on His Shoulders: Rev. Buford F. Gordon in South Bend, Indiana." In *The Negro in South Bend: A Social Study*, edited by David H. Healy, 1–14. South Bend, Ind.: Wolfson Press, 2009 [1922].

Herbeck, Dan. "Buffalo's Crimes of the Century: Mayhem, Murder and the Mafia—Darker Moments in the City's History." *Buffalo News*, December 27, 1999. Last updated July 12, 2019. https://buffalonews.com./author/dan_herbeck/.

Heuser, F. J. "Presbyterians and the Struggle for Civil Rights." *Journal of Presbyterian History* 90, no. 1 (Spring/Summer 2012): 4–15. http://www.history.pcusa.org/sites/default/files/Heuser_Civil_Rights_optimized.pdf.

Hill, Marc Lamont. *Nobody: Casualties of America's War on the Vulnerable, from Ferguson to Flint and Beyond.* New York: Atria Books, 2016.

Holley, Peter. "A Segregated Cemetery Divides a Texas Town: 'That Should Have Been Taken Out 75 Years Ago.'" *Washington Post*, June 7, 2016. https://www.washingtonpost.com/news/post-nation/wp/2016/06/07/a-segregated-cemetery-divides-a-texas-town-that-should-have-been-taken-out-75-years-ago/.

Huggins, Nathan Irvin. "Afro-Americans." In *Ethnic Leadership in America*, edited by John Higham, 91–118. Baltimore: Johns Hopkins University Press, 1978.

Johnson, Lyndon B. "Voting Rights Act Address." March 15, 1965. https://www.law.jrank.org/pages/Lyndon-B-Johnson-Voting-Rights-Act-Address.

Jones, Robert P. *White Too Long: The Legacy of White Supremacy in American Christianity.* New York: Simon & Schuster, 2020.

Katz, Andy. "Cobble Hill Health Center 40th Anniversary Rocks Aging." *Brooklyn Eagle*, November 18, 2016. Accessed December 5, 2016. https://brooklyneagle.com/neighborhoods/cobble-hill/page/11/.

Khan-Cullors, Patrisse, with asha bendele. *When They Call You a Terrorist: A Black Lives Matter Memoir.* New York: St. Martin's Press, 2017.

King, Martin Luther, Jr. "Facing the Challenge of a New Age." In *I Have a Dream: Writings and Speeches That Changed the World*, edited by James Melvin Washington, 14–28. 1957; reprint ed., San Francisco: Harper Collins, 1992.

Kraus, Neil. *Race, Neighborhoods, and Community Power: Buffalo Politics 1934–1997.* Albany: SUNY Press, 2000.

Lang, Clarence. *Grassroots at the Gateway: Class Politics and Black Freedom Struggle in St. Louis, 1936–75.* Ann Arbor: University of Michigan Press, 2009.

Lewis, John, with Michael D'Orso. *Walking with the Wind: A Memoir of the Movement.* New York: Harcourt Brace, 1998.

Looker, Benjamin. *BAG: "Point from Which Creation Begins"; The Black Artists' Group of St. Louis.* St. Louis: Missouri Historical Society Press, 2004.

MacLean, Nancy. *Freedom Is Not Enough: The Opening of the American Workplace.* Cambridge: Harvard University Press, 2006.

May, Gary. *Bending toward Justice: The Voting Rights Act and the Transformation of American Democracy.* Durham: Duke University Press, 2015.

McFadden, Robert D. "Brawley Made Up Story of Assault, Grand Jury Finds." *New York Times*, October 7, 1988.

McInnish, Sue. "Ministers Relate Williams Case to Parable of Good Samaritan." *Montgomery Advertiser*, March 1, 1982.

Mitchell, Henry H. *Black Preaching: The Recovery of a Powerful Art.* Nashville: Abingdon Press, 1990.

Norsen, Francesca. "Seminar Explores Islamic Connection to Judeo-Christian Traditions." *Brooklyn Daily Eagle,* February 17, 2000.

Oluo, Ijeoma. *So You Want to Talk about Race.* New York: Seal Press, 2018.

Oppel, Richard A., Jr., Derrick Bryson Taylor, and Nicholas Bogel-Burroughs. "What We Know about Breonna Taylor's Case and Death. *New York Times,* September 24, 2020.

Pearl, Andrea. "Paul Smith Takes Over as New Reverend of 1st Presbyterian." *Heights Press,* September 25, 1986.

Powers, Ann. "A Two-fold Mission of Piety and Pop." *New York Times,* October 27, 2000.

Pratt, Robert. *Selma's Bloody Sunday: Protest, Voting Rights and the Struggle for Racial Equality.* Baltimore: Johns Hopkins University Press, 2017.

Prugh, Jeff. "White Church in South Picks Black Pastor." *Los Angeles Times,* December 8, 1979.

Rector, Kevin. "Charges Dropped: Freddie Gray Case Concludes with Zero Convictions against Officers." *Baltimore Sun,* July 27, 2016.

Rivers, Prince Raney. "A Good Pastor at the Hour of Death." Faith & Leadership blog, Duke Divinity School, June 7, 2010. https://www.faithandleadership.com /prince-raney-rivers-good-pastor-hour-death.

Roberts, Sam. "Jon Lester, Convicted in Howard Beach Race Attack, Dies at 48." *New York Times,* October 23, 2017.

Robinson, Gabrielle. *Better Homes of South Bend: An American Story of Courage.* Charleston: History Press, 2015.

Robles, Frances. "New Ferguson Chief Sees Challenge and Vows Change." *New York Times,* May 9, 2016.

Rothstein, Richard. "The Making of Ferguson: Public Policies at the Root of its Troubles." *Economic Policy Institute Report.* Washington, D.C.: Economic Policy Institute, 2014.

———. *The Color of Law: A Forgotten History of How Our Government Segregated America.* New York: Liveright, 2017.

Sapong, Emma. "Cultural Changes Hitting Area's Black Funeral Homes." *Buffalo News,* April 19, 2015. Accessed June 4, 2016. https://buffalonews.com/news/ local/cultural-changes-hitting-area-s-black-funeral-homes/article_15942b6a- 968c-5c64-8eee-18150328b0a1.html.

Scanlon, Leslie. "Unrest in Ferguson: A Conversation with Mike Trautman." *Presbyterian Outlook,* October 6, 2014. Accessed February 2, 2016. http:// pres-outlook.org/2014/10/unrest-ferguson-conversation-mike-trautman.

Severson, Kim. "Helpful Hands on Life's Last Segregated Journey." *New York Times,* June 23, 2012.

Shelton, Jason E., and Michael O. Emerson. *Blacks and Whites in Christian America: How Racial Discrimination Shapes Religious Convictions*. New York: New York University Press, 2012.

Smith, Ellis. "Funeral Home Offers Itself as Crossing Racial Lines." *Times Free Press*, October 22, 2011. Accessed June 4, 2016. http://timesfreepress .com/news/business/aroundregion/story/2011/oct/22/funeral-home-offers -itself-as-crossing-racial/62106/.

Smith, Greg B., and Bill Hutchinson. "Gristedes Says 'Sorry' to Reverend." *New York Daily News*, March 22, 1999.

Smith, Luther E., Jr. *Howard Thurman: The Mystic as Prophet*. Richmond: Friends United Press, 1991.

Smith, Paul. "A Comparison of the Baptist and Congregationalist Denominations." Senior thesis, Talladega College, 1957.

———. "The Black Church: Our Heritage of Faith." *Proud* 7, no. 2 (1976): 4–8.

———. "The Relation of Black and Jewish Students Living in the Residence Halls of a Multi-Racial Midwestern University." PhD diss., Eden Theological Seminary, 1977.

———. *The Deep Calling to the Deep: Facing Death*. Brooklyn Heights: Coat of Many Colors, 1998.

———. Smith, Paul, Shaykh Ibrahim Abdul Malik, and Jeremiah Wright. "Theological Perspectives on Death and Dying for African Americans: Christian & Islamic Perspectives." In *Key Topics on End-of-Life Care for African Americans*, edited by Richard Payne, Gwendolyn London, and Sharon R. Latson. Durham: Duke University Divinity School, 2007. http://www.rwjf.org /en/library/research/2007/09/duke-institute-publishes-electronic-guide-on -end-of-life-issues-.html.

———. "Something to Think About." Paul Smith Blog, March 4, 2014. http://www .revdrpaulsmith.org.

———. "I'm Back and What a Mess." Paul Smith Blog, August 1, 2014. http://www .revdrpaulsmith.org.

———. "In Search of Common Ground." Paul Smith Blog, August 23, 2014. http:// www.revdrpaulsmith.org.

———. "The Need for Constancy, Not Consistency." Paul Smith Blog, September 27, 2014. http://www.revdrpaulsmith.org.

———. "When Your Cup Runneth Over." Paul Smith Blog, June 25, 2015. http:// www.revdrpaulsmith.org.

———. "OPINION: In Support of End-of-life Options. *Brooklyn Daily Eagle*, May 24, 2016.

Southall, Ashley. "Daniel Pantaleo, Officer Who Held Eric Garner in a Chokehold, Is Fired." *New York Times*, August 19, 2019.

Still, Larry. "Preacher Who Uses Jazz to Attract Teens." *JET* (January 10, 1963): 16–19.

Stolberg, Sheryl Gay. "At Historic Hearing, House Panel Explores Reparations." *New York Times*, June 19, 2019.

Sugrue, Thomas J. *Sweet Land of Liberty: The Forgotten Struggle for Civil Rights in the North*. New York: Random House, 2008.

Sweets, Ellen. "Laclede: An Experiment in Ethnic Harmony." *Seattle Times*, November 9, 1997.

Thompson, Heather Ann. *Blood in the Water: The Attica Prison Uprising of 1971 and Its Legacy*. New York: Pantheon Books, 2016.

Thornbrough, Emma Lou. *Indiana Blacks in the Twentieth Century*. Bloomington: Indiana University Press, 2000.

Thurman, Howard. *Jesus and the Disinherited*. 1949; reprint ed., Boston: Beacon Press, 1976.

———. *Footprints of a Dream: The Story of the Church for the Fellowship of All Peoples*. 1959; reprint ed., Eugene: Wipf and Stock, 2009.

———. *The Luminous Darkness: A Personal Interpretation of the Anatomy of Segregation and the Ground of Hope*. 1965; reprint ed., Richmond: Friends United Press, 1989.

———. *Deep River: The Negro Spiritual Speaks of Life and Death*. Richmond: Friends United Press, 1975.

———. *With Head and Heart: The Autobiography of Howard Thurman*. New York: Harcourt Brace, 1979.

———. "The Sound of the Genuine." *Spelman Messenger* 96, no. 4 (Summer 1980): 14–15.

Toner, Robin. "Abortion Marchers Gather in Capital." *New York Times*, April 9, 1989.

Tucker, Todd. *Notre Dame vs. the Klan*. Chicago: Loyola Press, 2004.

U.S. Department of Justice, Civil Rights Division. *Investigation of the Ferguson Police Department*, 2015. https://assets.documentcloud.org/documents/1681213 /ferguson-police-department-report.pdf.

Vaughn, Billy E. "The History of Diversity Training and its Pioneers." *Strategic Diversity & Inclusion Management Magazine* 1, no. 1 (Spring 2007): 11–16. https://diversityofficermagazine.com/cultural-diversity-factoids/historical -issues/.

Waldon, Alton R., Jr. "Deep like a River." Review of *The Deep Calling to the Deep: Facing Death*, by Paul Smith. *Boulé Journal* (Spring 2000): 63–64.

Weiser, Wendy, and Max Feldman. *The State of Voting 2018*. Brennan Center For Justice Report. Accessed August 19, 2019. https://brennancenter.org/sites /default/files/publications/2018_06_StateOfVoting_v5%20%281%29pdf.

"What to Know about the Death of George Floyd in Minneapolis." *New York Times*, March 23, 2021.

Wilkerson, Isabel. *Caste: The Origins of Our Discontents. New York: Random House, 2020.*

Wilmore, Gayraud S. "Identity and Integration: Black Presbyterians and Their Allies in the Twentieth Century." In *The Diversity of Discipleship: Presbyterians and Twentieth-Century Christian Witness*, edited by Milton J. Coalter, John M. Mulder, and Louis B. Weeks, 209–33. Louisville: Westminster/John Knox, 1991.

———. *Black and Presbyterian: The Heritage and the Hope.* Louisville: Witherspoon Press, 1998.

Wilson, Michael. "Trump Draws Criticism for Ad He Ran after Jogger Attack." *New York Times*, October 23, 2002.

Wright, George C. *Racial Violence in Kentucky, 1865–1940: Lynchings, Mob Rule, and "Legal Lynchings."* Baton Rouge: Louisiana State University Press, 1990.

Yarrow, Andrew. "In Brooklyn Heights, Wisps of Victorian Age." *New York Times*, March 8, 1991.

Young, Andrew. *An Easy Burden: The Civil Rights Movement and the Transformation of America.* Waco, Tex.: Baylor University Press, 2008.

Young, Jennifer. "The Persistent Racism of American's Cemeteries." In *Atlas Obscura*, September 7, 2016. https:// www.atlastobscura.com/articles/the -persistent-racism-of-america's-cemeteries.

Younge, Gary. *Another Day in the Death of America: A Chronicle of Ten Short Lives.* New York: Nation Books, 2016.

Index